Using her deep knowledge of Kenya, Ambreena Manji wrestles with the country's original sin – the dispossession of land from those who owned and worked it ... she argues that unless and until the land question is addressed as a justice issue, the postcolonial state in Kenya will remain on a dangerous precipice ... an important and intellectually transformative work on land in Kenya.

Makau Mutua, SUNY Distinguished Professor, Floyd H. & Hilda L. Hurst Scholar, SUNY Buffalo Law School, The State University of New York

Land is at the heart of Kenya's postcolonial politics, as Ambreena Manji's masterly book shows. Her meticulous treatment of decades of wrangling over 'the land question' conveys the fractured politics of efforts 'from above' by state authorities and politically connected elites to shore up electoral support and 'from below' by citizens to secure their access to land for their livelihoods ... a must-read for scholars, policymakers and activists.

Professor Ruth Hall, PLAAS, University of the Western Cape

A major contribution ... on the inextricable nexus between the history of land law and land reforms on one hand, and the constitutional change in Kenya on the other hand, while emphasising the importance of embedding constitutionalism in land governance.

Dr Francis Kariuki, Strathmore University

An important and timely contribution to knowledge – both in the empirical detail provided and in the analysis of land injustice in Kenya and inadequacies of current approaches.

Professor Gabrielle Lynch, University of Warwick

The Struggle for Land and Justice in Kenya

AMBREENA MANJI

JC JAMES CURREY

James Currey
is an imprint of
Boydell & Brewer Ltd
PO Box 9, Woodbridge
Suffolk IP12 3DF (GB)
www.jamescurrey.com
and of
Boydell & Brewer Inc.
668 Mt Hope Avenue
Rochester, NY 14620–2731 (US)
www.boydellandbrewer.com

First published in World excluding East and South Africa by James Currey in 2020
Paperback edition 2022

Published in East Africa (Kenya, Uganda, Tanzania, Rwanda, Burundi, South Sudan)
and South Africa in 2021 by Vita Books

British Library Cataloguing in Publication Data
A catalogue record for this book is available from the British Library

ISBN 978-1-84701-255-5 (James Currey hardback)
ISBN 978-1-84701-344-6 (James Currey paperback)
ISBN 978-9914-9875-8-4 (Vita Books paperback)

Typeset in 10 on 12pt Cordale with Gill Sans MT display
by Avocet Typeset, Bideford, Devon, EX39 2BP

For my dear friends, Yash Pal Ghai and Jill Ghai

Where all your rights become only an accumulated wrong; where men must beg with bated breath for leave to subsist in their own land, to think their own thoughts, to sing their own songs, to garner the fruits of their own labours – and even while they beg, to see things inexorably withdrawn from them – then surely it is a braver, a saner and a truer thing, to be a rebel in act and deed against such circumstances as these than tamely to accept it as the natural lot of men.

(Roger Casement's speech from the dock, 1916)

Contents

Foreword

In their chapter on land in a landmark text entitled *Public Law and Social Change in Kenya* published in 1970, Yash Ghai and Patrick McAuslan wrote: 'No part of the law of Kenya has raised stronger emotions over the years than the law relating to land and its administration, and none is of more importance at present'. This remains true today as Kenya marks the tenth anniversary of the inauguration of 2010 Constitution. In this book, Ambreena Manji explores our seemingly intractable land problems, including inequitable concentration of land in the hands of the wealthy, a propensity for land grabbing, unresolved historical land injustices and landlessness. She seeks to develop a theoretical framework for our discussions of land which, to adapt Upendra Baxi, himself adapting Ronald Dworkin, takes justice seriously.

Manji argues that land reform's tenacity as a key idea in Kenyan history is beyond doubt. Nonetheless, land reform can mean many things. Manji shows that land reform has in fact been reduced to land law reform. This has excluded critical debates. It has prevented us from thinking about more radical possibilities. It has foreclosed discussions of redistributive politics. Drawing on constitutional and land law, and on history, literary theory and political science, Manji calls our attention to the dangers of such a limited debate about land reform and argues that we must attend to insurgent knowledge and ideas of change. She uses the term 'land archive' to describe the accretion of land knowledge by formal and informal means. She shows that authoritative, official archives combine with legal folk memory to record the many land wrongs of the colonial and post-independence periods. The official archive of the land mischiefs committed by the state, politicians and the elite has been made available in a series of official reports. But beyond this, Kenyans have not been shy to develop a peoples' truth on land, creating what Grace Musila describes as alternative 'epistemic registers'.

Manji shows that demands for constitutional change and land reform have become intricately connected in Kenya and draws attention to some of the dangers inherent in this. She takes land as an exemplar of Kenya's constitutional optimism and argues that we have focused too much on how to achieve institutional change in relation to the management and administration of land. This has distracted from deeper – and more difficult – questions of how to achieve fairness and equity in the land domain. Land redistribution has been carefully and diligently excluded from discussions of what is possible. Indeed, Kenya's gini co-efficient on land has worsened since the inauguration of the 2010 Constitution. Manji suggests that we need to rethink the role of law in bringing about justice in relation to land.

A nuanced and historically informed analysis of land injustices in Kenya and the struggle against them require us to understand the consequences of what Manji terms 'land wrongs'. Reconceptualising historical land injustices, she argues that it is impossible to envisage the present-day economic structure of Kenya without acknowledging its roots deep in regimes of land ownership that were facilitated first by a settler political economy and then, post-independence, by an elite that reserved for itself access to and ownership of land on a massive scale. We must recognise that land wrongs in Kenya do not fit the neat temporal categories of law and policy constructed around terms such as historical land injustice. The proceeds of land wrongs circulate and recirculate in the economy. Current land injustices shape the country's political economy.

As we mark the tenth anniversary of the Constitution, Manji's book should be read by all those committed to what Atieno-Odhiambo characterised as 'African struggles for civil liberties, human rights, democratic participation, workers' rights, peasant independence, spiritual space, elective representation and civic responsibility'.

Dr Willy Mutunga
Chief Justice and President of the Supreme Court of Kenya 2011–2016

Acknowledgements

This book is the culmination of a decade of work on land issues in Kenya. I have had the good fortune to work closely with colleagues on constitutional and land law and across a range of disciplines including history, political science, law and literary studies. My thanks to John Osogo Ambani, Catherine Boone, Ngala Chome, Carli Coetzee, Alex Dyzenhaus, Achiba Gargule, Emily Kinama, Jackie Klopp, Gabrielle Lynch, Patricia Kameri-Mbote, Grace Musila, Ibrahim Mwathane, Raphael Nge'tich, Collins Odote, Mutuma Ruteere, Florence Shako, Connie Sozi, Ndirangu Wachanga, Hannah Waddilove, Justin Willis, and Liz Alden Wily for their collegiality and support.

Davinder Lamba, Gabrielle Dolan and Zahid Rajan have shared my interests and concerns. Patricia Kameri-Mbote, Gitobu Imanyara and Wachira Maina were hugely generous in making sure materials reached me. Waikwa Wanyoike talked to me about the ideas contained here and Makau Mutua asked me probing questions at a crucial point in my writing.

I discussed the ideas contained in Chapter 2 in the 6th CB Madan Memorial Lecture in December 2018, and I am most grateful to Gitobu Imanyara, Sylvia Kangara and Luis Franceschi for the honour of delivering the lecture.

A workshop at the Centre for Law and Society at the University of Cape Town in March 2019 afforded me an important opportunity to learn from Sanele Sibanda, Joel Modiri, Tshepo Madlingozi and Heinz Klug and I am grateful to Dee Smythe for bringing us together.

Colleagues at CODESRIA invited me to teach on its Gender Institute in Dakar in June 2019 and I discussed some of the ideas contained here on that occasion, for which I thank Godwin Murunga, Ibrahim Oanda, Divine Fuh and Ndoffene Diouf.

For their friendship and encouragement, my thanks to Lyla Latif, Faith Simiyu, Martha Gayoye, Barbara Hughes-Moore, Celine Tan, Faathima Mahomed, Dickens Olewe, Mulugetu Sissay, James Smart, Lizzy Willmington and Issa Shivji. Grateful thanks to Salim, Navida and Tehmeena Manji and to John and Greta Harrington for their support. Special thanks to Smith Ouma for our many conversations. It is difficult to imagine this book without his presence in Cardiff.

Cardiff Law School granted me research leave in the 2018–19 academic year to complete this work for which I am grateful. I am grateful to the anonymous reviewers of my manuscript for their expert suggestions, and to Jaqueline Mitchell and Lynn Taylor of James Currey for their support of this project.

My thanks to Chief Justice Emeritus Willy Mutunga for providing the Foreword to this book and for his wise counsel.

This book was written at the kitchen table and around family life. My love and thanks to John, Rafik and Naima Harrington, who make everything possible.

I dedicate this book to Yash Pal Ghai and Jill Ghai in gratitude for the example they have set.

I

Introduction

What We Talk About When We Talk About Land[1]

> No part of the law of Kenya has raised stronger emotions over the years than the law relating to land and its administration, and none is of more importance at present. (Ghai and McAuslan 1970: 79)

In many parts of Africa since 1990, the desirability of land reform has been a defining feature of political debates. Debates have raged about the purpose and direction of land reform with citizens calling for change and many governments resistant to calls for land grievances to be addressed. Nonetheless, many African countries have witnessed the appointment of commissions of inquiry into land matters, the formulation of national land policies and ultimately the enactment of new land laws. These countries include Eritrea, Ethiopia, Malawi, Mozambique, Namibia, Rwanda, South Africa, Tanzania, Uganda and Zambia. I have argued elsewhere (Manji 2006) that this has been the age not just of land reform but of land law reform.

The main thrust of land-related legal change has been the liberalisation of land tenure and the facilitation of markets in land. I have shown (Manji 2006, 2015) that international financial institutions such as the World Bank, international donors such as the British Department for International Development, African governments, legislators, non-governmental organisations, legal consultants, commercial lenders, and the judiciary have all played a role in land reform, and that a defining feature of contemporary land reform has been the effective translation of various and often contradictory concerns into land law reform.

At the level of international land policy, the enduring effect of the economist Hernando de Soto's ideas must be recognised. These were elaborated in his book, *The Mystery of Capital: Why Capitalism Triumphs in the West and Fails Everywhere Else* (de Soto 2000) which significantly shaped the thinking of international financial institutions and

---

[1] With apologies to Raymond Carver: see *What We Talk About When We Talk About Love* (1981).

bilateral donors. According to de Soto, the lack of formalised property rights accounts for much of the failure of development. According to this viewpoint the poor are not without assets. Indeed their 'the entrepreneurial ingenuity ... has created wealth on a vast scale' (ibid.: 32). The reason why this has not translated into development is that the poor 'hold these resources in defective forms' so that ownership rights to land are not always properly recorded even when investments such as housebuilding have been carried out of it (ibid.).

It is important to note that the solution advocated by de Soto envisages a central role for the law. His most influential recommendation is that the assets of the poor need to be brought into the legal system through a process of land registration and titling to enable that land to be offered as collateral for loans. De Soto's insight is that 'law is the instrument that fixes and realises capital' (2000: 164). This approach to land was rapidly and enthusiastically taken up by the World Bank, the United Nations Development Programme and the British Department for International Development, and his work was closely watched by a number of African countries. The most influential dissemination of his ideas took place through his Foundation for Building the Capital of the Poor based in Accra, Ghana. Personally championed by Kofi Annan, the Ghana project provided African governments with first-hand insights into a property reform on an ambitious scale, triggering something of a competition amongst them to be seen as leading the field in land law reform. Now linked with underdevelopment, non-formalised property relations must be discouraged. In this way, the formalisation of property rights has become a central component of development policy, giving the law an important role in promoting economic development across the continent.

Whilst these developments were taking place in international land policy, land matters had remained one of the most explosive issue facing Kenya more than fifty years after independence from Britain. If the inauguration of a new constitution in 2010 marked the beginning of a 'second liberation' (Mutunga 2018), there are nonetheless many land grievances remaining unresolved. Perhaps the most important question in today's political economy is who should have access to land and where, and on what terms. These remains the fraught questions at the heart of Kenyan politics. In this chapter, I introduce the key questions which animate the land debate in Kenya. I explore different and often apparently irreconcilable understandings of the meaning of land and connect these to different expectations of the role of the state. I argue that the struggle for land must be read as a struggle for spatial and temporal justice, and set out the key ideas around which this book is organised.

'The tyranny of property'

Atieno-Odhiambo (2002: 225) has described as one of the main 'strands' or 'historical themes' running through Kenyan history, 'the tyranny of property' which 'pitt[ed] the haves against the have-nots and inform[ed] the nature of class formation' in Kenya. Individual and collective positions on land often reveal what seem like insurmountable epistemic gulfs between citizens. Different understandings of land have come to co-exist and sometimes dangerously to collide. Crucially for the wider political economy, these understandings are animated by different conceptions of the role of the state. On one hand, land is viewed as a critical factor of production, an asset which brings both personal wealth and economic development, a commodity to which the state must guarantee secure access through its laws. In this neo-liberal model, what is needed is 'an institutional framework characterized by strong private property rights, free markets, and free trade. The role of the state is to create and preserve an institutional framework appropriate to such practices' (Harvey 2005: 2). On the other hand are those who conceive of land not as a commodity but as incarnating and expressing a set of other attachments including 'identity, home, family, heritage, livelihood and many other meanings' (Kepe and Hall 2018: 134). Okoth-Ogendo, in his writing on the African commons, explored how land meanings derive from historical and community connections with a given territory. He put it thus:

> We use the term 'Commons' to identify ontologically organized land and associated resources available exclusively to specific communities, lineages or families operating as corporate entities. The Commons are thus not constituted merely by territoriality, or by the temporal aggregation of members of any given entity, but are, in addition, characterized by important ontological factors among which is their permanent availability across generations past, present, and future. (Okoth-Ogendo 2002: 2)

This conception is vividly summed up by Krog's (2015: 219) suggestion that rather than seeing land as 'owned' by people, we need to consider how people might be 'land-owned', a perspective she describes as requiring us to 'map a new ethos of being land-owned as opposed to landowner'. Krog's suggestion, made in the South African context, shares much in common with the perspectives Okoth-Ogendo (2002) sought to elaborate throughout his scholarship on Kenya, drawing our attention to non-hegemonic ontological positions that viewed land as a factor of reproduction to which access also enabled connections to tradition, heritage and spiritual space. Land is understood as vested in members of the community rather than in individual landowners.

Deliberately relying on a pun, we might describe the different, and often opposed, ideas held by Kenyans about land as 'land values'. Both

Okoth-Ogendo and Krog encourage us to look for these alternative visions and in this way to promote a spatial reordering in thinking about land. Krog calls for 'a radical decentering' (2015: 219) and Cross (1992: 305) for a search for 'alternative legalities'. According to Krog, it is necessary 'to cross ontological and epistemological frontiers in thinking about land in a way that permits freedom from the essence of a self that is only possible with land possession' (2015: 219). This is a conception of land and self that a centralising Kenyan state, obsessed with landowners and landowning, has sought to snuff out.

Elaborating on how the expropriation of the commons (widely called communal or community land) required a denial of their proprietary nature, Okoth-Ogendo (1975) provided an account of the legal mechanisms by which this was achieved. I explore this in greater depth in Chapter 2, but a brief account can be given as follows. The Foreign Jurisdiction Act 1890 purported to give Britain imperial authority over overseas territories. Ghai and McAuslan (1970) describe how this was followed by making English law the basis of administration as well as the relevant law in determining civil and criminal matters. An 1899 Advisory Opinion from the Law Officers of the Crown then ruled that the effect of the Foreign Jurisdiction Act 1890 was to 'bestow upon the "sovereign" the power of control and disposition over waste and unoccupied land in protectorates where there was no settled form of government' (Okoth-Ogendo 1975). This land could be declared Crown Land or granted to individuals. The effect of this was to appropriate the commons by vesting it in the Crown. In 1923 a Supreme Court decision in the case of *Wainaina v. Murito* confirmed that

> the annexation of most of the protectorate had had the effect of destroying all African rights in the land of the new colony as follows: 'all native rights in such reserved land, whatever they were ... Disappeared and natives in occupation of such Crown Land became tenants at the will of the Crown.' (Ghai and McAuslan 1970: 89)

Much of the work of the colonial period and of the post-colonial Kenyan state has thus been directed at spatial reordering in relation to land. We can understand this by considering the history of radical title. A great deal of the power of Okoth-Ogendo's scholarship on the African commons derived from its insights into how colonialism disrupted understandings of radical title. Indeed, radical title was relocated several times as a result of colonial occupation. What we might describe as the kinetic history of radical title in the commons is critical to our understanding of this model of land. Okoth-Ogendo (2002: 2) argued that before the advent of colonial occupation, land had been held, managed and protected 'by a social hierarchy organized in the form of an inverted pyramid with the tip representing the family, the middle the clan and lineage, and the base, the community'. Each of these levels of decision making were concerned with questions of allocation, use and management of resources. Crucially,

> Decisions made at each level are not necessarily taken collectively. Rather, they are made by reference to common values and principles internalized at any such level. Decision-making at the base of the pyramid, however, further entails responsibility for the protection of the territory of the group as a whole; a function which does not entail appropriation of the radical title to the Commons. The location of radical title always was, and remains, in all members of the group past, present and future, constituted as corporate entities. (Okoth-Ogendo 2002: 2)

One of the effects of colonial occupation was to disrupt radical title, and to destabilise it by relocating it first to the Crown and then, in the 1930s, by using English trust doctrine as a mechanism for the administration of the commons. The kinetic history of radical title did not end there. As Alden Wily (2018c) has shown, and as I explore in later chapters, following devolution in Kenya from 2010, county governments now have trustee functions over community lands as long as these lands are not registered.

It is clear from the above that the private property / common property models I have described have been marked by different expectations and experiences of state involvement or interference. The private property model relies on the protection of the state and on guarantees of strong private laws and institutions. This private landowner model is promoted as the governing land value of the ruling elite through what Atieno-Odhiambo (2002: 239) has termed their 'hegemonic enterprises'. In contrast, the commons have had to be insurgent. They have been subject to deprecation and expropriation by the state. Their governing customary law has been subject to suppression. These models are also animated by different temporal orientations for, as Keenan reminds us, property is productive of temporal and spatial order (2013: 464). In the neo-liberal model, *homo economicus* (Williams 1999) is governed by future time and by the foreshortening of temporal horizons into the future (Shivji 2009: 51). Kenya's Vision 2030, launched by President Kibaki in 2008, is the foremost example of this. A development programme to transform Kenya into a newly industrialising, middle-income country, which was enthusiastically embraced by the Kenyatta Government on its election in 2013, Vision 2030 is referred to by some commentators as 'the real Constitution of Kenya' (Malombe 2013; see also Manji 2014). Vision 2030 richly suggests to us how Kenya 'sees like a state' (Scott 1999). The ideal citizen is also future oriented in their relationship to property. Time is measured by the tools made available by property ownership: freeholders are future oriented. Governed by what we might call 'title time' they perceive time as running from first registration. They are committed advocates of the right to exclude and adherents of ideologies of land improvement (Bhandar 2018). They are keen observers of the shrunken horizons of sale, speculation and debt (Shivji 2009). In the commons (or community land / communal land) model, in contrast, the relationship to land is temporally past-oriented. Claims are based on past connections, on occupation and use. Land is less property than territory (Cooper 1998). Crucially, as Okoth-Ogendo's analysis suggested, land in the commons is conceived of and held 'as a transgenerational asset' (2002: 3).

In Kenya, a state intent on centralised power has projected itself as a strong guarantor of private property rights. As I show in Chapter 2, one of the tasks of the post-independence period was to put an end to nationalist visions of land reform which sought a restoration of lands to the landless who had partaken in the struggle for independence (Ogot 1996). Instead, President Kenyatta sought to snuff out demands for land reform and to reassure European settlers of his regime's determination to follow 'an accommodationist course' (Mutua 2008: 279). An anti-nationalist vision of land valorised individual effort, most especially where this could be evidenced by improvements to land. This was encapsulated in the mocking terms in which Kenyatta addressed his former comrade Bildad Kaggia whose attempts to keep alive a nationalist vision of cooperative farming and the resettlement of the landless clearly rankled:

> Kaggia, we were together with Paul Ngei in jail, if you go to Ngei's farm, he has planted a lot of coffee and other crops. What have you done to yourself? If you go to Kubai's, he has a big house and a nice shamba. Kaggia, what have you done for yourself? We were together with Kung'u Karumba in jail, now he is running his own buses. What have you done for yourself? (Cited in Illiffe 2005: 334)

Mutua (2008: 277) has written that, with these words, Kenyatta 'established the benchmark for the elite's political morality' (see also Berman et al. 2009). In Illiffe's reading of this infamous 'what have you done for yourself' speech, the failure to amass property is deployed by Kenyatta to suggest 'indolence' and a lack of 'probity'. Conversely, the accumulation of wealth was a 'central element of heroic style' that underpinned notions of 'political honour' (2005: 334). But despite their formal adherence to neo-liberal tenets of individual hard work and reward, Kenya's ruling elite has not been above organising themselves as robber barons and acquiring land through little if any effort save for 'unlimited "eating" … at the public trough' (Berman et al. 2009: 474). Mutua (2008: 277), has characterised Kenya's elite as a 'betrayer class' that, although it suffers from its own cleavages and factions, is 'a resilient group that selectively reproduces itself' and which has deprecated (sometimes in the most personalised terms) redistributive demands in favour of a deeply conservative politics. Attempting to trace the elements of this conservatism, Murunga (2006) has argued that politics in Kenya is characterised by a powerful gerontocratic impulse and Musila (2009: 281), taking this analysis further, has written that 'at the core of Kenyan social imaginaries across the cultural, political and intellectual landscapes, lies a particular trope of veneration of both age and masculinity'. But what we might term the ideology of 'what have you done for yourself' should not be taken at face value. The elite's morality has not been organised around effort and hard work as Kenyatta's speech seemed to suggest. Instead, at independence and since, the plundering of land has led to accumulation on a grand scale, as I show in Chapter 3. Dispossession and displacement lie at the heart of Kenyan history.

Strictly future oriented temporally, the state has also shown a marked preference for being centralised spatially. This has been most apparent in its attitude to the technologies of property information: as I show in this book, decentralised institutions of land management, including land registries, have been taken as a threat to the state's centralised and monopolised control of property knowledge, symbolised for Kenyans by Ardhi House, the building that houses the Ministry of Lands. ('Ministry of Lands' and 'Land Ministry' are common parlance for the Ministry of Lands, Housing and Urban Development – later the Ministry of Lands & Physical Planning – and are used interchangeably throughout the book). Resisting decentralisation has also meant resisting the communal model of land traced above. Impatient with ways of seeing and dealing with land that do not view it primarily as an asset and which are not reliant on its commodification, the centralising Kenyan state has worked remorselessly on the 'normative inculcation' (Cooper 1998: 156) of its own land values.

Developing an adequate anthropology of the Kenyan state (Sharma and Gupta 2006) requires us to show how the state's conception of the citizen is first and foremost of a property-owning subject. Because, as Shivji has elaborated in his account of *Accumulation in an African Periphery* (2009: 77), 'the mantle of the settler was taken over by the yeoman farmer or politicians and bureaucrats turned farmers' ideologies of property in Kenya have been shaped by a newly emerged compradorial class. They have moulded the state in accordance with their own ideas of temporal and spatial ordering, work that since independence 'has had effects that are constitutive of subjectivity' (Keenan 2013: 490). When they have considered the commons at all, they have done so in order to treat it as a residual category which stubbornly endures and must in time be converted to more productive use. Resistance to commodification – demands for ontological and spiritual space in land (Okoth-Ogendo 2002), for democratic participation, and against exploitation – goes against the grain of Kenya's forward thrust as a market economy. The claims of indigenous peoples, which I discuss in Chapter 7, perplex the courts and provoke disdain. Nonetheless, land held under communal tenure constitutes a bounty, a rich reserve of land for accumulation by grabbing. Those resident on this land have long been a 'reservoir of cheap labour whether as a squatter or as a semi-proletarian in his reserve' (Shivji 2009: 82).

Read in this way, the struggle for land and justice with which this book is concerned has been a struggle for spatial and temporal justice. In accounting for this, we can draw important insights from ongoing debates about decolonisation, land and constitutionalism in post-apartheid South Africa (Hall and Thembela 2017; Klug 2018; Le Roux and Davis 2019; Madlingozi 2017; Modiri 2018). Although, as Mutua (2008: 168) reminds us, South Africa suffered extensive traumas under apartheid that fundamentally shaped its constitution-making process, and 'Kenya's cleavages had not been nearly as sharp', it is instructive to read South African reassessments of what has been achieved by constitutional reform from today's vantage point as Kenya approaches the tenth anniversary of the inauguration of its Constitution.

A great deal can be learned from a country further along the road of constitutional reform which, like Kenya, invested huge energy and optimism in the Constitution as marking a break with the past. After all, having borrowed substantively from South Africa in forging the 2010 Constitution (in relation to social and economic rights for example), Kenya has been deeply informed by its jurisprudence since that time. More specifically, in relation to land, South African debates have particular purchase. If in South Africa the critique of the Constitution is that it has in fact functioned to preserve rather than overturn apartheid, that claim has become increasingly plausible in the face of slow change in the land arena (Hall and Thembela 2017). The emergence of the Economic Freedom Fighters party has brought this argument from the margins of the debate around 2008 to the centre of political discourse in the 2019 elections as Le Roux and Davis (2019) have recognised. For them, the lack of progress in carrying out meaningful land reform has resulted in the Constitution being seen as an obstacle or even the means by which the material gains and privileges of the apartheid era are held on to and consolidated. In Kenya too, frustration with existing structures of property relations is similarly palpable, as the discussion of land mischiefs in Chapter 3 shows.

In his powerful critique of the limits of decolonisation in South Africa, Modiri (2018) draws on Wolfe (2006: 388) to urge us to consider settler colonialism as 'a structure not an event'. Taking that observation as a starting point, I wish to argue that in Kenya too we should pay attention to the structures of land dispossession which has been the legacy of colonialism and its aftermath. Refusing to see decolonisation as an event enables us to trace the continuities of land politics in the neo-colonial state. This structure is a legacy of racial domination in a settler economy followed by ethnic domination in a neo-colonial state with the coming of independence from Britain. In Kenya, 1963 was the beginning of settler colonialism by other means. As well as a material reality, land dispossession has also had to be a central ideological project of the state. It has taken what Blomley (2003: 114) calls 'sustained enactment' to project a commoditised model of land relations as common sense. This has been necessary in order to obtain the consent of the ruled to a structure of land relations which is exploitative and domineering. Intense ideological labour has been done to present land ownership as a marker of success, a way to distinguish the deserving land rich from the indolent land poor and wretchedly landless. Kenyatta was doing that labour in his stinging words to Bildad Kaggia. Hegemonic ideas of property relations have broken down only when they have been met with challenges from below. Intermittently, there have been attempts to call into question the elite's land values. Although a radical redistributive land agenda has not been promulgated in modern Kenya, claims such as those by indigenous peoples keep alive counter-hegemonic ideas of land.

Organising ideas

Kenya's constitutional reform process – and its success in enacting a progressive constitution which seeks to guarantee social, economic, political and civil rights – is well known around the world (Mutua 2008). Although the place of land reform in this wider constitutional context has received some attention (Alden Wily 2018a; D'Arcy and Nistotskaya 2019; Boone et al. 2019; Harbeson 2012; Kanyinga and Long 2012; Kariuki et al. 2016; Klopp and Lumumba 2017) there has been little sustained analysis which offers a critical schema for understanding the last decade of developments in the land domain and provides a review of where we have reached (but cf. Wanjala 2000). This is the aim of the present book. It is animated by several interrelated theoretical concerns which I elaborate here.

'Accumulation by dispossession'
In his study *Accumulation in an African Periphery*, Shivji (2009: 34) describes 'accumulation by dispossession' (see Harvey 2005) as 'very perceptively us[ing] Rosa Luxemburg's proposition of the continued existence of primitive forms of accumulation' to explain present-day neo-liberalism. Harvey's task has been to show how what Marx characterised as 'original' or 'primitive' accumulation at the start of capitalism continues and proliferates in the present day, such that they can be described as 'accumulation practices' (Harvey 2005: 159).

In his *A Brief History of Neoliberalism*, Harvey specifically refers to processes of commodifying and privatising land; to 'the conversion of various forms of property rights (common, collective, state, etc.) into exclusive private property rights'; and to the 'suppression of rights to the commons' (ibid.). Most important for our purposes is Harvey's analysis of the period between 1970 and 2000 which he presents as the hegemony of neo-liberalism. By this he means that in this period neo-liberal ideas, values and constructions come to dominate such that they became 'common sense' in economic and social thought (Shivji 2009). For Harvey, neo-liberalism is 'in the first instance a theory of political economic practices' (Harvey 2005: 2). In neo-liberal economic theory, what is needed is the liberation of innate entrepreneurial skills of human beings 'within an institutional framework characterized by strong private property rights, free markets, and free trade. The role of the state is to create and preserve an institutional framework appropriate to such practices.' But more than this, 'if markets do not exist (in areas such as land, water, education, health care, social security, or environmental pollution) then they must be created, by state action if necessary' (Harvey 2005: 2).

As I show in Chapter 2, Kenya's land question was marked from the start by its status as a settler economy. Shivji (2009: 77) has written that Kenya, like Zimbabwe, experienced 'massive alienation of land to settlers under the hegemony of the colonial state'. In this schema, peasant labour subsidised settler capital. The 'massive alienation of land to settlers' has meant that agriculture has developed not only in a capitalist pattern but 'as an enclave of super-exploitation and racial privilege under the overall domination of imperialist capital' (Shivji 2009: 78). This has meant that 'settler agriculture is subsidised by semi-proletarian labour in the reserves and communal lands'. After independence, market-led land reforms led to the 'Kenyanisation' of land ownership but 'did not change the fundamental relationship or the pattern of disarticulated accumulation in agriculture. Racial privileges were replaced by ethnic preferences underwritten by the neo-colonial state' (Shivji 2009: 78). Accumulation by dispossession has been underpinned by accumulation by ethnicisation. As Shivji (2009: 77) notes, the aim of market-led land reforms in Kenya before independence (discussed in Chapter 2) was 'to create a yeoman farmer class, which would be the bulwark against radical change'. For Shivji this simply 'paved the way for the transition from colonialism to neo-colonialism ... it ethnicised the land question'. In Harvey's (2005) account of the evolution of capitalism in the present day, he argues that, as well as extracting surplus value as Marx recognised, there is also predatory practice in which naked plunder and theft take place. As the discussion of unlawful and irregular land appropriation in Chapter 3 suggests, this plunder transfers capital to a privileged few. But it is important to stress that there is a connection between plunder and the market itself, between primitive accumulation and accumulation through the market, between what is taken by force and what is acquired legitimately (Harrington and Manji 2013). This is the tenor of comments by Githongo on the notion of state capture in Kenya (which I have previously sought to explore by referring to the 'grabbed state' (Manji 2012)) – that we must recognise that corruption *is* in fact the economy (Githongo 2019)). I elaborate on this in Chapter 8.

'Ideologies of order' and the limits of law
This book develops a socio-legal analysis of the struggle for land and justice in Kenya. If its organising ideas have their starting point in law, I nonetheless draw on a range of disciplines (history, political science and literary studies) to develop critical perspectives on the long-running struggle for land and justice that continues to occupy Kenyans in the present day. The complexity of the land question defies analysis in any one disciplinary framework. No single disciplinary approach can alone adequately offer us understanding of the multi-faceted land arena as it has changed and evolved trans-historically. This book takes seriously Ghai and McAuslan's critique of narrow legal studies. (For the wider intellectual context for this critique see Loughlin 2017; McEldowney 2017). As Ghai (2017: 161) reminds us, in order 'to understand the dynamics and functions of constitutionalism, one has to uncover its social and economic bases, and thus transcend the formal boundaries of the law'. Readers seeking a guide to land law in the present book will be disappointed (many such excellent texts are available, notably Kariuki et al. 2016). Instead, this book seeks to explain the often difficult politics of land (law) reform in both the colonial state and its successor, showing the continuities between different eras of reform. Klug, in his account of constitutional reform in the post-apartheid era, tracing the conflicts and the eventual compromise that led to the property rights clause in the new Constitution, shows how that debate 'was substantially framed by the available intellectual resources' (2000: 124) that affected and constrained the choices of parties to the change. My aim in this book is similar. I am interested in the ways in which ideas get mobilised, for example, the ways in which demands for constitutional reform and land reform became harnessed to each other. But equally interesting are the limits and constraints that characterised the debate in these two critical spheres. What was not admitted into the debate and why? In this respect the present book builds on a longstanding interpretation I have adopted in studying land reform since I first began to write in this area in the late 1990s (see Manji 1998). Then, as now, I was interested as much in revealing what is left out of or unsaid in wider policy and legal debates as I was in explaining the direction that land law reform had taken.

Ten years after the inauguration of the new Constitution in 2010, which promised fundamentally to alter the structure of land relations, I show how these promises have become increasingly difficult to fulfil. I ask whether we have placed too much faith in law and in legal change, including in new institutions. Were strong land institutions perhaps the wrong answer to the right question, a question articulated by Kenyans when they demanded of the Constitution of Kenya Review Commission a way to resolve land inequality? In order to propose a way to assess the 2010s, I consider the Constitution not only as 'a formal law-text' (Modiri 2018: 305) but just as importantly as an artefact. Modiri (2018: 305) has written of the South African Constitution that it has embedded a 'hegemonic public grammar, political imaginary and a form of historical and social consciousness'. I am similarly interested in the politics of citation (Ahmed 2013) as it relates to the 2010 Constitution. What stories have we told about that document and its role in aspects of our national life? What does it mean to invoke the Land and Environment chapter of the Constitution (Chapter 5) in different fora such as the courts, the land registry or Land Ministry, or in everyday life? My concern is to take a critical look at the work the 2010 Constitution has done in the land arena.

This book is concerned with accumulation by dispossession and with struggles against exploitation. In his 2013 study, *Land Law Reform in Eastern Africa: Traditional or Transformative?*, McAuslan set out an encouragement to scholars to develop a justice framework for understanding land issues in the region. In doing so, he argued that there has been a marked reluctance of scholars of Eastern African land issues to confront questions of justice and fairness in relation to land. McAuslan did not mark out any particular discipline for this criticism, but he was in my view directing his comments in particular at legal scholars who, distracted by the technical and the ameliorative, had neglected – perhaps avoided – to engage with the wider political and theoretical questions evoked by land inequality historically and in the present day. McAuslan contrasted what he saw as the dominant Eastern African approach with South African scholarship in which writing about the African National Congress land reform programme, the constitutional provisions on land, and the future of urban planning had manifestly committed to using a justice framework. He argued that what was needed in Eastern Africa was a 'transformative' rather than a merely 'traditional' approach to property. In making this argument, McAuslan was building on van der Walt's (2009) study, developed through a painstaking analysis of property doctrine and change in South Africa, that 'traditional notions of property do not suffice in transformational contexts, where the foundations of the property regime itself are or should be in question' (2009: 15). According to van der Walt, opportunities sometimes present themselves to 'rethink … the system …

the language, the concepts, the rhetoric and the logic' (ibid.) of the existing property regime. At these moments, the status quo property rules are 'stretched to the limit ... in the sense that they do not function "normally"' (ibid.: 21). At the time he was writing, van der Walt's analysis was based on the opportunity that seemed to be provided by a moment of revolutionary change, the break with the status quo constituted by the end of apartheid. His aim was to call into question the 'validity and justifiability of mainstream legal dogma from the unfamiliar vantage point of the margins' (ibid.: 23) and in so doing challenge the basis for accepted norms.

In my view, McAuslan was not entirely correct in claiming that land issues have not been framed in transformative terms in East Africa, or that justice has not been at the fore in land discussions. On the contrary, the very name given to the Mau Mau – the Land and Freedom Army – signals how intimately land and justice have been connected in Kenyan history. It would be more accurate to attempt to record, as I want to do here, how attempts to frame land as justice have been repeatedly and concertedly trumped at every stage. Marked by domination and exclusion from the start, with its roots in settler-colonial priorities, the heavy work of presenting Kenyan land issues in a justice framework has been attempted repeatedly, been defeated, evolved and attempted again. This book is in part concerned with tracing these efforts.

To do this, I build on van der Walt's suggestive framework, at once adopting and adapting it to cast a critical eye over our approaches to land questions in Kenya. I *adopt* a similar approach in that I too wish to question what is revealed when we ask questions about land relations, land reform and land inequality, paying special attention to notions of justice and fairness. How does the history of land in modern Kenya look when it is seen through a justice lens? And what have been the implications of failing to frame land questions explicitly in terms of justice, if indeed this is what we find to be the case? I *adapt* the McAuslan / van der Walt framework in that the analysis offered in this book does not hinge on studying a sudden break or a challenge to the status quo. Instead, in the Kenyan context, we can describe a slow, painful grinding to a halt of property institutions, rules and norms. In Chapter 3, I show how, 'stretched to the limit' over time by improper use and by neglect, neither legal dogma nor legal institutions any longer function 'normally' (van der Walt 2009: 21).

This book is concerned with both continuity and change in the politics of Kenyan land reform. Perhaps the most significant characteristic of the most recent wave of land reform is the emphasis on the institutions of land governance. As I show in the next chapter, solutions to dissatisfaction with land were, in the past, redistributive in either practice (land consolidation and resettlement), intent (the Million Acre Scheme) or rhetoric (for example in the Moi era). Although redistribution was only limited, failed to happen in practice or was subverted by the ruling elite for personal enrichment, land could and did change hands in the immediate pre-independence and post-independence period. By contrast, redistribution of land is nowhere on the political agenda in the present day. Instead, the emphasis is on the architecture of land governance. This is not to say that the institutions of land governance have not in the past been the loci of debate and struggle. As Harbeson (1971) shows, the constitution drawn up at the Lancaster House Conference in 1962 sought to put in place a protective architecture in which Central Land Boards were given sole control over settlement programme areas. Designed to protect the interests of European settlers and smaller communities fearful of encroachment by central government, the Central Land Board was the regional institution that would insulate and protect the settlement schemes (ibid.). Their independence from central government would, European settlers thought, protect their interests and their predominant concern not to be prevented from achieving 'the full value of the land they wished so badly to sell' (ibid.: 155). The ruling party, the Kenya African National Union (KANU) moved quickly to challenge this purported autonomy: hard on the heels of the Lancaster House Conference it created a separate Ministry of Land Resettlement and Water Development in a move which Harbeson (2012) argues was a strong signal of its intention firmly to control matters. (I elaborate on this in Chapter 2).

But whereas in the past institutional change was envisaged in tandem with significant changes in the control and ownership of land, in the present-day debates over 'getting the institutions right' (Boone et al. 2019: 215) trump wider considerations, effectively suppressing redistributive demands by focusing on technicist and ameliorative changes to land governance architecture. Redistribution in this model is best left to market imperatives. Instead, the focus is on an institutional response to past injustices: Kenya's political reconstruction took the form of what Klug (2000: 119) described in the context of South Africa's constitution-making process as 'a plethora of institutional checks and balances' which 'attempt to fragment state power'. By reforming the structures of land institutions, the argument went, you will create a more transparent, efficient and fair system of land governance. I show that in Kenya's national context this approach to reforming land relations was not as radical a political project as it was perceived to be by those promoting a national land policy and the anchoring of land issues in the new Constitution in the form of a land and environment chapter. Instead, it remained rooted in what Atieno-Odhiambo (1987) has described as Kenya's 'ideology of order' which has held political order as the highest priority, and which was not overturned by but in fact survived the democratic transition. This points to a contradiction in Kenya's use of law for political reconstruction. According to Teitel

(1997) the role of law in political transformation is paradoxical because it is required both to guarantee order and to bring about transformation (Klug 2000). The aim of this book is to show how the desire to navigate order/transformation has affected approaches to land and severely circumscribed the terms of the land debate.

More broadly, I argue that the institutional-legal approach described above must be understood in the broader global context. Since the 1990s, international financial institutions and bilateral donors have embraced law reform as a means to address a range of land issues such that, in international policy prescriptions, land reform is often equated with legal reform. A number of Eastern African countries preceded Kenya in initiating reviews of their land laws and national land policies: Tanzania, Uganda, Mozambique, Rwanda, Somaliland, South Sudan and Zanzibar all introduced new laws from 1990 in what McAuslan called 'the era of land law reform' (2013: 46). Atieno-Odhiambo (2002: 225) argued that, as well as national political culture, we must also attend to global contexts and to the 'theatre of world citizenship, which links the individual and the state to an international discourse on democracy'. Klug (2000: 2) takes a similar approach, arguing that we need to study 'the emergence and development of an international imperative of rights' as well as pre-existing legal context, culture and struggles. In accounting for the rise of legal reform, including new constitutions around the world since the 1990s, he describes a 'globalizing constitutionalism' (ibid.) which emphasises a strong legal framework, including a justiciable constitution, as central to political reconstruction. Today, at the global level, rule-of-law reform has institutional change – which Ackerman (1997) describes as a desire to put limits on on the exercise of political power – at its heart. In the land arena, there is an abiding belief that if you get the institutions right, you will perforce address the land wrongs before you. I show that this has been the predominant spirit of modern-day land reform in Kenya.

My interest in the reasons for this institutional focus, and its limitations, informs the approach I adopt. I focus on the architecture of land administration in Kenya in the present day in order to show how it has been reformed and what was intended by these reforms. This means that I am attentive to the disciplinary functions being performed by institutions of land governance, the institutions on which Kenyans rely to do the work of administering land. If early land reform efforts in Kenya in the 1940s and 1950s 'contemplated economic answers to what were in large measure political and social problems of [tenure] insecurity' (Harbeson 1971: 236) and so advocated land consolidation, I argue that modern land reform purports to provide *legal* answers to what remain political and social problems relating to land. Legal solutions and legal institutions are 'front and centre' (Kennedy 2003: 18). Evidence of this is not difficult to find. The term 'land administration and management' is ubiquitous in current policy prescriptions (Republic of Kenya 2009c) and in the law. It appears repeatedly in both constitutional and statutory provisions. Important examples include Articles 62 and 67 of the Constitution of Kenya 2010; Section 5 of the National Land Commission Act 2012; and Section 8 of the Land Act 2012. But despite the ubiquity of this term, the precise meaning of land 'administration and management' is nowhere elaborated. How the architecture of land governance should look and what should be the roles and responsibilities of its various institutions turns out to be one of the great questions at the heart of modern land reform in Kenya. This question came to the Supreme Court in 2014. The court was asked to set out an advisory opinion to clarify the shape of Kenya's land management institutions. As I show in Chapter 6, intra-institutional wrangling has characterised the years since new land laws were passed in 2012, with the courts sometimes called upon to adjudicate.

How have these institutions functioned, or not? In this book, I study a number of key institutions past and present. Each has played intertwined roles in the administration and management of land. Some of them are longstanding and have endured, some have had only short lives, some have evolved in structure and purpose over time. As regards survival, Kenyan land institutions can be set along a spectrum: some show remarkable endurance, others last for only a short time. At one end of the institutional spectrum, the Ministry for Land is the supreme example of an institution with an audacious ability to survive. It has gathered to itself significant powers and responsibilities over land. With tenacity, it has endured as an institution despite widespread public distrust and a widely known record of corruption and irregular dealings. In contrast, an example of a Kenyan land institution which failed before it had begun properly to function is the Country Land Management Boards which, created under the Land Act 2012, lasted four years before being disbanded by the Land Law Amendment Act 2016. Similarly, the likelihood of the National Land Commission surviving and thriving in its role as an independent land governance institution is difficult to predict. Created in 2012 and mandated by the 2010 Constitution, it has had a tumultuous youth. The ability of a land institution to endure or not, however, tells us little about the functioning and effectiveness of that institution. Indeed, the example of the Land Ministry suggests that longevity and proper functioning are inversely related. Known for its inefficiency, corruption and propensity to manipulation, the Land Ministry and its registry survive but do not thrive. Studying the institutions charged with administering and managing land in Kenya, we can trace the politics of land and the ongoing struggle for land justice.

One of the aims of this book is to move beyond what, during the 2010s, has become a convention of the legal academy and of commentators on

Kenya's Constitution. This is the tendency to view it as a reified legal text to be cited, evoked and deployed as a shield. In relation to land, my task is to ask what work the Constitution has done for and on society in that decade. By reference to critical race theory, settler-colonial studies and African jurisprudence, Modiri (2018) has warned that, in the wake of the ratification of new constitutions, we need to guard against being lulled by what Nkosi (2016: 255 cited in Modiri 2018: 302) has termed 'false narrative of "national transcendence"' (see also Mutua 1997). Instead, Modiri urges us to ask how a constitution 'embeds particular cultural and ideological values into its fold and as such works to consolidate and preserve particular arrangements and relations of power and knowledge' (2018: 305). Modiri's project as he articulates it here shares similar concerns with this book. My approach is to ask: why have we opted for law and in particular legal institutions as a solution to long-standing land problems and what might be the consequences of opting for these institutions as a bulwark against the land wrongs with which we are concerned? Writing of South Africa's post-apartheid history, the Comaroffs (2004) have described 'a country in the grip of a pervasive culture of constitutionalism, legality and rights' (quoted in Modiri 2018: 307). As we approach a decade since the inauguration of the Constitution of Kenya 2010, it is important to identify similar tendencies and sensibilities in ourselves and to ask what might be foreclosed by such an approach. To what extent have we come to rely on the courts and on 'litigation and the judiciary as sites of democratic social change' (ibid.: 311). As Modiri argues forcefully, we need to query how far we have succeeded in using law to bring about the 'decommodification of basic necessities and redistribution of resources' (ibid.: 325).

This book is concerned with understanding different framings of the meaning and importance of land and, in particular, different claims for epistemological and ontological justice in relation to land. The tendency of legal scholars to view land law as a branch of private law has inhibited our understanding of this (and deeply marks the way the subject is taught in law schools) (but cf. Okoth-Ogendo 2002; and the assessments of his scholarship contained in Kameri-Mbote and Odote 2017). A private law model of land law dominates scholarship and policy making. Rooted in an economistic model, it sees land predominantly as a marketable commodity (McAuslan 2013). In this model, the role of law is to facilitate the market and to guarantee the rights of the individual to own and control land. Statutory law is designed with this aim in mind. Marketability and alienability of land is front and centre. Set against this liberal legal approach is a model that views land as part of social relations (McAuslan 2013). Law (often in the shape of customary law) is concerned with protecting the users and occupiers of land. With entirely different philosophical bases, these two models of land can nonetheless co-exist. Indeed, as McAuslan (2013) pointed out, they co-existed in English land law. Although the 1925 reforms were aimed at guaranteeing marketability and 'a commodity approach to land in the market economy' (McAuslan 2013: 5–6; see also Bhandar 2018), McAuslan suggests an older philosophy, which regarded the protection of occupiers and users of land as most important, nonetheless sometimes breaks the surface of the law. McAuslan reads both case law and some legislative changes since that time as attempts to prioritise users and occupiers of land. He provides the examples of equitable estoppel (a doctrine that can prevent someone from going back on their word), and of constructive trusts, deserted wives equity, the protection of mortgagors, and case law on the protection of the family home (Manji 2017a) as areas in which 'this older philosophy of protection of the user, a philosophy with roots going back hundreds of years' can be glimpsed. McAuslan urges us to acknowledge the existence – and importantly, the co-existence – of these two approaches. He does so in order to argue that whereas a private law model of land law has been allowed to predominate in our teaching, research and analyses (see Manji and Ouma 2019), it is time to recognise the crucial role of public law in this domain, to recognise the existence of 'land law as public law' (McAuslan 2003: 255) where:

> the allodial title to land is vested in either the state, the President (Tanzania), the Nation (Lesotho), or even a National Land Commission (Ghana); this means that the citizen has to obtain land from the state or its organs, with state officials managing the land as landlords or trustees … In cases such as these, land law ceases to be a matter of private law, but becomes part of public law; it is in fact administrative law. (ibid.)

Sing'oei made a similar observation in his analysis of the pre-2010 classification of land as trust land:

> Under Kenyan law, property in trust land is vested in a public body, to wit, County Councils, subject to the beneficial ownership of communities 'ordinarily resident' in the land. This implies that trust lands under Kenyan law (before the adoption of the new Constitution 2010) are quasi-public in character. (2011: 519)

I return to this point in the discussion of historical land injustices and of indigenous peoples' land struggles in Chapter 7.

This book extends McAuslan's analysis, which is primarily aimed at making the case for using the guiding principles of administrative law when drafting land laws, to the history and politics of land in Kenya. I read land struggles within this private law/public law framework. I argue that, before independence and after it, land politics has been about which model of land law will predominate in public policy, in legal practice and in public perception. By this I mean that a private law / public model of land law can be used as a lens through which to understand vastly differing and indeed opposed philosophical and practical approaches to land. As I argued above, for some Kenyans, land is a marketable commodity, to be traded and owned anywhere and by anyone, a critical factor of production that should be underpinned by strong private laws guaranteeing individual rights, including use, enjoyment and sale. For others, land has deeper ontological meaning. Community, tradition and history are connected to the land, spatially and temporally. Laws to protect this must also guard against lands alienability and tradability. This conception of land requires a public law framework: it relies on land being vested in communities or in trustees, governed by customary laws and focused on the prioritisation of use and occupation.

What is the empirical extent of land governed by this public law framework in Kenya? If we accept that administrative law governs all land not held under private title but held instead in trust by public officials, then administrative law is the right framework for understanding two of the three land classifications in Kenya: public land and community land. As I show in Chapter 3, it is these categories of land that have most suffered from 'grabbing', the word commonly used to describe the illegal and irregular allocation of land by the state, by politicians and by well-connected individuals (Klopp 2000; Southall 2005). According to Alden Wily (2018b) we can estimate the extent of community lands by deducting private and public land from the overall area of the country to reach the conclusion that community land probably encompasses up to 60 per cent of Kenya and that this land lies largely in twenty-one of the forty-seven counties. The Constitution at Article 63 defines community lands as including those registered in the name of group representatives (group ranches); lawfully transferred to a specific community or declared to be community land by an Act of Parliament; lawfully held, managed or used by specific communities as community forests, grazing areas or shrines; ancestral lands and lands traditionally occupied by hunter-gatherer communities; and land lawfully held as trust land by the county governments (trust lands).

According to Alden Wily (2018b) the community land sector is unique in being made up largely of resources that have hitherto been neglected in analyses of property relations, such as forests, rangelands and swamplands. She notes that most community land is located in the dry northern half of Kenya, which is occupied mostly by pastoralists. This is where the largest areas of former trust lands are located. She points out that a rough estimate of the number of people on community lands is somewhere between 6 and 10 million people (which amounts to 20 per cent of the estimated total population of Kenya in 2017). Alden Wily shows in her work that it is ancestral lands and lands traditionally occupied by hunter-gatherer communities, and also land lawfully held as trust land by the county governments (trust lands) that are

likely to give rise to contests between communities and state authorities claiming control over them. State authorities will seek to argue
that they are in fact public property. There is therefore a strong imperative to register community land as a way to ensure that this valuable
resource is protected. This is especially the case as public land becomes
a scarcer resource due to land grabbing. This will increase the attrac-
tiveness and value of plentiful community land and lead to skirmishes
with the state as it tries to assert that the land in question is in fact not
community land but public land which it should control (Alden Wily
2018b).

Alden Wily's analysis suggests that the struggle over land in this
tenure regime – community land – will in the future be to some extent
a definitional struggle. This will take place at the point of adjudication.
By this I mean that it will entail the state arguing that a given piece
of land – often of significant size – is public land, and communities
countering that that land is in fact community land. A good example is
ancestral lands and land on which hunter-gatherer communities live.
Here, the state has always been bent on internal colonisation, claiming
control over land on which forest dwellers rely. Similarly, following
devolution, battle has been joined between the national and devolved
county governments over some areas of land historically held as trust
land by the latter. This trust land is considered by the state to be public
land over which it has control. Before the ink was dry on the Community Land Act of 2016 the definitional struggle had begun. This struggle
is not semantic or technical. It is one that will have a significant impact
on communities and their land over the coming years.

Struggle
My choice of the word struggle in connection with the politics of land in
Kenya is deliberate. In using it, I wish both to recognise the importance
in Kenyan history of the struggle for *Uhuru* – freedom – and to draw
on a rich seam of Kenyan historiography concerned with how ideas of
justice and fairness are constantly contested, not least by those who
'have continually urged the politics of vision as an attainable reality
within our lifetimes' (Atieno-Odhiambo 1995: 1). In his essay *The
Invention of Kenya*, Atieno-Odhiambo argues that one of the tasks of
the post-colonial historian of Kenya has been to forge a new history,
one which 'had to be invented, assembled together, arranged around
the metaphor of struggle' (ibid.: 2). I set out to write this book with a
similar idea in mind. How to assemble and bring together in one place
an account of struggles for land and justice in Kenya? What have been
these struggles since independence and what forms have they taken
(policy, political and legal)?

Writing specifically about the land domain, Cliffe (2001) offered a
typology of land struggles which provides a helpful frame for under-

standing the overlapping and multi-faceted ways in which access to land, land rights, land policy and land politics have been contested since independence. Cliffe provides a five-part description of overlapping struggles. The first he describes as 'the ceaseless daily and seasonal struggle for livelihoods' (ibid.: 10). Smallholder agriculture remains a significant part of daily life outside the city (Hornsby 2013) and women, small farmers and others are engaged in daily struggles to derive their livelihoods from this form of work, sometimes diversifying out of farming to access other forms of income to petty trading or casual labour (ibid.: 2001).

The second broader struggle identified by Cliffe (2011: 10) relates to property rights more specifically and concerns the 'struggles by households and communities to obtain access to land and to define systems and procedures for so doing'. This part of the typology is concerned with definitions of land rights, with struggles over tenure rules. Here we might think about changing approaches to types of land tenure, for example community land, or about how groups have used the courts to assert claims to land. This category we might label legal struggles over land.

Cliffe's third category concerns struggles over the politics of land. Here, he is concerned with

> 'Struggle' in the sense of the Swahili word for it (*siasa*) ... 'politics'. The 'politics of land' has covered two different kinds of contestation over land: those between and within communities, and those that have been part of a liberation struggle. (2001: 10)

The nature of this struggle is 'political mobilisation of people in the fight for land' and can range from struggles for liberation and against racial injustice (struggle 'on a grand scale') or take the form of 'low key, on-going tension between communities' (ibid.). As Hornsby has pointed out, the idea of communal land rights still has a powerful hold over the imagination of Kenyans: 'the idea of land as the specific entitlement of one ethnic community remains strong' (2013: 800). But I would also include here struggles to defend land, from land grabbing and other corrupt practices for example.

Fourth, Cliffe refers to struggles over the process of policy making which requires us to consider debates over such matters as land reform, rules of land tenure and redistribution. Finally, Cliffe is concerned with what he calls 'contending perceptions and models about land' and 'false conceptualisations, like the assumption that transfer of land from commercial, large-scale to African smallholder production is always a retrograde step' (2001: 10).

This book is concerned to some degree with each of these intertwined types of struggle. Its starting point is an exploration of struggles over the making of land law and policy – essentially struggle over the nature and purpose of land law reform (land struggles from above). But I am equally concerned with struggle 'on a grand scale' as Cliffe (2001: 10) puts it, and this book will explore the political mobilisations that have taken place around land since independence, most prominently the struggles of a varied range of civil society groups to resist land corruption and continually to guard against land mischiefs (land struggles from below).

History, sources, archives

Much of what we know about the sedimented history of land in Kenya we owe to formal archives. These archives are made up in large part by official reports directly on land and also reports primarily about other matters, but which are closely tied up with land issues and so raise and record them. Together these reports have, over time, become assembled into an archive. The practice of their regular citation by Kenyans keeps that archive – which Stoler (2002: 87) is at pains to emphasise is not a thing or a place but a practice – accessible. These reports are often cited in strikingly similar ways: at the opening of a paper, a newspaper article, a law case, they are mentioned serially and in neat temporal order. Kenyan's incantation of the Ndung'u report (Chapter 3), the Truth, Justice, and Reconciliation Commission (TJRC)'s report (Chapter 3) and so on has become almost ritualistic. Set out in this way they give authority to what is about to be said by invoking a political and legal folk memory, but in turn they cement the place of the reports as authoritative, official archive. In this regard, they may serve less as source (Stoler 2002) than as a reminder to the reader or listener of 'law's memorial function' (Motha and van Rijswijk 2016: 1). That memorial function is summed up in the words of the TJRC's report's self-referential opening:

> This is a Report. It is written with words and printed on paper or converted into electronic bits and bytes. Yet it is the product of, in some cases literally, the blood, sweat and tears of the stories that were told to us as we travelled the country. (TJRC Report, Chapter 1, Vol 1, note 9 pp. iii–iv)

In this book I rely on a series of reports documenting land wrongs as the official archive of the land mischiefs committed by the state, politicians and the elite. Thus, in Chapter 3 I draw on a longstanding and authoritative archive of official reports to explore the land grabbing, dispossession, irregular land dealing and land-related violence which Kenyans have endured, and which have been visited on them with great regularity by a predatory state. Acts of sovereign violence and the consequences for ordinary citizens are available to us to read in these reports. But the long history of state attempts to block the publication of reports (Kenya Human Rights Commission – henceforth KHRC – 2011) or to redact their content (Slye 2018) also points us to contestations over archives. They are a reminder to view archives not as things but as practice and process (Stoler 2002: 87). The struggle to have reports released and to see them published has been the valiant business of civil society (the composition of which is discussed in Chapter 4) since independence. The publication of the Ndung'u report and the intrigue and delay surrounding the release of the TJRC report are just two instances of contestation over official reports that have come in time to memorialise land and other truths. In the process of struggling for access to these reports, civil society has been able to ensure that a vibrant citizen's archive came into being in which content, persona and implications are richly debated and become the stuff of an everyday 'radio trottoir' (Ellis 1989: 321).

In Chapter 3, I consider the effects of this 'counter-archive' (Motha and van Rijswijk 2016: 1) which we might describe as constituting the peoples' memorial function. I argue that we need to pay attention to our 'counter-archival sense' (ibid.: 8) in relation to land. We should ask: what roles do stories and rumours play in developing counter-hegemonic accounts and in creating a peoples' archive on land? Musila (2017) has written perceptively about the difficulties we confront when doing research on issues 'framed by multiple epistemic regimes' (2017: 694). She makes the case for rumour as 'an influential genre of knowledge production, contestation and critique ... what has been termed a form of "community intelligence" – that challenges single-lens conceptions of credible knowledge' (ibid.: 695). Musila urges us to excavate 'the place of rumour as an important genre of social truths that enjoy epistemic authority' (ibid.). I suggest that an unstable, porous archive made up of subaltern narratives supplements official reports on land grabbing. In a state designed by and for a 'propertariat' (Baxi 1985: 112), how might law reformers and the courts adjudicating on land issues be put into conversation with this counter-archive?

Overview and structure

In Chapter 2, I provide an intellectual history of the idea of land reform in Kenya. If land issues have been the cause of both simmering discontent and violent conflict throughout Kenya's colonial and post-colonial history as scholars including Ogot (1976) and Okoth-Ogendo (2002) recognised, these problems nonetheless defy easy description. Kenya's land issues are complex and multi-faceted but we can say with certainty that they have resulted in massive and worsening inequalities in access to resources. A deep-running inclination to land grabbing and personal accumulation have characterised modern Kenya. There are continuing conflicts over who is and who is not entitled to occupy land. Chapter 2 is an attempt to locate present-day debates about land reform in the long arc of Kenya's land history since independence. My aim is to historicise our present debates. This is necessary if we are to confront existing patchy knowledge of the historical context within which current debates are located. The chapter seeks to present a history of ideas by asking: what has land reform meant at different times and to different people?

In Chapter 3, Making Mischief: Land in Modern Kenya, I set out to explore the multi-faceted land problems that have been experienced since independence in order to show what are the many land mischiefs with which land reform – when it returned to the political agenda from 2000 – was concerned. I draw on the work of political scientists to argue that official reports document the many wrongs associated with land and that Kenya thus possesses a powerful but neglected land archive built up over many years. This archive, I argue, is scattered and fractured but if brought together in one place by our analyses, it can constitute an important source of information about the many mischiefs associated with land. I show that Kenyans expended considerable labour in maintaining an informal archive about land mischiefs: the many wrongs associated with land can be traced, too, through attention to these stories from the margins. I explore the role of what I describe as Kenya's 'land rumours' in creating and sustaining a living 'land archive' that plays an important role in the public's imagination, knowledge and demands about land injustice. If Wasserman's (1976) cutting observation that, in the immediate post-independence period, land was the opium of the masses has been proven correct in the intervening years (not least as each election cycle reaches its peak), it is important not to overlook both the history and the contemporary evidence of significant challenges to this from the margins. I explore struggles over the legal protection to be afforded to community land. I argue that, although there has been progress in recognising the endurance and effectiveness of this form of tenure, land held in this category is endangered and future struggles over its preservation will be important. Community land is the one domain in which transformative land relations can be seen to have occurred in the 2010s. Here, ideas of what is suitable and modern as a form of land tenure have shifted: since 1990 we have gone from international and national land policy prescriptions which deprecated community land to ones in which such tenure regimes are seen as valuable, workable and indeed desirable. I argue that community land is the new battleground in Kenya's land politics. Public land – previously a plentiful resource and one available to powerful elites to use as a patronage resource – has been exhausted. The patronage machine's hunger for land now seeks to be satisfied in new ways. Law and other disciplines need to be alert to the fact that community land will be the new ground on which much of Kenya's land politics will be played out over the next decade.

In Chapter 4, I show how land reform and constitutional change came to be intricately connected in Kenya. I explore Kenya's elongated process of constitutional reform and pay particular attention to the demands made in relation to land (what the people told the Constitution of Kenya Review Commission in relation to land (Supreme Court Advisory Opinion No. 2 of 2014: para. 82); and see Constitution of Kenya Review Commission – hereafter CKRC – Final Report: 270–71, 279, 280, 284). I draw on historical and legal accounts of this period to show how reform in the land arena became a marker for the wider success of the 2010 Constitution and argue that there are some dangers inherent in this. Disillusionment with progress on land matters risks becoming more widely associated with constitutional disappointment. I argue that the anchoring of land in the Constitution should not lull us into overlooking the structural harm done in the land arena by colonialism and its successors in the post-independence period. I argue that as we reach the anniversary of the Katiba Constitution, we must not be compelled by 'constitutional optimism' (Modiri 2018: 325) to overlook this. A clear-sighted assessment of the last decade in the land arena demands instead that we are 'cognisant of the limits and limitations of the law in bringing about decommodification of basic necessities, redistribution of resources' (ibid.: 324).

Chapter 5 explores the new architecture of land governance envisaged by the reforms of 2009–17. I discuss the most important elements of the institutional architecture of land that has been constructed through the law and provide an assessment of their workings and prospects. I assess the idea of devolved institutions of land governance as a key change produced by the modern land reform movement and show the extent to which it has been driven by an 'ideology of order' (Atieno-Odhiambo 1987: 1). I show that, to date, the ambitious experiment to devolve land administration has had a patchy record, and that a powerful recentralising tendency can be discerned.

In Chapter 6, I explore in further detail the politics of the National Land Commission. I argue that institutional change was initiated which it was hoped would ameliorate Kenya's longstanding problem of unclear, overlapping and contradictory land governance. More particularly, I discuss the creation of the National Land Commission. As I show in Chapter 2, the idea of an independent body to manage public land was contained in the report of the 1999 Njonjo Commission. The Commission recommended that public land should be held in trust and managed by a body it called a National Land Authority. Radical title to such land should be vested in the National Land Authority. The idea of such a body entered the National Land Policy in 2009 and, as Chapter 4 demonstrates, was a key demand in the constitutional review process, by which time the label National Land Commission had been adopted. The long-awaited body came into existence in the National Land Commission Act 2012. Drawing on both political science and legal analyses, I show that significant hope was invested in the National Land Commission: as an independent constitutional commission, it was hoped that it would be an institutional challenge to the centralised corruption of the Land Ministry. I provide a detailed analysis of the Supreme Court's intervention when in 2014 it had an opportunity to discuss the role of the National Land Commission vis à vis the Ministry for Lands. This important analysis by the Supreme Court, which it was keen to stress was of a binding rather than a merely advisory nature (Supreme Court Advisory Opinion No. 2 of 2014: para. 316), will have important implications for the management and administration of land.

In Chapter 7 I explore the promise of the new Constitution to address longstanding grievances over land. To do this I study the term 'historical land injustices' which has firmly entered Kenya's constitutional lexicon. Both the National Land Policy 2009 and the 2010 Constitution (see Article 67(1)(e)) use the term to assert the connection between land and justice. The report of the Truth Justice and Reconciliation Commission (2013) provides perhaps the best illustration of the links made between land issues and claims to justice, although the term 'historical land injustice' does not appear in the legislation creating the Commission. I argue that through its repeated use by activists and campaigners for constitutional reform and human rights, the term has become part of the everyday language of politics. The National Land Commission is responsible for initiating investigations into and responding to complaints about historical land injustices and is charged with recommending appropriate redress. The new laws passed in 2012 (the National Land Commission Act as amended through the Land Laws Amendment Act 2016) provide a framework for this. I argue that we must be alert to the interaction of historical and present-day land injustices and to the ways in which the economy of land grabbing and corruption and the regular economy have come to be intricately connected, such that it is surely right to speak in the present day of 'a grabbed state' (Manji 2014) or, as is becoming increasingly common, of 'state capture' (Maina 2019). I argue that the struggle for land and justice must confront the ways in which the irregular and the regular economy interact.

I conclude in Chapter 8 with an assessment of the future prospects for land and justice in modern Kenya. Bringing together the book's interdisciplinary insights, I argue that, whilst land professionals have been concerned with developing and making effective a new architecture of land governance, a significant movement from the margins has kept up considerable pressure on land issues. They have inherited the mantle of earlier, radical movements that, in the immediate post-independence period, had challenged a conservative elite on land issues (Bates 1989). Harbeson (2012) is surely right to argue that it was the work of an autochthonous civil society, not international pressure, that bore fruit in the National Land Policy and the constitutional provisions on land. In Kenya, and more widely across the continent, the enactment of new land laws cannot be understood apart from these wider political and sometimes constitutional struggles. Land can be understood as a significant category around which progressive struggles have been – and will continue to be – organised. In contrast to Hornsby's bleak assessment that 'Kenya's land policy has failed' (2013: 800), I try to recoup the role that land struggles have played in wider political and constitutional struggles since independence, and argue that these land struggles have been an integral part of what Atieno-Odhiambo characterised as 'African struggles for civil liberties, human rights, democratic participation, workers' rights, peasant independence, spiritual space, elective representation and civic responsibility' (1995: 2).

2

Land Reform in Kenya: The History of an Idea[1]

The history of land reform is as long as the history of the world, extending back into medieval, ancient and biblical times. (Tuma 1965: 3)

The Kenyan political story over the past century has been one of a rapid march from the creation of the conquest state, to its high noon of settler ascendancy during the interwar years, to the deep colonial crisis precipitating the Mau Mau war between 1952 and 1956. This was followed by the brief period of mass nationalisms between 1957 and independence in 1963, which was succeeded by a contested statehood whose future continues to be uncertain. (Atieno-Odhiambo 2002: 225)

Introduction: The long arc

Land issues have been the cause of both simmering discontent and violent conflict throughout Kenya's colonial and post-colonial history (Ogot 1976; Okoth-Ogendo 1975). They remain a 'key fault line' in modern Kenya (Hornsby 2013: 787). Historians of Kenya and commentators on her politics continue to find patrimonialism, ethnic favouritism and corruption at play, nowhere more so than in the politics of land. Kenya's problems with land defy easy description: they remain complex and multi-faceted and include massive and worsening inequalities in access to land, a propensity to land grabbing and continuing conflicts over who is and who is not entitled to occupy land. Efforts to address these problems have since before independence been erratic at best. This chapter is an attempt to study present-day efforts at land reform in the long arc of Kenya's land history since independence.

This chapter seeks to place modern-day debates in the context of Kenya's long history of land reform. My aim is to historicise them. There

[1] An earlier draft of this chapter was presented as the 6th Annual CB Madan Memorial Lecture, Strathmore Law School, Nairobi, in December 2018.

are two reasons why I think this is an important task. First, it is in part my response to what I perceive to be the existing patchy knowledge of the historical context within which we are debating contemporary land reform. A concrete illustration of this is the common occurrence of lawyers and others such as activists and journalists citing key reports of commissions of inquiry by name but rarely elaborating on their content. The practice of listing the names of critical inquiries touching on or centrally concerned with land matters has become commonplace. It is a practice of incantation. But this bare form of citation has substituted for detailed discussions of the history of land debates and reform proposals in Kenya. It limits our knowledge. Most analyses provide only partial accounts of longstanding pressures for a constitutional response to land problems (but see the accounts provided in Lumumba 2017 and Kanyinga 2017).

A second, more positive reason to rehearse the history of land reform as an idea is a recent statement by the Supreme Court which expresses a desire, and indeed a need, to understand the country's history. In an important judgment on land issues handed down in 2014 (and discussed in Chapter 6), the Supreme Court argued that there is a 'need for a historical and cultural perspective when interpreting the Constitution' because it is only by this means that it can fulfil its mandate set out in Section 3 of the Supreme Court Act, 2011 (Act No. 7 of 2011) to 'develop rich jurisprudence that respects Kenya's history and traditions and facilitates its social, economic and political growth' and to 'enable important constitutional and other legal matters, including matters relating to the transition from the former to the present constitutional dispensation, to be determined having due regard to the circumstances, history and cultures of the people of Kenya' (Supreme Court Advisory Opinion No. 2 of 2014: para. 97). The Supreme Court, alert to its own legal history, here makes a commitment to bring history to bear in its decisions. In so doing it draws on an earlier Advisory Opinion in which the Chief Justice sought to elaborate on his understanding of Section 3 of the Supreme Court Act 2011:

> In my opinion, this provision grants the Supreme Court a near-limitless and substantially-elastic interpretive power. It allows the Court to explore interpretive space in the country's history and memory that, in my view, goes even beyond the minds of the framers whose product, and appreciation of the history and circumstance of the people of Kenya, may have been constrained by the politics of the moment. (Sup. Ct. Advisory Opinion Reference No. 2 of 2013: para. 157)

If 2002 marked the beginning of a period of intense debate and pressure over land reform, it must also be understood as the return of an idea to the political agenda. In one way or another, land reform has had its advocates in Kenya since as long ago as 1920. Indeed, land has often been the lens through which historians, political scientists and latterly lawyers, not to mention economists and students of development, have sought to understand the country's fraught politics and to propose solutions to its perceived ills. In this chapter, I seek to show the significant continuities that today's politics of land reform share with the past and, equally importantly, to distinguish past debates and perspective from present-day efforts. As such, this chapter uncovers the history of an idea. Mutating, evolving, turning back on itself, the idea of land reform has meant different things at different times and to different people. Its tenacity as a key idea in Kenyan history is beyond doubt.

As in the past, the struggles for land reform and for political and constitutional settlement – or reform – have been intricately related. Telling the story of land reform debates in Kenya leads us inevitably onto the ground of demands for political and constitutional change, including decolonisation. In its most recent phase, which dates from around 2002 and the inauguration of the Kibaki Government, land reform came explicitly onto the political agenda for the first time since independence. The findings of the 2004 report of the Commission of Inquiry into Illegal and Irregular Allocation of Land (popularly known after its chairperson as the Ndung'u report) brought into sharper focus widespread and multi-faceted grievances that had nonetheless remained unarticulated in Kenyan official and public life (although not in the everyday talk of Kenyans whose 'radio trottoir' or pavement radio (Ellis 1989: 321; see also White 2000) had long known and talked of wrongs associated with land). The Ndung'u report directed and gave shape to land-related anger. Its publication was an impetus for change, but the articulation of what we might call its 'land truths' was alone not enough to bring such change about. Only with the violence and upheaval of the 2007 election did significant pressure from civil society result in an official commitment to look again at Kenya's land grievances (Harbeson 2012; Republic of Kenya 2008).

The National Land Policy was agreed in 2009 after sustained pressure by civil society groups (Klopp and Lumumba 2017). Long suppressed questions of land injustice – barely able to be articulated for the first thirty years of independence during which dissenting voices (on land and on much else) were quieted by authoritarianism – slowly took shape in this progressive and rather utopian policy document. As I show in Chapter 3, the struggles of civil society and citizen engagement from the margins had created a rich but informal archive that had carefully recorded and remembered the injustice associated with land. In time, as the arc of Kenya's history bent towards what was widely called her second liberation (Mutunga 1999), this informal archive had a profound influence on the process of negotiating, drafting and agreeing the National Land Policy. In the aftermath of its publication, Kenya enshrined the Land and Environment chapter in the new

Constitution inaugurated in August 2010 (Constitution of Kenya 2010). Between 2010 and 2017, Kenya experienced an intense period of law making in relation to land. In 2012 alone, it passed three new pieces of legislation, the Land Act, the Land Registration Act and the National Land Commission Act. Thereafter, in 2016, it enacted the Community Land Act and the Land Law Amendment Act. These rapid changes in the legal framework governing land marked the first time since independence that Kenya revisited land policy and land law questions in a comprehensive fashion. But Kenyans have never rested on their laurels as regards land. They have not been permitted to do so, not least because the political elite has embedded in their practices an intimate and negative association of land with electoral politics, manipulation, patronage and reward (Kanyinga 2017).

Despite official policy that land in Kenya should be a symbol of national unity rather than 'a symbol of unity for divergent African communities' (Harbeson 1973; see also Hornsby 2013), the associations of land with ethnicity and autochthony grew in the post-independence period. Inequalities in land access and ownership also grew. President Kenyatta had to work hard to suppress protestations over his distribution of vast amounts of land to his allies (Republic of Kenya 2004), instead of to the land poor in the Rift Valley (Hornsby 2013). The grabbing and misallocation of land meant to have been redistributed under the Million Acre Scheme (noted below) has long rankled. A specific example is the acquisition by Kenyatta's closest allies of so-called Z plots consisting of one hundred acres of land and farmhouse (Hornsby 2013). For his part, President Moi was a master of channelling the anger of the landless and land poor towards 'ethnic others' and away from the elite's own land mischiefs (Klopp 2000). In his mouth, articulating the intricate connections between land, ethnicity and belonging became an art form. Drawing on Lynch's (2008) work, Boone (2012: 85) argues that Moi 'became progressively more active in using land allocation and the land restitution issue as tools to forge a cohesive ethno-political constituency out of the Kalenjin groups and the other ethno-cultural groups claiming to be native or indigenous to the Rift Valley'.

Histories of land reform

Before we explore the history of land reform, the history of the acquisition of protectorate and the colony must be elaborated. Law and administration were key to the colonial endeavour. In their analysis of the legal framework of colonial power in Kenya, Ghai and McAuslan (1970) discuss the intertwined laws governing control over indigenous people and over land. From 1895, East African protectorate status meant that the local inhabitants were foreigners not British subjects, but nonetheless sufficient powers were needed 'to ensure effective government could be assumed in a protectorate' (ibid.: 19). Gradually, through the East Africa Orders in Council in 1897, 1899 and 1902, power was acquired to administer the protectorate. An important obstacle however remained that protectorate status did not automatically allow the alienation of land in that territory and so the ability of the British Government to attract settlers by alienating land and providing incoming settlers with parcels of land was impeded. In 1896 therefore the Indian Land Acquisition Act was extended to the East Africa Protectorate. This permitted land to be acquired compulsorily for public purposes such as building a railway. Land Regulations passed in 1897 stipulated that outside of the ten-mile-wide coastal strip which was in the control of the Sultan of Zanzibar, in the remainder of the protectorate, certificates of occupancy for a period of ninety-nine years could be issued. Ghai and McAuslan argue that this was largely unattractive offer, 'a mere license to use land' (1970: 26) that did not lead to great interest in European settlement and so, in 1899, a different interpretation of the principle of unoccupied lands in a protectorate was offered by the British Government's Law Officers. This new interpretation amounted to saying that by assuming the protectorate, the Crown assumed the right to deal in 'waste and unoccupied land' (ibid.: 25; and see the discussion in Chapter 7), a change in the 1833 advice given to the British Government that had cautioned that the acquisition of a protectorate did not lead to the power to alienate land there unless rights to waste and unoccupied land had been specifically reserved in a treaty or agreement. In 1901, the East Africa (Lands) Order in Council was promulgated and had the effect of vesting Crown Lands in the protectorate in the Commissioner and Consul-General. They held it in trust for the Crown and could make it available as grants or leases. A year later, a further extension was accomplished through the Crown Lands Ordinance which laid out that sales of land and ninety-nine-year leases could be offered, opening the way for large-scale European settlement (ibid.). In 1915 the Crown Lands Ordinance extended the definition of Crown Lands beyond just public land acquired by the monarch by virtue of treaties and agreements or acquired under the Land Acquisition Act 1894, to 'land occupied by native tribes' (Ghai and McAuslan 1970: 27) as well as land reserved for their use by the Governor, whilst providing that this reservation did not amount to allowing members of a tribe to alienate that land (ibid.). In the course of just a few years, control over land in the protectorate had been comprehensively acquired such that 'complete legal power' was exercisable by the Crown. Land could be widely and easily alienated for settlers and 'the disinheritance of Africans from their land was complete' (ibid.: 28).

Kenyan land policy was thus racialised at its inception. Its structure was bifurcated. Ghai and McAuslan described the pattern of land and agrarian administration from 1902 as a 'dual policy' (1970: 80). Between 1902 and 1960, law, policy and administrative practice maintained one policy for European settlements and another for African reserves. Racial exclusivity in the colony centred on European control of land in the Highlands. Towards the end of this period, Ghai and McAuslan show, 'there was a slow move away from the dual system' (1970: 124) as Africans began to find representation in political institutions and the value of and need for African agriculture in its own right came to be recognised. But from 1902 until the Second World War, the demands of Europeans dominated: for land on attractive terms; for spatial controls on Africans and their herds, and for policies to hinder their agricultural competitiveness with European farmers (predominantly in growing maize and coffee); and for cheap and plentiful labour (ibid.).

Kenyan land politics was in essence redistributive in this period in the sense that in a 'conquest state' (Atieno-Odhiambo 2002: 225) dispossession of some was necessary for the accumulation of land by others. Redistribution of land occurred with colonial conquest: the colonisation of Kenya centred on the redistribution of land from Africans to Europeans, the banning of Africans from owning the most fertile and productive land, and the disbarment of Africans from growing cash crops that might compete with colonial agriculture. In particular, the racial exclusivity of the Highlands became 'sacrosanct': Ghai and McAuslan describe it as 'the arc of the European covenant' (1970: 102). This political and economic project was underpinned by the creation and consolidation of bifurcated land policy and land law.

On this reading, efforts to address the resulting skewed ownership and control of land that was a legacy of colonialism were necessarily a part of the political settlement entailed by decolonisation. It was tied up with ending colonial subjugation, asserting rights to territorial space and, importantly, demanding ontological recognition. By this I mean that land reform demands in Kenya cannot be understood without some recognition of the ontological assault occasioned by colonialism. If the colonial project forcibly took land and deprived Kenyans of their livelihood, it also delegitimised ways of being, of seeing territory and of relating to land. Ways of relating to land that did not conform to Western notions of ownership and exclusive possession, and that contained notions such as intergenerational rights and obligations (Okoth-Ogendo 2002) were deprecated. This is an important context in which to understand law reform to recognise and protect customary (or communal) land rights, discussed below.

Writing of Zimbabwean land reform, Hanlon et al. (2013) identify different phases of land reform in that country. The first, in the mid-1980s, took place as a result of the Lancaster House agreement on independence, and compelled the government to engage in a willing-buyer/willing-seller scheme for land resettlement. They point out that in general the land sold was of poor quality and estimate that 75,000 families were resettled by this means (see also Moyo 2011). The second phase of land reform – fast track land reform – began in 2000 in response to widespread dissatisfaction with the slow pace of change and resultant land invasions and occupations by the landless and unemployed (ibid.). In Kenya too, we can identify a series of land reform phases. Although these overlap in time, they can be broadly character-ised as land consolidation (1953–54); land resettlement (1960–68) and adjudication, registration and titling (from 1959).

First wave land reform: Land consolidation
In Harbeson's magisterial (1971) book on land reform between 1954 and 1970, he identifies two distinct but related efforts at altering land relations. The first of these, initiated during the Mau Mau insurgency beginning in 1953, is widely described a period of consolidation (see also Wasserman 1976). It aimed to provide Africans with individual legal title to land, encourage consolidation of land parcels and promote the use of collateral for loans to support cash crop farming. Long promoted and shaped by the ideas of agricultural officers in colonial Kenya, the aim of these reforms when they were adopted by the colonial admin-istration was two-fold. They were advocated by economists and agri-culture specialists as a way to stimulate economic productivity and by colonial administrators faced with a nationalist uprising as a way to take the sting from the tail of nationalist politics that was explic-itly connecting tenure insecurity and the unjust acquisition of land by European settlers (Bates 1989). The consolidation programme only got underway when agriculture specialists were finally able, after at least three decades of recommending the consolidation of land parcels and the issuance of land titles over land held under customary tenure by the Kikuyu, to persuade the colonial authorities that this was the way to address simmering disaffections over land.

On this reading, the arguments of economists and agriculturalists came to be heard when they seemed to offer an opportunity to solve a burning political problem. They were able to enrol the interests of the colonial authorities faced with an insurgency with land injustice at its heart (Manji 2006). Their work paid off in 1954 when the first consolidation schemes were initiated. This was Kenya's first wave of land reform, reluctantly embraced by the colonial authorities rather too late, as land grievances gave rise to a nationalist movement amongst people who had experienced the loss of the fertile lands of what became the 'White Highlands' and the loss of their access to land in the 'native reserves'. The settlement of European farmers on Kikuyu land over which they then exercised exclusive control put land injus-tice at the heart of Kenyan nationalism in this period: 'the redress of this grievance became a fundamental article of the nationalist political faith in Kenya' (Harbeson 1971: 232). Agricultural development was the priority in this period, with technical education and direct loans provided to smallholder farmers as a way to address land hunger and the expressed anxieties over insecure tenure. The agricultural extension officer Swynnerton gave his name to the scheme (van Arkadie 2016). First wave land reform in Kenya was endorsed by colonial politicians but driven by agricultural experts and economists.

Second wave land reform: Land resettlement

Kenya's second wave of land reform, which followed hard on the heels of the first, took the form of a land resettlement programme. Rolled out in haste, the programme was also reactive. Again, it offered economic solutions to a political problem, leading politicians by the nose as the latter sought an effective way to avert unrest, forestall political radicalism and prevent mass land grabs. A ready response to the announcement in 1960 that independence would be forthcoming in the near future (Boone 2012) and promoted by 'technocrats' working in the Land Development and Settlement Boards, Kenya's resettlement programme was rapidly constructed:

> By the time that revolutionary forces from below and the pressures from Whitehall from above had made independence inevitable, the Department of Lands and Settlement had crafted plans for the transfer of lands from European to African ownership in such detail that they could be circulated in international capital markets, appraised, and funded to the tune of over £20 million – all within a few months' time. (Bates 1989: 58)

The aim was to address European anxieties about impending independence (Kyle 1999; Wasserman 1976). The result of intensive lobbying by European farmers with significant illiquid assets, the settlement schemes became a means to 'underwrite European farm assets and/or allow them to sell their land at what they considered a reasonable price' (Harbeson 1971: 241). Their origins however lay in public relations. Kyle (1999: 152) reminds us that the schemes 'had started out as a means of diluting the bad impression created abroad, especially in the United States, by the European monopoly [of land in the Highlands]; they were not designed specifically to respond to the problem of landlessness'.

Under this scheme, land was chosen that would enable small holders with experience of successful farming to expand onto high quality agricultural land with high potential. A 'Yeoman scheme' and a 'Smallholder' scheme were created (Kyle 1999: 153). At a later stage, as intelligence reports suggested that a Land and Freedom Army was active in the Rift Valley, the British Government sped up its attempts to address landlessness with a New Smallholder scheme in which marginal, poorer land was made available to inexperienced, landless Africans (ibid.).

The question of how to fund these programmes was a considerable issue for the British Government. It hoped that the assistance of the World Bank would provide funds and, as importantly, also release Britain from the responsibility of having to oversee the repayment of any loans after it had departed Kenya (Kyle 1999). The World Bank required that any loans be for 'the development of the economy and not mere transfer of ownership' (ibid.: 153) and so land with high potential (to grow tea, coffee or pyrethrum) was prioritised for transfer to 'men with farming experience, managerial capacity and adequate finan-cial resources – in other words, members of the African middle class' (ibid.). The World Bank agreed a loan for the scheme in 1961. The British Government announced that it would also provide loans and grants through the Colonial Development Corporation to enable the transfer of a million acres of land farmed by Europeans to 250,000 African farmers (the 'Million Acre Scheme').

The financing of the scheme played an important symbolic role. If in financing the scheme the World Bank insisted the programme was concerned with economic development not the transfer of land owner-ship, the British for their part saw payment for land as strongly signal-ling that Africans were not to be permitted under any circumstances to acquire former European land for free (Harbeson 1971; Kyle 1999). This structure was accepted and endorsed by Kenyatta in the face of more militant insistence, by Karamogi Odinga and Bildad Kaggia for example, that Africans should not pay to get back land in the White Highlands and that it was not for Britain to play any part in the making of land policy (Harbeson 1971; Kaggia 1975; Odinga 1967). They 'argued that Kenya should not be saddled with any debts for regaining African land from Europeans' (Kyle 1999: 153) and called for a boycott of the schemes. To accept that Britain could call the shots on the terms of Europeans departure from the White Highlands was, to Kenyatta's opponents, an unacceptable compromise (Kaggia 1975). As Kanyinga notes, there were significant divisions within Kenyatta's Kenya African National Union (KANU) party about the direction that land reform should take:

> a radical faction rooted in the nationalist position on land championed *nyakua* (a Kiswahili word meaning seizure – referring to wholesale seizure of expropriated land) in the White Highlands to settle the landless and the squatters who had lived in the Rift Valley for decades. (2017: 198)

The radicals opposed the very principles of land reform as presented by Kenyatta, chiefly the requirement that the landless raise deposits and loans to reacquire property which was theirs. But 'Kenyatta was deter-mined to pursue an accommodationist course' (Mutua 2008: 278) and the radical position on land was quickly suppressed. Although the politics of loan repayment rankled for many years, the political thought of Kenya's land radicals is mostly submerged and awaits its historians. (For an interesting contrast, see the debate on the payment of 'land annuities' in Ireland. This was the label given to funds the Irish Government was compelled to reimburse Britain for financial loans which had been given to tenant farmers to enable them to purchase farmland from landlords under the Irish Land Acts. The requirement to repay Britain was part of the 1921 Anglo-Irish Treaty. In 1932, Éamon de Valera refused to make the land annuity payments, triggering an economic war with Britain; see Lee 1989). For colonial administrators departing Kenya, great symbolic significance was attached to the honouring of the loans: the insurgent nationalist demand that land forcibly and unjustly taken should be returned for free could not be seen to be indulged. For the new Kenyan Government, concerns about the country's credit rating made it critical that they be rid of the debt. On all sides, those involved knew that 'the loan had been contracted by a colonial administration in deference to European rather than African interests' (Harbeson 1971: 248) and, worse still, accepted by Kenyatta and his party.

After independence, in 1965, the Kenyatta Government introduced a land purchase programme, promoting the market as a way to access land rights. To distribute land in the Highlands, it established the Agricultural Development Co-operation to purchase the land of private owners and make it available for sale to African farmers (see Kanyinga 2009) consolidating the position of a salaried middle class able to pay for land, and establishing them as a significant political constituency. As Hornsby (2013: 247) argues, unequal access to finance also had 'ethnic implications' because the Kikuyu community was more able to command access to finance with 'better access to loans and better protection from default'. This meant that the first wave of land purchases and thus the first transfer of land ownership from white owners in the Rift Valley was marked by class and ethnicity. Wealthy Kikuyu and Meru were the new owners of land, embedding from the very start inequalities that would deepen and widen in the coming years. Kanyinga provides an account of the formation of land purchase companies in this period and traces how this enabled different groups to access finance by acquiring loans from the Agricultural Finance Corporation. According to Kanyinga, settler farmland turned into 'primary sites of intense competition between and among different land purchase groups' (2009: 332). Noting that a majority of these land purchase groups were characterised by ethnic or class uniformity, Kanyinga argues that the competitive process of bidding for and acquiring the best land and most productive farms 'spilled over into intense inter-ethnic conflict' (ibid.). In this fraught process, 'each of the bidding groups mobilised support from their respective supporters and ethnic regions to bring political influence to bear on the land control boards, which authorised transactions in the land market' (ibid.). Kanyinga's analysis demonstrates that the re-Africanisation of the Highlands was marked by bitter contestations and that it resulted in significant ethnic blocs mobilising to try to gain land, with the Kikuyu and the Kalenjin making land purchase offers and wrangling over whose offer would be favoured, whilst expending significant effort in mobilising politicians to support their particular proposed purchase. For Kanyinga, the roots of later conflict can be traced to this period:

> The programme transformed the highlands into a prime site of ethnic and class competition over European-occupied land; competition that later spilt into class and ethnic conflict over control of Africanised land. The most significant effect of the resettlement efforts is that it provided the state elite with the necessary political and economic conditions for demobilising the various groups – Mau Mau detainees and radical politicians. While this was a relief for the government, it created the basis for inter-ethnic conflicts. (2009: 333)

Kanyinga shows how land and political representation became deeply intertwined in this period. Notably, there was a concerted struggle by different ethnic groups to access the settlement schemes as a way to provide for their hitherto landless constituencies. This 'opening of the highlands' promoted competition amongst competing ethnic groups each seeking to address 'the land hunger of the people on whom their political security depended'. In this way, the landless became an 'indispensable constituency in the struggle for political power by various groups and individual politicians' (2009: 335).

Third wave land reform: Land adjudication, registration and titling

In 1954, the Swynnerton Plan had proposed that giving African farmers security of tenure through providing 'indefeasible title' would provide both an incentive for investment of labour and effort in farming and also enable the land to be used as security to raise financial credit. The 1953–55 East Africa Royal Commission had recommended the adjudication and registration of individual titles. As a result of this thinking about the role of titling and registration, the Native Lands Registration Ordinance was passed in 1959. This introduced 'a system of registration of title based on the English model' (Coldham 1978a: 91).

Kenya 'has had the longest history of experimentation with formal titling in the region' (Nyamu-Musembi 2007: 1457; see also Cliffe 2001). But the history of land is marked, from its beginnings, by exclusion and domination. As Harbeson (1973: 327) notes, if the main aim of European politics in colonial Kenya was the '[e]nlargement of the European farming enclave in the White Highlands', land reforms in the decade before independence were dominated by the interests of European and colonial political leaders:

> The basic political significance of these land reforms has been that their timing, structure and objectives have been decisively influenced by European settlers, the colonial administration, and international lending agencies, rather than by the African political leaders who made land reform nearly as important an element of African nationalism as political advance itself. (Ibid.: 328)

Ngugi (2002) has argued insightfully in his assessment of the changing political economy of colonialism in this period that the Swynnerton Plan framed the land question in specific ways so as to avoid pointing to colonial expropriation of land as the root of ongoing land problems. Instead of focusing on the shortages of land that had resulted directly from expropriation, the report portrayed the African land tenure system as the problem. In doing so, it refused to admit that there was a 'causal relationship between the imperialist occupation and the colonial land policies and the problems facing African agriculture' (ibid.: 337). The disciplinary techniques of the plan were directed towards Africans. It allowed European policy in Kenya to aim at modernisation. The diagnosis that African tenurial arrangements were to blame led to the recommendation that what was required was the promotion of individual tenure. Ngugi (ibid.) argues that this construction of a perceived problem should not obscure the fact that 'the real aim of the Swynnerton Plan was to create a conservative, newly landed class of Africans: 'It was here that the first seeds of the eurocentric Post-colonial State in Kenya were planted' (ibid.: 338) Crucially, the Swynnerton Plan, by emphasising tenure reform rather than redistribution as the essence of land reform was able to maintain the status quo as regards a by-now severely skewed land distribution. The Swynnerton Plan was essentially a securitisation of the land question. As Ngugi points out, Okoth-Ogendo (1991) recognised this when he noted that the project itself was directed as tenure reform amongst African peasants in 'Mau Mau districts' (Ngugi 2002: 338). The aim was to diffuse a security threat and to construct as rapidly as possible through granting individual tenure, a stakeholder class of conservative cash crop farmers. For Ngugi (ibid.) 'individualization of tenure was a political tool that came in handy to blunt Africans' demand for land redistribution ... The overriding aim was to retain the economic basis of colonialism.' For Ngugi (ibid.):

> The impact of the so-called tenure reforms was the creation of a class of conservative nationalists who, though eager for political independence since that would ensure them the powers of the State, were not inclined to support radical policies or politics. This way the problem of the Mau Mau uprising was skillfully navigated and the stage was set for cautious conservative politics. The colonialists had succeeded in their primary approach to systematically diffuse political nationalism by creation of a social class within the African ranks having similar interests, aspirations and ideals as those of the ruling colonial elite.

Land reform was thus a 'European-colonial defence strategy' (Harbeson 1973: 329) from the start. Land reform was also political settlement. Kenya's leaders who emerged out of this settlement would cooperate in the preservation of European interests and could be relied upon to check any more militant demands, such as those that had appeared in their own KANU party demanding the seizure of land. As Kanyinga (2017) rightly points out, this period saw the defeat of a radical movement by an emerging liberal elite which consolidated its power through controlling both land and the dominant ideologies of land. Importantly for later debates on provisions in the National Land Policy and the 2010 Constitution on confronting historical land injustices and the necessity of a legal framework for restitution (which I discuss in Chapter 8), Kanyinga reminds us, land transfers in this period took place on very specific terms. The transfer of rights to land to Africans in the former White Highlands was not founded in considering historical claims of ownership. Rather, land was simply offered for sale as private property with financing being made available by the government. The Swynnerton Plan was not organised around possible historical territorial claims by the different ethnic groups or individuals. Having organised the transition to decolonisation around private property, the task was to talk populist talk, but always to walk a conservative path. Navigating that path would take some skill. How to divert protest about landlessness and land shortage, or the migration of ethnic outsiders, and say just enough to garner electoral and wider support by decrying these ills, whilst in practice avoiding meaningful redistribution? Hornsby argues that, although Kenyatta boasted of his government's record in acquiring European farms, 'the numbers settled were modest' (2013: 195). This is not apparent when the acreage of land transferred into African hands is measured. At first glance, the achievement seems substantial. Assessing settlement schemes and the willing-buyer/willing-seller programme, Hornsby writes:

> Between 1960 and 1968, more than 2 million acres (800,000 hectares) of former European farms were taken over; 45,000 to 50,000 families … were settled on 1.1 million acres of settlement schemes. By 1970, when most schemes ended, more than two thirds of the original European mixed farming area was African owned. (2013: 195)

But this redistribution had the effect of quieting demands because it could be presented as an achievement and twinned with a promise of yet more to come. In truth, policy preferences leaned strongly the other way. Kenya in this period 'quietly favoured larger farms' (Hornsby 2013: 195) and agricultural policy was strongly informed by international preferences which deprecated subdivision of land and small-scale farming as harmful to productivity and as economically inefficient. In reality such was the scale of landlessness by this time that '[o]nly a complete end to the large farm sector could have made a real inroad on landlessness' (ibid.). That would not come to pass. But Kenya's leaders became astute at using land to promote populist messages whilst overseeing land policies which ensured that distribution of land was, from the very start of independence, structured inequitably.

Part of my argument in this book can be summarised as the idea that in the present day too, solutions to land problems are again formulated to deliver just enough 'to take the steam from the kettle' to use a phrase from the period of land consolidation (quoted in Harbeson 1971: 196). They seek to satisfy a long-running 'strong egalitarian element in popular culture' (Hornsby 2013: 196; Monte 2018) as regards land whilst at the same time avoiding more difficult debates about distributional choices (Kennedy 2003). Still less are they centred on ideas of justice, equity, restitution and the putting right of past wrongs. Indeed, land policy in Kenya's colonial and immediate post-independence period was forged with as much attention to its symbolic meaning as to its practical effect. At no cost should land be perceived to be restored, for free, to its rightful owners. It was critical not just materially but also symbolically that the inverse be achieved: European settlers must be compensated for their losses, 'at prices they could not refuse' (Bates 1989: 59), and no impression must be given that this was a concession to an uprising.

Taking racial form in the colonial period, after independence an African elite did not institute a radical break with this model of land relations, but instead maintained a significant continuity in which they sought to seal their power and domination with control of land (Shivji 2009). Shivji has written that 'control and coercion rather than management and persuasion were the hallmarks of the colonial legal order' (1991: 8). We need to understand, from a political and sociological and not just a legal point of view (Ghai 2017) how the nature of the colonial state 'without a trace of constitutionalism' (Ghai 2017: 161) is linked to the subsequent 'predatory nature of its descendant, the independent state'. Bates (1989) has convincingly shown in his study of rural transformation in the 'White Highlands' and the 'native reserves' that political struggles over land rights were also family struggles over kinship. For Bates, by the 1950s, the legal struggles that took place over entitlements to land were overseen by, and benefited, 'those families with a foot in the new social order' (ibid.: 39): rural entrepreneurs, those able to read and write, clerks and colonial bureaucrats, and those with urban jobs. A conservative bent about property rights (and by extension about family), was built into the new order as it was under construction. After the Mau Mau, 'power was seized ... by the conservative faction of Kenya's rural society: those with a commitment to accumulation, investment, and private property' (ibid.) In the early days of independence, radical alternatives to the nation's land policies were still being voiced as Harbeson's (1973) account of the views of more

militant KANU members shows. These have been quieted in the intervening years.

The politics of the Ten Mile Strip, which runs the entire length of
the Kenya coastline took a different form than those outlined above.
Legally the territory of the Sultan of Zanzibar (Brennan 2008), the
ten-mile-wide strip existed in a state of exception from the 1920s and
then in a state of legal limbo in the early 1960s. This is because when
British East Africa achieved the status of Colony in 1920, the strip
was not included and remained a protectorate. This gave the coast an
'uncertain legal position' (Willis and Gona 2013: 50). As Willis and
Gona argue, the status of the ten-mile strip was complicated by the fact
that it belonged to a larger Coast Province, which constituted a much
larger and inland administrative unit. Between 1962 and 1964, during
the debates about federalism (*majimboism*) that took place at independence (Anderson 2005b), the question of the strip's status was a cause of
disagreement. Should it, like each of Kenya's provinces, assume the new
status of region with devolved responsibilities or 'should [it] continue
to be no more than administrative units of a centralized state' (Willis
and Gona 2013: 50)? In 1963, it was decided that, although the strip was
legally still the property of the Sultan, it would become a full part of a
newly independent Kenya (Hornsby 2013). The centralising tendency
we continue to see in the present day was exercised and the provinces
remained only administrative units in a powerful central state, with
the Ten Mile Strip collapsed into this structure. According to Hornsby
(2013: 78), 'Kenya needed the coast, and particularly Mombasa, too
much to risk a federal model'. This led to 'the entrenchment of Arab
land ownership in the coastal strip' and was at the root of grievances
over African, specifically Mijikenda people's, access to land which have
continued to simmer in the present day (see Chapter 7). At the root of
the problem was the fact that, during the rule of the Sultan, people of
Arab, Swahili and Asian origin acquired land on the strip and had the
support of land titles to prove their ownership. In spite of this, much
of the land was settled by Mijikenda families who took the land to be
unoccupied or government land (Hornsby 2013). Effectively squatters
without any guarantees of rights to remain on the land, when land
registration began to take place in Kwale and Kilifi between 1971 and
1973, it was inevitable that they would be declared illegal and the superior land title of landowners confirmed by their eviction. As Hornsby
(2013) points out, land was growing in value on the open market, tourist
development was booming and favouring landowners, and the government used coastal land to make grants. The Mijikenda were evicted
as the commercial value of the land increased and more powerful and
well-connected individuals in possession of land titles sought to assert
their rights. In an early echo of personalisation of presidential power
over land, which I discuss in Chapter 3, Kenyatta ordered that no beach

front land could be sold without his approval. As Hornsby (2013: 252) notes, 'the result was to move control of these assets entirely into presidential favour, a process administered by Coast PC Eliud Mahihu, who could now decide who could and who could not buy coastal plots' (see Kamau 2009). As I show in the next chapter, this reservation of administrative control over land to the President and the 'administrative elite' (Hornsby 2013: 252) with whom he surrounded himself led to abuse, dispossession and deep grievances.

The nature of property law in the present day – the way in which social relations are structured and by whom (Gluckman 1955) – cannot be understood apart from the country's conservative transition explored above. For Bates, 'Kenya's conservative core runs very deep … it had been laid down in the very political struggles that brought the nation to independence' (1989: 40). When modern-day land reform was mooted and then finally embedded in a national land policy and a new Constitution in 2010, it was no doubt motivated by a desire amongst some to break with longstanding associations of land with domination. But the long history of land policy changes that I have traced here suggest that such changes have strongly favoured the powerful and been finely calibrated to deny the existence of deep-running land injustices. Subsequent land reform was unlikely to have justice and fairness as its aim. It is to this land reform that I turn next.

Land reform or land law reform?

The emergence of land reform onto national political agendas in the late 1980s must be understood in the context of wider pressures for the liberalisation of African economies. By the 1990s, many African states were under pressure from rural constituents to deal with grievances over land matters, to address historical wrongs or to resolve problems of conflict and displacement. But this does not fully account for the thorough overhaul in land relations that resulted across the continent. Below I explore and try to explain the rise to prominence of land law reform. Before that, however, it is important to put Kenya's land reform efforts since 2010 in the wider context of land reform discourses and projects on the continent. In order to do this, I explore Africa's land questions in the contemporary period and ask why land reform has been perceived to be important. In this light, I explore what has been meant by the term 'land reform'.

Both socialist and non-socialist states have attached importance to land relations as a marker of broader economic and political relations. Byres, arguing that land tenure has often been perceived as a possible impediment to growth in the post-1945 period, cites an early United Nations report on land reform in evidence:

for many countries the agrarian structure, and in particular systems of land tenure, prevent a rise in the standard of living of small farmers and agricultural labourers and impede economic development, both by preventing the expansion of the food supply and by causing agriculture – usually the major economic activity – to stagnate. (Byres 2004: 2)

According to this view, the economy as a whole, not just the agrarian sector, is adversely affected by inequitable or inefficient tenure. Unsatisfactory land tenure is held responsible for a lack of economic growth. It restricts food supplies to the urban workforce and affects industrialisation as well as allowing the countryside to stagnate. Since the 1990s, international land policies and development aid policies have explicitly linked access to secure property rights with poverty reduction. The World Bank formulated the idea that unclear tenure rights hinder the development of agricultural and wider credit markets, a perspective that came to be shared by bilateral donors such as Britain. Land issues became clearly visible on international aid agendas in the 1990s as international development policy encouraged private, individual and registered property rights.

As I have shown above in relation to the colonial period, different meanings are capable of being attached to the term 'land reform' at different times. Similarly, in modern times, it is important to clarify what is meant by its use in varied contexts. Bernstein has traced the transition from the state-led development perspectives of the 1950s and 1960s to contemporary land reform. He describes the latter as 'self-styled "new wave" agrarian reform in the age of neo-liberalism' (2002: 433) and shows that the end of the developmental era also marked the cessation of major redistributive land reforms. These had lasted from 1910 to 1970. For Bernstein, these reforms were part of the transition from feudalism to capitalism. A transition occurs from an agrarian to an industrial economy in which generalised commodity production is the norm. In the classic bourgeois view, agrarian change is overseen by the state in order to ensure the modernisation of farming and overall economic growth. In contrast, contemporary land reform takes place in an era of globalisation in which the state is taken to play a diminished role, and the liberalisation of trade has integrated third world farmers into global commodity chains and markets (ibid.).

In the immediate post-independence era redistributive reform was, in Bernstein's view, very much on the political agenda. But when it returned to the political agenda in the 1990s, it reappeared in a significantly altered economic and political context. In its new guise, land reform no longer signifies redistributive reform with its emphasis on the possibilities of transferring larger operational holdings to those with little or no land, such as wage labourers or the landless. Instead, land reform has come to mean tenurial reform. Such reform is concerned with the terms on which an operational holding is controlled and worked (Byres 2004). The current focus is not on redistributive reform but on altering land tenure. Specifically, as Sam Moyo (2001) pointed out, discussions of land reform have focused on the problems of land administration systems and the need for their reform rather than on redistribution. Land reform has reappeared on the policy agenda in economic circumstances quite different to those that prevailed in the 1960s and 1970s. Most notably, economic globalisation has forced countries of the South to open up their national economies to trade, as well as to privatise productive state enterprises.

Byres (2004) explains the critical distinction between redistributive land reform and tenurial land reform. Contrasting the different elements of each approach, he has argued that redistributive reform is concerned with the possibilities of redistributing operational holdings, transferring land from those with larger holdings to the landless or to wage labourers for example. It thus has the potential to be more radical than tenurial reform, which is concerned with the terms on which an operational holding is controlled and worked. It focuses on those aspects of tenure which it is thought affect incentives, investment and efficiency. Both redistributive reform and tenurial reform focus on obstacles to agricultural productivity. The former holds that access to land will bring about increases in output and provide a source of subsistence and access to credit, whilst the latter emphasises how certain aspects of tenure, such as tenancy arrangements, can act as impediments to growth. Calls for redistributive reform also tend to follow a period of political upheaval, for example on the achievement of national independence or as a result of peasants demands. Similarly, Albertus (2015) has argued that land redistribution tends to occur more often under dictatorships than under democracies. According to Byres, the beneficiaries of tenurial reform tend to be larger peasants, whilst those of any redistributive measures are generally the landless and waged labourers.

Although Byres' analysis does not focus on the role of law, his elaboration of the elements of tenurial and redistributive reform has important implications for our discussion. Redistributive reforms clearly require that, after the allocation of land, tenure reform be undertaken to consolidate or guarantee changes. Although its initial impetus is political rather than legal, redistributive reform still implies and eventually attracts law reform because legal changes will be necessary in order to consolidate its achievement. In contrast, tenurial reform, although it may indeed have political motivations (such as addressing the grievances of rural constituents as in Tanzania or as part of constitutional change as in Kenya), can be seen to be much more closely linked to legal change. Seen in this light, tenure reform is in fact land law reform. It does not in fact require redistribution of land holdings. It is simply dependent on the alteration of the terms on which such holdings are owned, controlled and dealt in. This will not only require changes *in* the law but will in fact be achieved *through* law.

The relative desirability of redistributive reform and tenurial reform has been much discussed by theorists of agrarian relations over the past twenty-five years. Bernstein (2004) argued that debate was reignited in the 1990s when the idea of poverty alleviation became prominent in discourses of international development. In a key example of this approach, a paper by Griffin et al. (2002) explicitly linked issues of poverty and land distribution. This thesis on redistribution held that the solution to enduring rural poverty is redistributive land reform that transfers land from landlords to peasants with little land and landless labourers. This, they argued, would set up an agrarian structure dominated by peasant owner-cultivators using family labour to cultivate the land. The authors argue that tenure reform alone cannot tackle poverty or substitute for redistribution because it is possible for powerful landowners simply to ignore or find ways around tenurial changes such as the imposition of land ceilings. Their thesis is founded on the idea of the inverse relationship. This holds that, whereas large landholders have plentiful access to land and capital, they find themselves short of sufficient labour, whereas the opposite is the case for small farmers for whom land and capital are in short supply but labour is abundant. According to this model, large landowners respond to shortfalls in labour supply by employing expensive hired labour and by relying on mechanisation to cultivate their land in an extensive manner. In contrast, small farmers cultivate their land intensively, and generate more 'employment' per unit of land. In the absence of economies of scale, this means that small landholders achieve more per unit than large ones. It is based on this perceived efficiency of small farms that the authors frame their argument for redistribution. They contend that land should be redistributed to small farmers who make more efficient use of labour and who, given greater access to capital, are likely to be more productive overall than large landholders. The position of Griffin et al. (2002: 280) is summed up in the statement that 'the case for land reform rests not on the existence of defective tenure contracts but on the concentration of land ownership rights and the inefficiency, inequality and poverty that this creates'. Byres (2004) disagrees with this position on a number of grounds. Most notably, he argues that tenure reform alone has the potential to achieve a great deal, by abolishing landlordism for example, and should not be wholly dismissed.

The salience of the redistribution versus tenurial reform debate was also reaffirmed by the emergence of rural movements in the 1990s, with struggles to access land through extra-legal means such as occupation or squatting. As a result of land occupations, calls for redistribution came once again to political prominence not just in Africa but globally. They have signalled the political and economic importance of land reform. This has not been lost on the makers of international land policy such as bilateral donors and financial institutions. The strategies adopted by Brazil's *Movimiento Rural Sem Terra* (Landless Workers Movement) in the south and south-east of the country since the 1980s – including the invasion of land and its settlement, the setting up of cooperatives to oversee production, and the nurturing of alliances with the Workers' Party – is thought to have elicited a response from the World Bank and the United States Agency for International Development (USAID) in the form of accelerated titling programmes to counter the confiscatory methods of the movement (Bernstein 2002).

A number of scholars have sought to capture the range and complexity of Africa's land problems. In general, they have pointed to insecurity of tenure, subdivision of land, informal land markets, the alienation of land and its concentration, and the role of undemocratic structures of local government in dealing with land disputes. Peters summarised the main land issues facing the continent as follows:

> Competition over land for different purposes intensifies due to growing populations and movements of people looking for better/more land or fleeing civil disturbances; rural groups seek to intensify commodity production and food production while retrenched members of a down-sized salariat look for land to improve food and income options; states demarcate forestry and other reserves, and identify areas worthy of conservation ... representatives of the state and political elites appropriate land through means ranging from the questionable to the illegal; and valuable resources both on and under the land (timber, oil, gold, other minerals) attract intensifying exploitation by agents from the most local (unemployed youth or erstwhile farmers seeking ways to obtain cash) to transnational networks (of multinational corporations, foreign governments and representatives of African states). (2004: 291)

Moyo has written that 'the essence of [the] land question ... has never been adequately conceptualised' and asked 'whether Africa has a land question, and if so, what is the nature of its land question' (2003: 8). He argued that theorists have focused too narrowly on the root of possible land questions, seeking evidence of historical land alienation under colonialism as their first point of reference. In doing so, they have neglected the range of ways in which land concentration has taken place over time and failed to recognise the glaring empirical evidence that land inequalities continue to increase due to such concentration. Moyo points in particular to emerging rural movements as evidence of the existence of pressing African land questions. Focusing specifically on the politics of emerging rural movements and on processes of illegal land occupation or squatting, Moyo presents the following analysis:

> Pressures for the growing marketisation of land reflect both external interests in economic liberalisation and foreign access to land and natural resources, as well as the increasing internal class struggles over primitive accumulation by a broadening African indigenous capitalist class. New land policies justify these tendencies of unequal land control, but generate growing conflicts over land allocation and use across class, gender, nationality and ethnic lines. (Ibid.: 1–2)

For Moyo, 'variegated struggles at varying scales and localities over escalating unequal access to and control of land represent a real land question in ... Africa' (2003: 2).

Broadly speaking, African land questions can be distinguished by region. Whereas North Africa has experienced severe shortages of arable land, in West Africa the problem is predominantly one of land administration and conflict between the state and local communities. In former settler colonies, the land questions arising can be seen to be connected with the concentration of resources and therefore with the issue of redistribution. Although it is thus possible to describe African land problems by employing a series of generalised and distinct explanatory categories – such as conflict arising from historical injustices or from concentration and commercialisation – land issues have rarely lent themselves to such tidy portrayals. Instead, considerable overlaps can be found in the experiences of any one region or country. In Kenya, for example, the land claims being asserted by the Maasai might be categorised as arising from historical injustices, as much as from the concentration and commercialisation of land for the purposes of tourism. Encapsulated in the story of the Maasai land claim is the desire to resolve historical grievances (the alienation of ancestral land by members of the community in the form of long leases to the British colonial power) and ongoing dispossession due to commercialisation (the longstanding development of ranching and luxury tourist facilities in Maasailand). In the country as a whole, a chaotic state of land administration and management facilitates land grabbing and deepens grievances, as I show in Chapter 3.

Ghai (2017) has described how in the present day an international focus on constitutionalism can be ascribed to the end of the Cold War as well as the end of a number of conflicts. This has resulted in a proliferation of new constitutions 'inclining towards forms of democracy, liberalism and market' (2017: 150) and a rise in comparative constitutionalism as the decisions of superior courts influence other, similar jurisdictions, and international norms find expression in national constitutional texts. This puts lawyers, draftspersons, the judiciary and legal academics at the centre of political change. Similarly, modern law reform of land in the period since 1990 has been driven by the involvement of law and lawyers. The contemporary interest in using law in these ways is not new. Its roots can be traced historically. In the immediate post-independence period from the late 1960s, the scholarship and practice described as 'law and development' attributed a similarly important role to law (see Ghai 1987; Vyas et al. 1994). In its early manifestations, the aims of the law and development movement, comprising scholars and practitioners, were to provide technical assistance to government ministries and thus to boost their administrative efficiency in such a way as to bring about development. In this period, the law and development movement had a pragmatic and instrumentalist view of the role of law (Trubek and Galanter 1974). Samir Amin (2000: 32) characterised this as a 'bourgeois national project' of developmentalism. The project had lawyers at its heart. By the mid-1970s, both as an area of scholarship and as a policy-oriented practice, the methods, outlook and objectives of the law and development movement had been thoroughly critiqued and its limitations as an instrumental project with shallow theoretical roots revealed (Merryman 1977). It was largely abandoned as an approach.

By the 1990s however, law and development scholarship and practice were widely reinvigorated. This has been explained as a consequence of economic globalisation. In this period, the dominant development model was market-oriented (Spalling 1992). It was imposed on peripheral and semi-peripheral countries which were required to open up their national economies to trade and to privatise productive state enterprises. They were also required to address their property rights systems and make sure that private property rights were clear and inviolable, inaugurating what de Sousa Santos (2002) called a new legal common sense. The formalisation of property rights was at the core of this neo-liberal economic programme (Kennedy 2003; Manji 2006). Law in development had come once again onto the international agenda. Central to its objectives was the promotion of good governance and the rule of law and, in the words of de Sousa Santos (2002: 167), 'formal democracy as a political condition for international assistance'.

This emphasis on the rule of law has given the renewed project of law and development – of which the emphasis on constitutions that Ghai (2017) notes is a part – its contemporary flavour. The first law and development movement had a remote relationship with redistributive land reform. Both shared an overall concern with state-led development but law and development did not play a key role in the alteration of land relations in the immediate post-independence period. A revived law and development movement from the 1990s enjoyed a more intimate relationship with land reform: scholars located in the broad field of law and development have taken a leading role in thinking about the purpose and direction of land reform as well as frequently being involved in the technical task of drafting new land laws (McAuslan 2003). In the land domain, this has taken the form of an assumption that, without the formalisation of the legal rules governing property, economic growth will be held back. This perspective is summed up in Posner's (1998: 2) observation that 'a modernizing nation's economic prosperity requires at least a modest legal infrastructure centred on the protection of property and contract rights'. In the late 1990s, the World Bank's then General Counsel, Ibrahim Shihata, elaborated the elements of the rule of law as follows: a set of rules known in advance; rules that are actually in force; the existence of mechanisms to ensure the proper application of rules but which allow controlled departure when necessary; the existence of an independent judicial or arbitral body to make binding decisions when conflicts in the application of rules arise; and procedures for amending rules (see Shihata 1997) When the former US secretary of state Colin Powell declared that it is 'the rule of law that permits wonderful things to happen' (see Institute for Liberty and Democracy 2002) it was clear that the promotion of the rule of law was to be a priority of foreign aid. Rule-of-law aid or rule-of-law reform became a central feature of development assistance.

This emphasis on the rule of law has had its critics. Based on empirical and historical evidence from the United States and Japan, Upham (2001) has argued that the rule of law defies attempts to create a universal template and that it cannot be transplanted from one country to another. For Upham, the intricate connections between law and politics should not be denied. They should be made explicit, and it should be recognised that the formalisation of rules ignores the workings of informal agreements and social control. Upham argued that the rule of law has been misconceived as a path to development when it should in fact be viewed as a desirable consequence of development. In his turn, Kennedy offered an insightful characterisation of the contemporary embrace of the rule of law. Echoing Upham's analysis, Kennedy argues that there has been a failure to interrogate 'the idea that building the rule of law might itself be a development strategy' (2002: 17). By closing down rather than promoting 'contestation over economic and political choices', advocates of the contemporary law and development movement with its rule-of-law inclinations have given law inordinate power. They have ensured that 'law, legal institution building, the techniques of legal policy-making and implementation – the "rule of law" broadly conceived' is now 'front and centre' (ibid.: 18).

Thus, although an instrumentalist view of law fell out of favour in the 1970s, economic and political neo-liberalism provided the necessary conditions for a new law and development from the 1990s onwards. Land law reform has been central to this new law and development. Many African countries – amongst them Eritrea, Ethiopia, Malawi, Mozambique, Namibia, Rwanda, South Africa, Tanzania, Uganda and Zambia – have been involved in land reform projects in one form or another. What the seemingly inexorable rise of land reform projects may obscure however is the difficult distributional choices which any land policy must entail. Just as Ghai (2017) has argued that the rise in interest in constitutions is in part due to networked lawyers, drafters and judiciaries, so with land reform we have witnessed the emergence of legal drafters and consultants who have put legal solutions as the heart of land matters (McAuslan 2003).

As Byres (2004: 3) has reminded us, '[l]and reform [does] not reach policy agendas in a political vacuum'. Cutler's work on the role on law in neo-liberal globalisation offers a means to explore the wider context for land law reform. From a historical materialist position, Cutler has argued that the significance of law's role in the process of neo-liberal globalisation has not been adequately understood and critiqued. Cutler notes that law links global and local political and economic orders in complex ways, forming 'a juridical link between local and global political-legal orders' (2002: 231) so that, despite being neglected in most scholarship, 'the globalisation of law is an integral aspect of the globalisation of capitalism.' Law plays a crucial role in the globalisation of capitalism in two interrelated ways. First, the globalisation of law promotes certain values:

> the law that is globalized is essentially American or Anglo-American in origin, promoting the values of neo-liberal regulatory orders. These values and beliefs are in turn embodied in legal rules that provide the foundation for the expansion of property relations based in the private appropriation of surplus value. (Ibid.)

Second, the cultural effect of the process of globalising law 'is integral to the internalisation of neo-liberal discipline by elites' whilst also ensuring that this discipline is in turn reproduced in local laws as well as transnational laws. Cutler argues that '[g]lobalized law advances the interests of a transnational class whose members function as the "organic intellectuals" for the globalization of capitalism' and that a transnational class 'advances a particular legal culture informed by neoliberal values and the privileging of private ordering as the most natural, efficient, consensual, and just means of regulating commercial and productive relations' (2002: 231).

Cutler's elaboration of law's importance to the globalisation of capitalism contains important insights. Her characterisation of law can assist in understanding the functioning of African land law reform in a number of ways. First, her theoretical approach allows modelling of the different levels at which land law reform has been debated and enacted. Law forms the link between the many levels of land law reform, starting at the global level with international financial institutions and moving through national governments down to peasants in the fields. The notion of a 'juridical link' allows us to see the phenomenon of land law reform in its global and local aspects. The globalisation of law, as Cutler reminds us, is fundamental to the globalisation of capitalism. The idea that the problems of economic development lie in non-formalised land relations (de Soto 2000) can only take place in an era of neo-liberalism, and the solution – that land relations must be formalised – likewise has its political and economic context.

Cutler further urges us to be alert to the ways in which the globalisation of law promotes certain values. For example, the replacement of communal tenure with private tenure is achieved not simply by the spread of a network but by the globalisation of law. Across Africa, remarkably similar new land laws will seek to replace complex and varied forms of communal tenure with private land tenure. Local elites internalise the globalisation of law, naturalising and privileging private ordering and portraying the process of its triumph over other forms of social and economic life, such as communal tenure, as consensual. In accounting for the role of a transnational elite, the members of which act as 'organic intellectuals for the globalisation of capitalism', Cutler's account allows us to explore the role of powerful actors in the land reform process.

Little attention has been paid to that which is excluded by opting for one approach to African land tenure rather than another. Debates about the purpose and direction of land reform have taken place within strictly proscribed parameters. The liberalisation of land is treated primarily as a technical exercise and, with the exception of a few commentators (see Bernstein 2002; Shivji 1997a) its ideological nature remains unexposed. At least two alternative perspectives have been neglected as a result of the dominance of legal solutions to land. First, as Kennedy (2002) argues, the difficult distributional choices entailed in any debate about land have been overlooked. According to von Benda-Beckmann, this amounts to treating property law as 'scapegoat and magic charm' and ensures that the political aspects of property and vexed issues of redistribution are not confronted (2003: 187). Cutler has summed this perspective up by urging us to pay attention to 'the political significance of law, in terms of determining who gets what' (2002: 231).

There are important implications flowing from Kennedy's observation that we have been persuaded to overlook a range of political and economic choices by relying on the law. How land should be distributed and accessed, and by whom, is a question of critical social, political and economic importance. If contestation over the meaning and precise content of land reform has been excluded or severely circumscribed by resorting to law and to building legal institutions, we need to excavate the content of other narratives and to consider excluded alternatives (I return to this in Chapter 8).

Conclusion

For Shivji (2009: 31), '[t]he land question was central to the struggle for national liberation. Formal independence from colonialism never fully resolved the land question'. Such attempts at resolution as we have seen have remained within narrow parameters. A reliance on law to reform how land institutions work has predominated. In the discussion that follows, I will show that the consequences of legalistic approaches to land reform are starkly evident in Kenya's new land laws. The process of land law reform foreclosed debates about redistribution, prioritised land law reform as the most effective way to address land problems and so evaded more difficult questions about who controls access to land and how a more just distribution might be achieved. Since the new laws were passed, we have seen significant land grabbing, allocation of valuable land by politicians to their allies, and continued distress as a result of land shortages and land-related violence.

3

Making Mischief: Land in Modern Kenya

What we have been examining is the rapid emergence of a patrimonial state on the legal foundations of the constitutionalist state, some transformations secured through the manipulation, trivialisation, and disregard of the law. (Shivji 1991: 106)

Introduction

In this chapter, I explore how a number of official reports have over the years since independence recorded the multi-faceted land problems that Kenya has experienced and made recommendations for reform. The many land mischiefs that have characterised the land domain have been comprehensively recorded by these reports. This meant that land reform – when it came onto the political agenda from 2000 and began to seem achievable – was able to draw on a dense archive of official reports documenting the many land wrongs to be righted. I argue here that Kenya possesses a powerful but neglected 'land archive'. This archive records what citizens have labelled 'Kenya's land grabbing mania' (Klopp 2000: 7). It is made up of a series of official reports published by commissions of inquiry, each charged with different mandates but which have contributed cumulatively to a land archive which has been built up over many years. Because it is scattered and fractured, it is rarely brought together in one place by our analyses. Indeed, the reports are often cited in isolation rather than treated as comprehensively recording in their entirety the many problems associated with land since independence and the demands for change in this domain. But these reports explain a great deal about Kenyans' estrangement from the state.

The aim of the present chapter is to correct this and to show that official reports, read together, provide critical insights into the *longue durée* of land reform demands in Kenya. Only by a comprehensive reading of these reports, side by side and with an acute sense of their history and inter-relation can we hope to find insights into the task of land reform and its ambitions through time. We can also, by reference to this official archive, assess the limits of what has been achieved by land reform to date. In this chapter, I show how a series of reports, not all of which are exclusively concerned with land matters, constitute a detailed and nuanced archive of land mischiefs and of concrete recommendations for legislative and constitutional change. This provided an important source of information and a reference point as the struggle for constitutional change made headway from 1992 onwards, intertwining demands for constitutional and for land reform in important ways, as I go on to show in Chapter 4.

In what follows, I study this accumulated land archive. In doing so, I distinguish between reports directly concerned with land issues and those which, although they had a wider remit, raised land relations as an important concern. Good examples of the latter are the Waki report published in the wake of the post-election violence of 2007, and the report of both the Truth Justice and Reconciliation Task Force in 2003 and the resultant Commission in 2013. Neither of these commissions were exclusively mandated to report on land matters but their necessary incursions into this area and their analyses of land problems demonstrate how inequality along this axis is tied up with political disenfranchisement and how land has been used to mobilise political and ethnic constituencies in ways that have led to violence, dispossession and loss of life.

Kenya's accumulated land archive

In this section, I explore the key inquiry reports that have gone to make up Kenya's official archive on land matters. Some of these reports have been directly concerned with land issues, others raise land as an aspect of their wider remit. I argue that these official reports, collected together, reports contributed to the momentum for constitutional reform. The difficult land problems to which they pointed ensured that land reform came to be seen as a fundamental demand in the wider constitutional movement when this began to gather pace after 1992.

The Njonjo Commission

The first significant land inquiry in the post-independence era was the Presidential Commission of Inquiry into the Land Law System of Kenya (known as the 'Njonjo Commission' after its chairperson) which reported in 2002. The appointment of the Njonjo Commission by President Moi in 1999 has been interpreted as a response to an increasingly vocal civil society and ordinary citizens expressing their dissatisfaction over the state of land relations and, in particular, land grabbing. It was seen as an attempt by President Moi to diffuse pressure over land wrongs which had been building up for decades (Klopp and Lumumba 2017). The Commission was mandated to consider the policy and legal framework for land and to consider how this might be reformed. Although it is less well known than the 2009 Ndung'u report which I discuss below, it can be described as one of the most important initiatives in the arena of land reform in Kenya.

The Njonjo Commission was given a narrow mandate to explore policy and legal options, rather than specifically to inquire into land grabbing as the Ndung'u Commission later was. Its findings are considerably less 'juicy' (Southall 2005: 142) than those later recorded by the Ndung'u Commission. This may account for its relative neglect by Kenyans. Nonetheless, the comprehensive report produced by the Njonjo Commission marked the beginning of post-independence land reform debates and very clearly brought land issues onto the ground of constitutional, public and administrative law. Appointed in 1999, it was required to make recommendations for administrative and legislative reforms needed in order to address longstanding land problems in Kenya. It was mandated to set out the principles of a National Land Policy Framework; to recommend what might be the constitutional position to be afforded to land and to set out in detail a new institutional framework to govern land administration.

The report of the Commission recognised that at the heart of Kenya's land question lay complex questions of tenure, access to land and skewed distribution. It pointed out that how use of land is regulated and how control of the land is exercised forms the basis of the exercise of administrative and political power. It argued that land must have a status in law and in the Constitution. In doing this, the Commission was laying an important emphasis on land as a matter of public and administrative land rather than of private law. This recognition that the legal status of land is an important question beyond the purview of questions of private law (such as contracts for sale of land for example) but in fact also raises critical questions about the scope of the public exercise of administrative law (Manji 2017b; McAuslan 2003), gave the report much of its power. (I elaborate on the importance of studying land from a public law perspective in Chapter 5.) In the words of the report:

> Land-rights delivery is a process which entails the mobilization of institutional mechanisms and personnel for ascertainment of rights ... These are processes which, in Kenya, are run as part and parcel of public administration. (Republic of Kenya 2002: para. 179)

The Commission recommended the formulation of a land policy to provide a framework for the governance of land. Recognising the political, social and cultural complexity of the land question, it strongly recommended that a policy framework be drafted which would guide future law making. The Njonjo Commission also opened the way for a reconsideration of the tenure regime as a whole, recommending that land should be categorised as public land, common land and private land. Importantly, the Commission recommended that radical title to land be vested in an independent land body and in so doing enabled important questions about powers of radical title in land to enter the nascent land reform debate. The wider context for the Njonjo recommendation on radical title is important. In 1992, the Tanzanian Presidential Commission of Inquiry into Land Matters (widely referred to as the 'Shivji Commission' after its chairperson) had submitted a two-volume report which, amongst other recommendations, urged that the radical title to land be divested from the government and vested in the village assemblies and an extra-executive body to be called the National Commission of Lands (United Republic of Tanzania 1994). (Significantly for future debates in Kenya about the architecture of land governance, which I discuss in Chapter 5, the Shivji Commission also recommended that a large and powerful part of the executive arm of the government, the Ministry of Lands, be abolished). The Tanzanian Government was deeply displeased (Shivji and Kapinga 1997). It was not prepared to implement a recommendation which it knew would have substantially altered the structure of the state by abolishing its monopoly of the radical title to land. An early draft of the National Land Policy therefore rejected the recommendation to divest the radical (or ultimate) title to land from the President. It argued that 'to detach the Head of state from land would be a radical departure from the present land tenure system. Such a change is just like making him and his government beggars for land' (see United Republic of Tanzania 1994). Shivji rightly pointed out that the feudal notion that there should be a relationship between sovereign and property thus reappeared in republican Tanzania (Shivji 1997b). Thus, the Njonjo Commission's work was taking place at a time when debates about the state's monopoly over land were also happening elsewhere in East Africa.

Crucially for the way in which the land reform efforts would later unfold in Kenya, the Njonjo Commission recommended an independent national land institution that it suggested be known as the Kenya National Land Authority to govern private land, as well as a body to be called the District Land Authority which would be entrusted with common (later to be known as community) land. This National Land Authority would be responsible for categorising land under different tenure regimes, mapping and recording all customary land rights, verifying land titles and preparing a comprehensive register. The National Land Authority could, further, create a network of decentralised land registries. Radical title would be vested in this body, thus removing control of radical title from the powerful and centralised control of the Commissioner of Lands. Given the influence successive presidents had exercised over the Commissioner of Lands, this recommendation would also indirectly curtail presidential powers over land. The Njonjo Commission envisaged that these bodies would be established by legislation and that their status would be entrenched in the Constitution. In so doing, the Commission hoped to open the way to the building of 'above politics' (Boone et al. 2019) bodies which by virtue of their constitutional status would be insulated from political manipulation. Crucially for what came to pass in the land domain in later years (see Chapter 6 in particular), it was envisaged that these independent land bodies would have control of their own finances but would be required to account for this expenditure to the Minister of Lands. More broadly, these independent bodies would have a relationship of accountability to the Minister of Lands (see Supreme Court Advisory Opinion No. 2 of 2014: para. 115).

The Ndung'u Commission
The Njonjo report was never implemented. Just after its publication in 2002, Kenya's new National Rainbow Coalition (NARC) won the election and the report was shelved. NARC recognised immediately that it would need to respond to rising disquiet over land mattes. It moved quickly to commission a new inquiry into land, this time with a different mandate. It promised that this commission would investigate and then ensure the recovery of all public lands illegally allocated by the outgoing government. In doing so, it stated that it was responding to the demands of ordinary Kenyans and of civil society groups aggrieved by land grabbing and misallocation of land by the Moi Government. Investigation of this issue was one of NARC's most important commitments, together with the replacement of Kenya's independence Constitution. Its focus on land was presented as part of a wider war to be waged on corruption (Branch et al. 2010; Wrong 2009). In this connection, the new government undertook thoroughly to investigate and then to ensure the recovery of all public lands illegally allocated by the outgoing government. A Commission of Inquiry into the Illegal and Irregular Allocation of Public Land (widely known after its chairperson as the 'Ndung'u Commission') was appointed.

The Ndung'u Commission's report (Republic of Kenya 2004) was presented to President Kibaki in December 2004. It was released six months later, only after protracted campaigning and pressure from civil society. There were widespread accusations of government censorship as a result of the long delay in making the report public (Africog 2009). Indeed, campaigns to have the report released had the effect of binding land-related and wider human rights civil society groups such as the Kenya Land Alliance and the Kenya Human Rights Commission (KHRC) closely together. When it was made available, it was clear that the 244-page report was much less directly focused on policy and legal framework than the Njonjo inquiry had been. Instead, it tackled the longstanding practice of land grabbing head on.

The Ndung'u report set out in forensic detail the illegal land awards made over the years to the families of Presidents Kenyatta and Moi, numerous former ministers, members of Parliament and civil servants, as well as to individuals in the military and the judiciary. Despite the enormous detail provided in the annexes (amounting to 976 and 797 pages each), the Commission stressed that the report was still incomplete because the it had encountered a widespread lack of cooperation when it carried out its work (Africog 2009: 29). The Commission warned that this meant that the report provided a snapshot of only a proportion of the illegal/irregular land allocations that had taken place over the years. The report recommended that a large majority of land titles acquired illegally or irregularly should be revoked and the rectification of others (Republic of Kenya 2009a: 117).

In the report, the Commission laid out in detail the illegal land awards made to powerful individuals and families. Kenyans quickly seized on this archive and in particular on the annexes to the report. Those able to acquire copies leafed through its contents, familiarising themselves with the detailed annexes and finding there confirmation of land grabbing on a huge scale. Kenyans had long suspected and in some cases knew in intricate detail the details of grabbed land, of the public clinics and government schools that were never built because the land reserved for such public purposes was mysteriously and irregularly or illegally allocated. The annexes laid out this information as never before. Details of the plots of land subjected to grabbing were provided in neat columns, with the registration numbers (known as the LR numbers) of the plots provided. This enabled citizens easily to search for specific land parcels subjected to grabbing and although the picture was incomplete, confirmed for them the scale of land wrongs committed since independence. The findings of the Ndung'u report were widely reported in the newspapers so that what would otherwise have remained complex legal and technical matters, as was perhaps the case with the Njonjo report, became widely known to the general public. It was reported that conveyancing lawyers began to use the report to carry out due diligence checks when they were involved in property transactions so that the report quickly established itself as the authoritative and definitive guide to land grabbing to date. The report was widely discussed in the Kenyan media and became the subject for some time of Kenya's 'radio trottoir' (Ellis 1989: 321). Its findings were taken up by leading human rights groups (see Africog 2009; KNCHR and KLA 2006) and discussed by academics studying land matters in Kenya.

The first volume of the Ndung'u report provided important information about the mechanisms by which public land was misallocated and showed how the doctrine that public land should be administered and allocated 'in the public interest' was consistently perverted. The report showed that land corruption was indulged in by bureaucrats, politicians, business people and lawyers who were able to employ their professional skills and networks to accumulate great personal wealth. It quickly became apparent that the scale of what had been uncovered meant that the economic and social costs of extensive land corruption were in total likely to be far higher than the overall costs of corruption scandals such as Anglo-Leasing and Goldenberg that had received widespread international attention and condemnation (Harrington and Manji 2017; Klopp 2000). Klopp (2000) is surely right to argue that local manifestations of land grabbing, damaging as they were, were not within the sights of the international donor community whose attention was drawn instead to large-scale financial scandals. As I argue in the next chapter, this has meant that struggles to protect land from grabbing and to ensure that the constitutional review process addressed the many land wrongs that marked Kenya history, must be understood as the result of grassroots citizens struggles and of the concerted work of civil society groups over time. Land corruption, unlike other forms of corruption, went largely unremarked by the international community.

Despite widespread public awareness of the report, Southall (2005) has nonetheless pointed out that discussions of its findings have not always been comprehensive. The Ndung'u report has received less academic attention than it deserves (but see Boone 2012; Kanyinga 2009; Klopp 2000; Southall 2005). Most analyses of the report have tended to focus on what Southall calls its 'juicy findings' (2005: 143). Commentators quickly became preoccupied with the 'what' and 'whom' of illegal or irregular land allocation, the forests, road reservations, school playgrounds and graveyards that have been misallocated and the individuals and families who acquired them, rather than the mechanisms, what we might describe as the 'how', of land grabbing. Although the report provided detailed information about the mechanisms by which public land was misallocated and the means by which the doctrine that public land should be administered and allocated 'in the public interest' (Republic of Kenya 2004: 8) was consistently perverted, this aspect of the report received much less attention. But Southall (2005: 143) pointed out that it was in fact

> the chapter and verse which the Report gives concerning the systematic way in which established procedures, designed to protect the public interest, were perverted to serve private and political ends which may well prove to be its most long lasting value.

I have argued elsewhere (Manji 2012) that one of the most significant issues raised by the Ndung'u Commission was the extent to which illegal or irregular transactions in public land in Kenya have been made possible through administrative and professional corruption. In his short assessment of the Ndung'u report, Southall (2005: 146) remarked that the 'extensive complicity of professionals (lawyers, surveyors, valuers, physical planners, engineers, architects, land registrars, estate agents and bankers) in the land and property market was key to the process of land grabbing'. This aspect of land grabbing was widely known in Kenya, and many of the rumours which circulated about land narrated stories of professionals involved in self-enrichment. The report became for civil society groups and for reforming lawyers an authoritative source for professional and institutional involvement in land grabbing and thus something of a manual for the reforms needed to address and stem land grabbing.

The findings of the Ndung'u report shaped the constitutional debates – which I will go on to describe in Chapter 4 – in important ways. This is because it set out the detailed mechanisms by which public land was illegally or irregularly allocated not for the purposes of development but as political reward (see Hunt 1984; Kanyinga 2000; Klopp 2012; Olima 1997; Onoma 2010). It revealed the intricate connections between land matters and Kenya's fraught electoral history (Anderson 2005b; Throup and Hornsby 1998). The Commission found that illegal allocations of public land escalated significantly before or soon after the multiparty general elections of 1992, 1997 and 2002. This was evidence that public land was allocated 'as political reward or patronage' (Republic of Kenya 2004: 83). For Southall (2005: 143), 'even a cursory analysis serves to confirm earlier analyses that corruption and patronage have become thoroughly embedded in Kenya's politics'. This confirmed the suspicions that citizens had long had that at each election improper allocation of public land had taken place as a way to raise electoral finance and to shore up political support, as well as to consolidate personal gain before losing office. Press reports had suggested that politicians would use public office to access key land institutions such as the Ministry of Lands and the land registry in order to identify profitable land to be grabbed or to sell land already acquired. Notably, because this category of land is almost exhausted and its availability as a 'patronage resource' (Klopp 2012) has largely come to an end as a result of widespread looting, community land stands to become the form of land most likely to replace public land as a new resource for looting and land grabbing (Alden Wily 2018b), a point to which I return below.

We can therefore trace the conjoining of the land and constitutional reform movements which I describe in the next chapter to the Ndung'u report. According to the African Centre for Global Governance (Africog 2009: 11), the Ndung'u report established that 'illegal allocation of public land is one of the most pronounced manifestations of corruption and political patronage in our society'. On a conservative estimate, some 200,000 illegal titles were created between 1962 and 2000. Of these, 98 per cent were issued between 1986 and 2002. The categories of public land affected include forests, settlement schemes, national parks and game reserves, civil service houses, government offices, roads and road reserves, wetlands, research farms, state corporation lands and trust lands. The report makes it clear that the illegal allocations took place either on the direct orders of the President or on the orders of prominent senior public officials and well-connected business people and politicians. Those who benefited from the illegal or irregular allocations of grabbed land included ministers, senior civil servants, politicians, business people, churches, temples and mosques.

The report distinguished between the illegal and the irregular allocation of public land (Republic of Kenya 2004: 57–67). The first category of wrongful allocation, when land is illegally issued, occurred when the legal safeguards governing the allocation of land were ignored or subverted. For instance, where a title was issued for a piece of land which was not in fact legally available for allocation, the title acquired was illegal. The report recommended that such titles should be revoked and stipulated that in certain instances, such as where the land had been sold on to a third party or is being held by a bank as security for a loan, decisions as to revocation should be made on a case-by-case basis by a Land Title Tribunal using clear criteria such as the number and classes of people financially affected and 'the public interest' (ibid.: 67). The second category of wrongful allocation was irregular allocation of land. According to the Ndung'u report (Republic of Kenya 2004: 49), this occurred when administrative procedures for dealing in land were not followed. Here, the land concerned was legally available for allocation, but the requisite legal standard was not met or the correct administrative procedure followed. For this second category of cases, the report recommended that irregular titles be rectified by following the administrative procedures that had been bypassed.

The Ndung'u report provided exhaustive details of the processes by which the wrongful allocation of public land was achieved. According to the report (Republic of Kenya 2004: 81), the abuse of the powers of allocation was central to the plundering of public land. It was therefore necessary to understand the allocation process and how it affected the three categories of land then in use and later reformed by the land law reforms of 2012. The first was government land, which included both alienated land (that is, land which had been leased to a private individual or company or reserved for use by a government department or corporation or institution, or which has been set aside for another public purpose), and unalienated land (that is, land that had not yet been leased or allocated). Second, trust land which was held by County Councils on behalf of local communities under customary law. Once such land was registered according to any of the land registration statutes, it became private land and was then regarded as the sole property of the individual or group in whose name it is registered (Republic of Kenya 2004: 147). Third, land which was registered in accordance with the land registration statutes in the name of an individual or a company was deemed to be private land. This category of land could be created from either government or trust land through registration after certain procedures had been followed (Republic of Kenya 2004; Southall 2005). The Ndung'u Commission investigated the illegal and irregular allocation of government land and, when cases came to its notice, of trust land affected by fraudulent practices. Taken together, government land and some trust land made up the category of 'public land' into which the Ndung'u Commission inquired.

According to the commission's findings, it was the very individuals entrusted with being custodians of public land who were involved in 'pilfering the public' (Klopp 2000). They did so by subverting or ignoring the legal safeguards in place to protect public land (Republic of Kenya 2004: 8). Thus, although the President had the right to allocate unalienated government lands (and could delegate limited powers to the Commissioner of Lands), he could not exercise his powers without taking into account the public interest. The report describes how in practice the Commissioner of Lands and his officials were given responsibility for public land: under the Government Lands Act they could allow township plots on unalienated land to be sold by auction if that land was not otherwise required for public purposes. However, neither the President nor the Commissioner of Lands had the authority to allocate alienated government land, that is, land that has been earmarked for a public purpose (such as road reservations) (ibid.: 51). As well as subjecting the President and the Commissioner of Lands to these legal safeguards, the law also controlled the process of allocation itself. A formal offer of sale had to be made to an approved purchaser by the Commissioner for Lands. Known as a letter of allotment, this was only made to the person to whom it was addressed, lapsed after thirty days, and had conditions attached. Significantly, a letter of allotment cannot be legally transferred to another person (ibid.: 5). Similarly, land categorised as trust land could only be removed from the communal ownership of local people by a process of adjudication in which local communities are given adequate notice and the opportunity to claim their ownership in accordance with customary law (ibid.: 52).

The commission investigated the illegal allocation of different types of land, including urban land, ministry land, national parks and museums, to mention a few. To take urban land as an illustration, the commission found evidence of widespread abuse of presidential discretion with regard to unalienated urban land. Both Presidents Kenyatta and Moi were found to have made grants to individuals without any reference to the public interest. The allocation was therefore done without following the correct legal procedures. Furthermore, both presidents also allocated alienated land despite the fact that this is not a category of land which they have any legal power to allocate. The Ndung'u report also found that a number of Commissioners of Lands had made direct grants of government land without any authority from the President. Often, land was quickly sold by grantees at very high prices to third parties without any adherence to the conditions laid down by letters of allotment, and despite the fact that such letters only have the status of letters of offer and cannot be sold. Far from being restrained by the principle of public purpose, the Commissioner of Lands and many local authorities completely disregarded it, and sold land reserved exclusively for public purposes such as schools, playgrounds and hospitals. Forged letters and documents were commonly used to allocate land. Records at the Ministry of Lands and Settlements were found to have been deliberately destroyed (Republic of Kenya 2004: 75).

The report also provided critical details of developments in the aftermath of illegal or irregular land allocations. It showed how those allocated land would move quickly to sell it, in many cases, to state corporations at hugely inflated prices. State corporations were in effect exploited as coerced buyers of grabbed land. Pressurised into making illegal purchases of public land, they become 'captive buyers of land from politically connected allottees' (Republic of Kenya 2004: 14). As the report makes clear, there was a further injustice created by the fact that state corporations were also sometimes the victims and not just the conduits of land grabbing. They could 'lose their land to grabbers for free, and then be pressured to buy other lands for millions of shillings' (Republic of Kenya 2004: 92). The primary state corporation targeted to purchase land was the Kenyan workers' pension scheme, the National Social Security Fund (NSSF). It spent about Ksh 30 billion (about US$300 million) between 1990 and 1995 on the purchase of illegally acquired property. The NSSF was set up in 1965 and regulated by the Minister for Labour, to whom a tripartite Advisory Council gives advice and assistance in connection with the implementation of the National Social Security Fund Act 1965 (Mullei 1988: 433). This legislation stipulated that the purpose of the NSSF is to provide for contributions to the payment of benefits out of the Fund and to provide social protection against old age, death and incapacitating physical or mental disability. Instead, the Ndung'u Commission found that the NSSF and other state corporations were simply abused as a vehicle for offloading grabbed land: 'State corporations were used as conduits for land grabbing schemes through which the public lost colossal amounts of money' (Republic of Kenya 2004: 87).

The implication of the Ndung'u report was that the economic and social costs of widespread land corruption would be felt for many years to come. Through its publication, Kenyans learned that land that should have been available for the public good – for the building of medical clinics and schools, for public parks and public transport facilities such as railways – had instead been transformed into private land. This privatisation, they now saw, deprived the public of significant social goods whilst generating large profits for the private consumption of well-connected individuals and families. Those involved in land corruption were able to ensure that their identities were carefully concealed. The two annexes to the Ndung'u report are filled with the names of companies clearly set up in order to shield the names of those involved in land grabbing from public scrutiny. There developed a thriving market in letters of allotment which came to be treated as tradeable land documents, although they do not have this status in law. Using their networks in the Ministry of Lands and Settlement, individuals in the know were able improperly to acquire changes of use that allowed land that had been reserved for public purposes such as schools and medical clinics, and most commonly for roads, to be sold for residential or commercial use. Lawyers often advised clients how to regularise land scams after the event.

By the time the Ndung'u report was published, the Ministry of Lands and Settlement was already widely known as one of Kenya's most inefficiently run public services. It had been cited in Transparency International's Bribery Index 2011 (Transparency International 2011) as Kenya's fifth most corrupt institution after the police, the Ministry of Defence, Nairobi City Council and the Immigration Department. The Ndung'u Commission found that one of the main reasons for the illegal allocation of public land was the 'chaotic record keeping system' in the Ministry and in the district registries (Republic of Kenya 2004: 188). In addition, it found that records were falsified or hidden in order to conceal the illegal allocation of land (ibid.: 188). The Ndung'u report found that surveyors employed by the Ministry would survey a piece of land 'from their desk' without ever visiting the site (ibid.: 80), and subsequently issue two title deeds to the same parcel of land, one under the Registered Land Act 1963, for example, and one under the Registration of Titles Act 1982: 'as part of an elaborate scheme of land grabbing and given the multiplicity of land registration laws, different titles would be issued to the same piece of land ... The double issuance of titles was meant to facilitate the illegal allocation of public land' (ibid.: 80) by enabling land to be dealt with under two systems simultaneously. The Commission also discovered quite early in its work that many illegal allocations of public land were made not to individuals but companies. These companies were ostensibly registered at the Registry of Companies in conformity with the requirements of the Companies Act. The Commission would not have fulfilled one of its Terms of Reference if it had not disclosed the names of the people (either directors or shareholders) behind these companies. This meant that in many instances, a single title of land required a painstaking double search at the Ministry of Lands and at the Registry of Companies. Despite the cooperation of the Registrar of Companies, the commission encountered problems in identifying the individuals behind companies that had been allocated land. In some cases, the companies holding allocated land did not exist in law. In these cases, individuals had acquired blank Certificate of Incorporation forms which they submitted to acquire public land but which had not been reflected in the records of the Companies Register. In others, companies that had not been fully incorporated acquired land. The Ndung'u report showed that most high-profile allocations of public land were made to companies incorporated specifically for that purpose, largely to shield the directors and shareholders of such entities from easy public view (ibid.: 40). The commission gives a list of companies which acquired land but whose individual owners are not immediately evident (ibid.: Annexe I: 22–5).

The report also showed that letters of allotment were widely used as land titles and changed hands quickly in sales of grabbed land, despite the fact that they cannot be properly used for this purpose. These documents confer no transferable interest or rights over land in favour of the person to whom they are addressed. Strictly, they only enable land to be allocated so long as the exact conditions set out on the face of the document are adhered to. As noted, these specify that the offer to allocate land is made only to the person named in the letter of allotment, that it expires after thirty days, and that the land allocated must be developed within a given period. Despite the fact that letters of allotment cannot function as titles, letters of allotment were transformed from letters of offer into land instruments to be transacted.

Another widespread practice involved changes of use. Improper changes of use enabled land reserved for public purposes to be privatised and developed or sold for large profits. In practice, this amounted to an illegal allocation of land reserved for public purposes by the Commissioner of Lands 'in total disregard of the law and the public interest for which they had been reserved' (Republic of Kenya 2004: 77). These lands were allocated following the submission of Part Development Plans prepared by lawyers and surveyors to the Commissioner of Lands, who then issued consents for changes of use under the relevant law, such as the Physical Planning Act 1996 or the Forests Act 1982. Land was often then swiftly sold on to third parties by the original allottees. The most prominent category of land allocated in this manner was land reserved for the future development of roads. Changes of use enabled this category of land to be grabbed throughout the country. In Nairobi, the City Council approved development plans for areas that were clearly set aside for construction of roads. According to the report, it was not unusual for the commission to see a development plan for a residence being prepared for land that was supposed to be reserved for a road (ibid.: 55). In addition, officials in the Ministry of Roads,

Public Works and Housing and the Nairobi City Council regularly wrote letters of no objection to problematic proposed developments (ibid.: 77). However, the report notes that neither the approval for change of use given by the Commissioner of Lands, nor the letters expressing no objection could properly result in valid changes of use. As a result, allocations acquired in this way were not legal (see ibid.: Annexe 1 Chapter 4 for a list of affected road reserves).

The Ndung'u report was met with enormous interest by the media and by civil society on its release. For many, it confirmed much that had been known about land crimes and constituted an official record of widespread dispossession. Amidst rumours that the report had been doctored before its release to protect the names of prominent individuals, a claim denied by the commission's chairperson, the press reported extensively on those who had been involved in land grabbing and the land that they had acquired (see Manji 2012). Given the period over which the illegal allocation of public land had taken place, many of the land titles investigated by the Ndung'u Commission were held by third parties who were not involved in the original transactions, many of whom had not committed any legal wrong: they might have been offered and bought the land from the original allottee, been offered the title to land as security for a loan, have inherited the land from a deceased friend or relative or received it as a gift. When considering the legal position of third parties the commission argued that such rights are extinguished since they were illegal from their inception. Third parties could be interpreted as being in the same position as the original allottee. However, it recognised the difficulties entailed in dealing with third parties who had acted innocently in acquiring land interests. They noted in particular the potential hardships endured by third parties who had made substantial developments, by state corporations which were coerced into buying land, and commercial lenders who had acquired the titles as security against loans. Although it was generally recommended that illegally issued titles that had been passed on to third parties should be revoked and the land repossessed, the commission recognised that where the land had been developed 'consideration should be given to all the circumstances of the case including the cost incurred in developing the land', the number of people involved financially, the economic value and the public interest (Africog 2009: 23).

Fundamental to the problems rehearsed in the Ndung'u report is the fact that the administration of land is intricately tied up with politics rather than sheltered from political interference. The Njonjo Commission had sought to address this critical issue in 2002 when it recommended the creation of an independent National Land Commission. This recommendation, which might have stemmed the land grabbing reported by the Ndung'u Commission, was never acted upon. It was restated in the Ndung'u report and when the movement for constitu-

tional reform gathered pace and became connected with the movement
for land reform, the creation of this new body, standing apart from the
executive, became an important demand.

Non-land reports

In this section I discuss a number of official reports which, although
they did not solely concern land matters, raised ongoing land injustices
as part of their wider mandate. This is important because it demonstrates the intricate connections between land and human rights
abuses and state violence and highlights how central land grabbing
had become to wider questions of economic disenfranchisement and
inequality. The land question was unavoidable across political, social
and economic domains. A good example of this is the report of the
Commission of Inquiry into Post-Election Violence (the so-called Waki
Commission). As the demands for constitutional reform gathered pace,
the work of this Commission followed in December 2007. Although not
directly mandated to investigate land matters, the commission's report
when it was published nonetheless had the effect of distilling many of
Kenya's ongoing land problems, and connecting them with ethnic-based
violence, exclusivity and dispossession. In its report, the commission
described how many districts of the country had become ethnic based
so that the provision that it is possible for any person to hold land in any
part of the country was simply not observed, and existed in principle
only. In practice there existed 'exclusive sub-national enclaves akin to
"native reserves" in which there are "insiders" (ancestral landowners)
and "outsiders" (migrants)' (Syagga 2015: 13 quoting Republic of Kenya
2008: 31). This finding had profound implications. It linked access to
land powerfully with violence, with ethnic mobilisation which peaked
during each election cycle and with the deliberate construction by
the country's leadership of ethnically homogenous areas. The Waki
Commission expressed grave concerns at what it saw as both overt and
covert policies to encourage ethnic homogeneity in land allocation and
in the acquisition of land. This had led over the years to 'residential
apartheid', for example in urban areas where concentration of ethnic
groups together had become commonplace. The report noted that this
approach to land had been pursued by successive governments.

These findings supplemented and reinforced the approach taken in
the Report of the Task Force on the Establishment of a Truth, Justice and
Reconciliation Commission (widely known after its chairperson as the
Mutua Task Force). In its report published in 2003, the Mutua Commission had recognised the role that had been played by successive regimes
in inflaming land tensions in order to gain electoral support and target
opposition to their rule. It noted that the Moi era had seen access to land
used as a pretext: the government 'instigated and at times directed
the ignition and execution of ethnic clashes' directed against oppo-

sition areas so that '[c]ommunities that had lived peaceably together for decades were suddenly turned against each other' (Mutua 2004). The report acknowledges the effects of these clashes on communities, noting the 'deep wounds have been left on the Kenyan psyche by these clashes' in areas such as Molo, Enoosopukia and Likoni; it urged that these land matters should be central to the terms of reference of a truth commission so that they could be investigated and some form of redress recommended.

The Mutua Task Force took an interesting approach to the historical span to be addressed by a truth commission, arguing that what was needed was an investigation into land and ethnic clashes that paid particular attention to historical claims that arose out of the colonial period. It suggested that the best way to achieve this was to expand the mandate of the newly appointed Ndung'u Commission discussed above and by this means require it to investigate and settle historical land issues. Relatedly, in its report the Task Force was clear that, although the land wrongs and human rights violations in the colonial period were grave, a truth commission should not be mandated to investigate these. Its argument was that these events were too remote in time and raised questions too difficult for the particular transitional justice mechanism being explored by the Task Force in the form of a truth commission. As well as problems of evidence and considerations of feasibility and cost, the Task Force recommended that the answerable party was in fact the United Kingdom rather than Kenya, and pointed out that truth commissions are not generally established to investigate departed powers. In its view Kenyans could only hold their own country to account and not the colonial British state. The report therefore concluded that the best course of action was for the government to consider the creation of a different mechanism, such as a committee of eminent Kenyans who could be given the responsibility of investigating issues relating to the colonial period and who would recommend redress that might be sought from the British, including in the form of recognition of those who fell in the struggle for independence. It was recommended that any commission should cover the period 1963 to 2002 (Mutua 2004).

The post-election violence of late 2007 and early 2008 and the intervention of Kofi Annan and the African Union's Panel of Eminent African Personalities finally led to the setting up of Kenya's Truth, Justice and Reconciliation Commission after many years of advocacy for such a forum (Branch 2011; Kanyinga 2011; Lynch 2018). The commission started work in 2009. Its hearings were widely followed (Lynch 2018). So too were the numerous controversies that surrounded its chairperson, Bethuel Kiplagat. A number of these controversies were connected with land. Most significantly, the chair of the commission had been named in the Ndung'u report discussed above as having benefited from land grabbing under the Moi Government (Bosire and

Lynch 2014). Those critical of his role in this latest commission argued this cast significant doubt on his integrity and, going further, that his appointment was designed to pervert the work of truth-finding with which the commission had been charged. In addition to this, the publication of the report when it eventually took place in 2013 was attended by controversy when it was alleged that political interference was involved in ensuring the final version was redacted to remove a critical section on land which laid out how and where land was acquired for personal use by the Kenyatta family from settlement land meant to be distributed to landless families at the coast (Slye 2018). There was little that was new in this finding. The Ndung'u report had laid out empirical findings on a similar scale (Warah 2019). The difference this time was that those who were thought to be responsible for the post-election violence had been reported to the International Criminal Court (ICC)'s Office of the Prosecutor (OTP) in 2009 and the ICC Pre-Trial Chamber had authorised the OTP to begin to conduct investigations. In 2012, the Office of the Prosecutor confirmed charges against four individuals, leading to an electoral alliance between two of these, former rivals Uhuru Kenyatta and William Ruto, in what quickly came to be labelled an 'alliance of the accused' (see Bosire and Lynch 2014; Lynch 2014) (in the 2013 election Kenyatta and Ruto went on to win). One of the international commissioners, the US legal academic Ronald Slye, has described the pressures surrounding the publication of the report and the influence exercised by key individuals in the government to ensure it was redacted. Slye and his fellow international commissioners published a dissenting chapter on the topic of land (Slye 2018) and also made available the report in its full extent at the Seattle School of Law website after the website of the TJRC was taken down in 2014 or 2015 (see Slye 2018; TJRC 2018).

As Warah (2019) has pointed out, there was little that was empirically new in the dissent. It was perhaps made more vivid because it reported the testimony of witnesses before the commission on wrong-doings associated with land and named names, but other than that it simply echoed the findings of previous inquiries such as the Ndung'u report. Timing accounted for the difficulties described by Slye (2018). As a result of these difficulties, the controversy surrounding the dissent to the land chapter was widely reported and keenly followed. For this reason, the dissent has come to form a counter-archive (Motha and van Rijswijk 2016: 1; White 2000; see also the account provided by Anderson (2015) of Britain's 'migrated archive'). Derrida (1996: 36) has written that we must be attentive to the ways in which archives might be future oriented, reminding us that 'it is the future that is at issue here, and the archive as an irreducible experience of the future'. The dissent, like the report of the TJRC as a whole, confirmed what Kenyans knew had been longstanding wrongs in relation to land and much else, as well as suggesting the shape of a future to be wished for. Knowledge of the past and guides to future change are in this way connected: 'the return to the archive is often informed by a quest for utopian futures' (de Jong 2016: 3) The attempts at its suppression simply confirmed Kenyans' popular memory. It became in this way part of a 'repository' (Stoler 2002: 97) connecting the state's secrecy with the exercise of undue influence and of violence and threats. By this means it contributed to Kenyans' 'cultures of documentation' (Stoler 2002: 88) in relation to land. It is to these wider practices of documentation and to the theme of popular memory on land that I now turn.

Land and popular memory

In a paper published before the commissioning of the Ndung'u report, Klopp (2000: 7–26) provided a perceptive account of the 'pilfering' of public land, focusing on the 1990s and the illegal allocations of public land that took place under the Moi regime. Her account of 'the irregular privatisation of public land' remains one of the few academic analyses to take seriously local or internal land grabbing. Of course, the extent and details of this were widely known amongst members of the public and civil society groups (Hirst and Lamba 1994). Many communities became victims of the predatory actions of land grabbers (Klopp 2000), and the land grabbing stories that regularly circulated in Kenya ensured that few people were ignorant of the scale of misallocation of public land. Indeed, a number of organisations vigorously resisted land grabbing, including through the courts. In October 1998, at the height of attempted land grabbing in Karura Forest, the Architectural Association of Kenya announced that it would take disciplinary action against any member found to be working with improperly acquired properties (Githongo 2000).

Much of the analysis presented by Klopp is confirmed by the Ndung'u Commission. Klopp (2000: 7) argued that, as Kenya's powerful political elite confronted the reality of declining 'patronage resources', it sought alternative ways to finance its patrimonial control. She sees the growth in the illegal allocation of public land of the 1990s as a 'creative counter-strategy to change'. These threats to patronage resources included the decline in foreign aid as a source of patronage, the greater scrutiny of some forms of corruption by the international community and, in the context of the introduction of multiparty elections, the increased political contests they faced (ibid.: 8). Public land, less visible to international donors and therefore escaping their scrutiny, was transformed into a valuable 'patronage asset' (ibid.). Kenya's 'land grabbing mania' (ibid.: 8) is for Klopp an unintended consequence of donors' periodic withdrawals of aid in the 1990s. The accuracy of this claim has subsequently been confirmed by the Ndung'u Commission's finding that illegal and irregular allocations of land peaked at election times (Republic of Kenya 2004: 2; Southall 2005: 146).

Klopp also argues that, with the increased competition entailed in the liberalisation of the political system, administrative officials feared for the continued access to land that they exercised, and sought quickly to maximise the rent they extracted from its (mis)allocation, as well as adding to their personal stocks of land resources. Key to this was the allocation of land to property developers. For Klopp (2000: 8), 'the intensification of irregular allocations of public land to well-connected individuals and land-buying companies ... is a particularly revealing and underscrutinised case of deepening corruption' which, despite being both widely discussed and resisted within Kenya, had 'largely failed to attract commensurate attention on the part of scholars'. Writers on developments in Kenya's political system in the 1990s and subsequent years privileged formal political practice over 'informal manoeuvring' (ibid.: 8). Citing the work of non-governmental organisations (NGOs) including Kituo cha Sheria (an NGO with a focus on human rights and the legal advice to the disadvantaged) and the Kenya Human Rights Commission Land Rights Programme in running Operation Firimbi ('whistle' in Kiswahili), which sought to document instances of land grabbing and to organise local resistance to these actions, Klopp (ibid.: 23) argued that such work created a 'realm of public scrutiny'. Since Klopp's paper, the Ndung'u report, by creating a permanent official record of the phenomenon, has made a lasting contribution to this scrutiny.

So much for the official archive of Kenya's land troubles, accumulated over many years and often going over similar ground. Its common themes of grabbing, ethnic mobilisation and violent election-related conflict have been recorded time and again in the reports studied above. There is no shortage of evidence of a sedimented history of land wrongs. In referring to these reports as constituting an archive, I mean to show that Kenya's accumulated land archive is not a thing or a place but rather a practice or a process (Stoler 2002: 87). Although official reports have been published over an elongated time period and are often scattered in different places, more often than not their publication and release has only taken place after protracted struggle (KHRC 2011). A state responsible for land wrongs on a massive scale has resisted at each step the coming into being of a land archive. Struggles to have official reports released or to resist attempts to redact or alter them have breathed life into the archive. Over time, these reports have come to constitute a political and legal folk memory. It could be said that in this regard they function less as source (Stoler 2002) than as a reminder to the reader or listener of 'law's memorial function' (Motha and van Rijswijk 2016: 1).

In the discussion above I drew on longstanding, authoritative official reports to explore the land grabbing, dispossession, irregular land dealing and land-related violence committed by a predatory state for which 'accumulation by dispossession' is central to its political economy (I return to this in Chapter 8). Through the years, important work to have official reports released and made publicly available has been undertaken by leading human rights and other civil society organisations. As I suggested in Chapter 1, the struggle to achieve the publication of the Ndung'u report, and the resistance to the manoeuvring and delay around the release of the TJRC report are two leading examples of the efforts to resist the suppression of critical report by the state. The Ndung'u report has become one of the most important ways on which Kenya's land truths have become memorialised, its annexes in particular exercising a fascination for citizens intent on uncovering who grabbed what and where. I would argue that the struggle for the release of official reports has itself played an important role in political and civil life. In the process of struggling for access to these reports, civil society has been put into conversation with citizens. Often detailed and technical material has had to be communicated to the wider public and political processes and implications explored. In mediating and communicating technical content, a vibrant citizen's archive has been brought into being. Indeed, in the years preceding the constitutional review process, Kenyans had become adept at maintaining this people's archive and at discussing and by necessity speculating on the content of reports. Stoler's (2009: 87) reminder to view archives not as places but as process enables us to understand the consequences of these struggles over meaning. When the Constitution of Kenya Review Commission came to hear evidence around the country in preparation for a new draft constitution, it was on a people's archive accumulated over many years that citizens were able to draw (see CKRC 2005a)

The maintenance of a people's archive, in dialogue with official reports, and brought into being as a result of these reports, is an important part of Kenya's land history. In relation to the politics of dispossession on the coastal 'Ten Mile Strip' from the late 1950s to 1964, for example, Willis and Gona (2013: 48) have explored 'the way that people now retell the history of earlier debates' and have shown how 'these retellings suggest both the power and the plasticity of claims to historical knowledge'. Studying the Mombasa Republican Council (MRC), Willis and Gona (ibid.: 50) explain:

> While some of these retellings of history evidence a familiar theme – the malleability of remembered historical knowledge and the flexibility of oral history – the centrality of written treaties suggests a rather different phenomenon. By citing such documents, the MRC offers a challenge to the esoteric knowledge that lies behind state authority, the distribution of which is profoundly inequitable, and it asserts a claim to an alternative authoritative knowledge of docu-

ments that can remake power – a subversive appropriation of what Sharon Hutchinson, in another context, has called the 'hidden powers of "paper"'. Levels of literacy on the Kenya coast are much higher than those in Hutchinson's study area in southern Sudan, but here too words on paper are attributed a special, sometimes magical, power that may be particularly compelling for those who cannot read them.

This suggests that we must also account for possible 'counter-archives' (Motha and van Rijswijk 2016: 1). Building on the observation (ibid.) that law has a 'memorialising function' we might consider how ordinary citizens have memorialised land mischiefs. Beyond their engagement with official narrative and documents, how might Kenyans have developed a 'counter-archival sense' (ibid.: 8) in relation to land? What part is played by stories and rumours in developing counter-hegemonic accounts of land mischief? What is the content of a peoples' archive on land? Here, we might offer as examples the struggle to preserve Karura Forest in Nairobi from excision and grabbing (Manji 2017b) and the *Shule Yangu* (My School) movement which sought to draw public attention to the grabbing of school land by powerful individuals and in this way to prevent the land being permanently lost. Both these movements were driven by ordinary citizens and relied on publicly circulating knowledge to identify land threatened with grabbing. In both these examples, the watchfulness of citizens made it more difficult to grab public land with impunity. Musila makes the case for 'rumour as an influential genre of knowledge production, contestation and critique – what has been termed a form of 'community intelligence' – that challenges single-lens conceptions of credible knowledge.' (2017: 695) She urges us to excavate 'the place of rumour as an important genre of social truths that enjoy epistemic authority' (ibid.). An unstable, porous archive made up of subaltern narratives supplements official reports on land grabbing. For Willis and Gona (2013: 71), people's experiences of official documents can be understood in the language and mobilisation of the MRC since 2005.

> The story of the MRC's success is in part a story of the peculiar vulnerability of arcane knowledge to subversive re-interpretation; it shows how the layered paper legitimacy of the colonial and post-colonial state can be challenged by interpretations whose popular appeal does not require them to obey the logic of that legitimacy. For people who do not expect documents to make sense, they can be made to mean anything. (Willis and Gona 2013: 71)

An important question for activists, policy makers and lawyers is: how might law reformers and the courts adjudicating on land issues might be put into conversation with this counter-archive? Macharia and Ghai (2017) have emphasised the importance of public participation in constitution-making. In this regard, it is important to recognise that people's participation in the creation of counter-archives and alternative land narratives was an entry point into the constitutional review process. Seen in this light, participation had begun long before the review process as citizen's kept alive a record of rumour and stories of land wrongs and politics more widely. This was distilled and given shape by the process of civic education that preceded constitutional drafting.

Struggles on new ground: Community land

According to Alden Wily (2018a) one of the most important recent developments in land and property in Africa has been the focus on improving the legal status of customary land interests. I would suggest that community land, or customary land or communal land – which are used as interchangeable terms – is one domain in which transformative land relations can be seen to have occurred during the 2010s. Here, ideas of what is suitable and modern as a form of land tenure have shifted in ways that are remarkable: we have gone from international and national land policy prescriptions which deprecated community land to one in which such tenure regimes are seen as valuable, workable and indeed desirable. The importance of legal interventions in this form of tenure is not limited to Kenya. Changes relating to community land have now taken place, or are under discussion, in Benin, Democratic Republic of the Congo, Ghana, Kenya, Liberia, Malawi, Mali, Morocco, Namibia, Senegal, Sierra Leone, South Africa and Zambia (Alden Wily 2018a).

Having explored the history of public land in Kenya and the many wrongs associated with it, it is important to be aware of what is likely to happen as patronage resources are depleted and increasingly unavailable. Alden Wily (2018a) has suggested that community land is the new battleground in Kenya's land politics. Public land – previously a plentiful resource and one available to the President and powerful elites to use as a patronage resource as explored above – has been exhausted. A finite resource, public land has been grabbed in a process of allocation and conversion in which it is has been transmogrified into private land. This reclassification of public land into private land happened under both Presidents Kenyatta and Moi, and there were already signs, by the time President Mwai Kibaki assumed office, that it was running out. The patronage machine's hunger for land now seeks to be satisfied in new ways. Community land, a new category of land which found its way into the National Land Policy in 2009 and into the 2010 Constitution, and thence came to take legal form in the Community Land Act 2016, will be the new ground on which much of Kenya's land politics will be played out over the next decade. Alden Wily (2018b) identifies a paradigm shift in which there has been a recognition that community tenure should be afforded respect and protection as opposed to being seen as backward and, through a teleological lens, as a form of tenure that would die out over time to be replaced with individual property rights (McAuslan 2003).

Conclusion

Over the years, a number of official reports, supplemented by the intimate, everyday knowledge of citizens' 'radio trottoir' about malpractices connected with land, had recorded how Kenya had become 'the President's plantation' (Ngugi wa Thiong'o quoted in Wachanga 2018: 17) because the Constitution empowered the President to make grants or dispositions of any estates, interests, or rights over public land. The Ndung'u Report Inquiry into Irregular/Illegal Allocation of Public Land revealed just how the President's authority was repeatedly misused. It is however difficult to find fault with the thrust of Southall's comment that one of the shortcomings of the Ndung'u report was that it did not tell us much about what happened to the land effectively redistributed by grabbing:

> [W]hat is lacking from its analysis, even if – strictly speaking – it may have gone beyond its terms of reference, is some assessment of what land grabbing may have had upon the economy, and whether, in particular, land which was illegally appropriated has been put to productive use. In this regard, no overall summary or analysis has been provided, even though, with regard to the majority of allocations, the Commission offers two columns which list, first, the officially intended use of the land, and in the second, its current use. Even so, even an unsystematic thumbing through the pages of the annexures suggests that the overwhelming majority of allocations have been utilised for residential, commercial, industrial or building purposes. (Southall 2005: 150)

The Report of the Task Force on the Establishment of a Truth, Justice and Reconciliation Commission was alert to this when it noted that the state had knowingly caused the marginalisation and exclusion of citizens and land injustices, including by skewing distribution and limiting access to economic resources. I return to the wider implications of this in Chapter 8 when I argue that we must be alert to the ways in which corruption and the 'normal' economy have become intertwined, and show that this raises critical questions about how we understand land wrongs and their effects in the past, present and future.

4

Land and Constitutional Change

_____

In an ideal situation, a constitution should set out the broad principles for the governance of land and establish an efficient and equitable institutional framework for land ownership, administration
and management. Land policy reforms are not likely to succeed in the
absence of such a sound constitutional framework. Accordingly, land
reforms should be accompanied by constitutional reforms if they are
to be effective. (Republic of Kenya 2009b)

Kenya's current constitutional moment has included both the first
popularly ratified constitution and its first post-independence comprehensive land reform policy. The roughly temporally parallel processes
that brought about these two signal achievements have inserted
the interests of ordinary Kenyans into this constitutional moment
in a way that elections and constitutional ratification alone would
not have, reflecting more than two decades of civil society pressure.
(Harbeson 2012: 15)

Introduction: Land as exemplar

In the 1990s, the struggles of civil society for constitutional reforms
and the demands of civil society for an end to kleptocratic land relations
became deeply interconnected. Constitutional reform became at once a
'struggle over the formulation of the norms, structures, and processes
to govern the state' (Mutua 2008: 117) and a struggle for 'legal text
and political culture' (Modiri 2018: 295). In this chapter, I explore the
part played by demands for land reform in the constitutional debate. I
show how the constitutional debate and the land debate became intertwined and ran alongside one another. Part of the explanation is that as
well as running alongside each other temporally (Harbeson 2012: 15),
they also shared the same _dramatis personae_. Members of civil society
campaigning on land issues were often also participants in wider
anti-government and pro-democracy movements. They often had what

Kenyans call 'struggle credentials' along more than one axis. For this reason, I think the place of the land struggle in the period of Kenya's new constitution-making was different to that occupied by 'specialized cadres' which Mutua (2008: 118) identified as 'clusters of reformers ... focused on single issues'. In the 1990s, as a result of the official reports and subaltern pressures that I describe in Chapter 3, those agitating for land reform succeeded in elevating land problems as typifying Kenya's national political culture and demonstrating the need for change. By trying to place land at the heart of demands for change, civil society offered it as an *exemplar* of the injustices that needed to be addressed. They did this by harnessing the findings of key reports such as the Ndung'u report and the Waki report discussed in the previous chapter to argue that land wrongs exemplified what was wrong with Kenya's wider political structures, institutions and culture.

What were the implications of this conjoining of land and constitutional struggles? In this chapter, I argue that the joining of constitutional and land reform struggles had some important advantages. It allowed those pushing for changes in the land sector to draw significant attention to key issues, often by translating them into language and claims suitable to and so audible by a wider constitutional struggle. I show that by making land wrongs relevant to constitutional debates over the *longue durée*, a committed land-related civil society succeeded in achieving important visibility for land questions. As pressures for constitutional reform built, they ensured that reform aimed at fairer land relations were also seen as part of the solution (Manji 2006). By their concerted work, they inserted land questions effectively into wider debates about the nature and purpose of constitutional change (Harbeson 2012). But I also argue that the dual reform movements on which Kenya embarked from around 2002 were each circumscribed in similar ways. Driven by an urban middle class, they were marked by a reliance on transformation through law, by insufficient scepticism of rule-of-law discourses and by the early foreclosure of more radical possibilities.

This chapter is structured as follows. In the section that follows, I provide an account of Kenya's path to its new Constitution in 2010 and explore how land reform and constitutional reform became conjoined. I suggest some implications of this. In the next section, I explore the composition and role of a vocal civil society that successfully framed the land question in a way appropriate to the political moment. The solution to longstanding land questions, they argued, lay in institutional control of an executive that had long preyed on the sector for personal enrichment and political gain. Resolving the land question was presented as a fundamental requisite of wider political change. Theirs was a task of translation, of making audible to the wider constitutional movement how the terms they employed to explain land wrongs could also be used to explain wider political wrongs to be cured by constitutional reform:

abuse of executive power, a despotic presidency, personalised corruption, a deep-seated tendency to kleptocracy, compromised institutions. In this section I also explore issues not admitted into the land debate and seek to explain why. I show how some topics and possibilities had to be placed outside the realm of debate. This was because the translation of land demands into constitutional demands presupposed a liberal constitutional framework which could read off those demands from history and society and incorporate them into suitable constitutional language in a settled and agreed document. More radical possibilities – for agrarian reform and for land redistribution – could not find a place within the liberal legal framework that appeared to be the agreed mode for a much needed political settlement. Recognising that the possibilities for change were circumscribed – and that the constitutional settlement that could be reached was necessarily a compromise – land-related NGOs nonetheless seized the opportunity to secure some gains through the constitutional reform process as it gained momentum. Land was treated as a constitutional category at various stages of the review process such that reform in the land arena became a marker for the wider success of the 2010 Constitution. I suggest that there are some dangers inherent in this. Disillusionment with progress on land matters risks becoming more widely associated with constitutional disappointment.

Land and the Constitution conjoined

The transition to democracy and the process of 'writ[ing] a new contract between the state and society' (Mutua 2008: 141) in Kenya took place over an elongated time period from the first multiparty elections in 1992. Given that the process was protracted (Brown 2004), how to account for the momentum for constitutional change that characterised the decade from 1990 to 2010? Harbeson (2012) traces the roots of change to demands from civil society backed up by the informal group of creditor nations known as the Paris Club, advocating strongly for multiparty elections from 1991. These demands were strengthened by the unrest of the 1992 elections (Hornsby 2013; Mutua 2008) and then were quickly seen as vital in the wake of the violent 1997 elections. The pressures that led President Moi to agree to the appointment of a constitutional review commission have been discussed in detail elsewhere (see Berman et al. 2009; Mutua 2008) and the outcome was a draft constitution which was 'uniquely participatory' and which 'sought principally to divide and limit executive power' (Harbeson 2012: 29). President Kibaki, by then accustomed to the untrammelled powers of office (Mutua 2008) resisted the proposals. A revised draft was put to a referendum in 2005 and rejected. A period of drift followed but the violence of the 2007 general elections gave fresh urgency to demands for constitutional change. This demand received backing from Kofi Annan in his headship of the African Union Panel of Eminent African Personalities whom the country relied upon to broker a solution to the post-election breakdown. In the end an agreement was reached between President Kibaki's Party of National Unity and Raila Odinga's Orange Democratic Movement (ODM). Organised around a power-sharing arrangement, the parties committed to addressing a number of long-standing issues at the root of the electoral violence. These included both constitutional reform and land reform. In the constitutional arena, the agreement was to renew the engagement with reform and in good faith to seek to draft a new document for approval at a referendum.

In the land arena, the commitment was to take seriously the reality that difficult land problems lay at the heart of the elections in 1992, 1997 and 2007. In concrete terms this meant that the process of adopting a national land policy, which was to be the country's first comprehensive land policy (Harbeson 2012), would have to be restarted so that a final document could be presented for approval to Parliament. Reform in the land arena can thus be said to have restarted with the approval of the National Land Policy in 2009. In 2010, the new Constitution, incorporating the principles of the National Land Policy in its Chapter Five, was passed at a referendum. As Harbeson (2012: 15) has observed: 'While many of Kenya's achievements since 2008 have been accomplished with international assistance (or because of international pressure), the principal driver of these reforms has been the energy and decades-long persistence of Kenyan civil society'.

Nonetheless, Kenya's history of constitution-making needs to be understood in the context of modern global constitutional history in which 'constitutional change was the preferred solution in processes of state reconstruction that swept the world in the last decade of the twentieth century' (Klug 2018: 473; see also Ghai 2017). What is striking when reading accounts of Kenya's constitutional movement is how clear sighted that movement was about the history of political and civil repression that needed to be remedied with a transformative constitution. There are several reasons for this. Leading names in the movement had long participated in oppositional politics: they had watched the dismantling of checks and balances and the increasing concentration of personal power in the President. They had a keen sense of the work to be done. Much of the work would involve addressing the constitutional amendments made by the Kenyatta and Moi regimes. According to Berman et al.,

> devolution of powers and checks and balances was emasculated by amendment over a period of only a few years. The amendments dismantled freedom and democracy, replaced the system of devolution of powers by a highly centralized administration, modified the parlia-

mentary system by a presidential system with an enormous concentration of power in one person, established one party rule, and enacted draconian laws including preventive detention. Under a facade of party rule and electoral processes, an authoritarian system of personal authority, ethnic favouritism, and patronage replaced liberal democratic citizenship with a system of patrons and their client subjects. (2009: 478–9)

On top of a clear agenda for reform of the state, the movement for constitutional review derived much of its legitimacy and its popularity from its responsiveness to the people. It argued that the impetus for constitutional change came from the people. The Constitution of Kenya Review Commission (CKRC 2005a) declared that their work would be informed by consultation with citizens. The guiding document of the movement became a chapter in the CKRC report (ibid.). As Diepeveen (2010) has shown, the CKRC process set out clear guidelines for civic education so that citizens were enabled to participate meaningfully in consultations over the review process. But as she shows, this also meant that they 'were confronted with political and social elites' perceptions of possible parameters for political interaction' (ibid.: 234):

The CKRC outlined its views on the parameters of good government in a national curriculum for civic education providers, and in two documents entitled Reviewing the Constitution (CKRC 2001a), and Constitutional Review Process in Kenya: issues and questions for public hearing (CKRC 2001b). The CKRC programme emphasised political legitimacy rooted in a democratic legal-rational authority. According to the 2001 curriculum manual, democracy was a system 'to promote self-reliance in decision-making ... and generally empower [people] to make decisions' (CKRC 2001c: 17), and government was the organ that 'carries out responsibilities and exercises power on behalf of the people' (ibid.: 51). This emphasis on popular sovereignty was coupled with the suggestion that a rule of law was necessary to maintain political stability; the constitution was described as 'the foundation of a house' and 'roots of a tree' (ibid.: 43). (Ibid.: 235)

A progressive civil society movement calling for constitutional change was determined to show both that Kenya's constitutional reform movement had grown deep roots through time and that those roots had been nourished by the concerns and the demands of ordinary citizens. Similarly, in the related arena of demands for land reform there was a clear sense of Kenya's land history. Here, the guiding documents were the Ndung'u report, which received widespread attention when it was published in 2004 and which, together with its companion inquiry reports, lent significant momentum to demands for a national land policy. The Ndung'u report set out in detail the abuse of power that had characterised the land sector and the legal mechanisms such as letters of allocation that had been misused. From its publication, pressure mounted for constitutional and legislative solutions to land issues. Ghai (2017: 157) reminds us that the CKRC draft and the final Constitution was 'a constitution replete with values of constitutionalism, but not only that, since major themes of the constitution are social justice for the present and future generations and redressing past injustices in matters pertaining to land'.

What were the implications of the twinning of the land and constitutional reform movements? Clearly, the linking of their demands to wider political debates lent impetus to the land reform movement. It enabled them to keep a spotlight on land issues and energised them after many years of struggle, for example, in pressing for the publication of the National Land Policy. When this finally took place in 2009 it was only after their determined insistence. The close affiliation between the land and the constitutional movements enabled Kenyans to read the constitutional moment holistically, to see how abuse of executive power had taken place across sectors and interrelatedly. In the struggle against illegal acquisition of land around the perimeters of Karura Forest in Nairobi (Manji 2017b), to take one illustration, questions of land grabbing, electoral politics, abuse of presidential powers over land and of administrative discretion were all evoked. This allowed Kenyans to see that land grabbing was about personal enrichments by the elite but also about that elite helping itself to public goods in order to use them as a patronage resource in the election cycle and so hold on to power. This perspective was given impetus by the key finding of the Ndung'u report that 'most illegal allocations of public land took place before or soon after the multiparty general elections of 1992, 1997 and 2002' (Republic of Kenya 2004: 83) which, as Southall pointed out, made an important connection between political office and land grabbing, confirming for ordinary citizens that public land was indeed being illegally or irregularly allocated 'as political reward or patronage' (Southall 2007: 147). Ndung'u made explicit for Kenyans how the vicious circle of 'land wrongs – political abuse – hold on power' had kept turning. Similarly, as the constitutional review process got underway, struggles in other arenas informed its debates and concerns. In addition, as Sing'oei (2011) has argued, considerations of the category of trust land with its roots in the colonial era were informed by the ongoing judicial struggles of the Endorois peoples first in the Kenya High Court and then through the African Commission for Human and Peoples' Rights. According to Sing'oei, the category of Community Land created by the 2010 Constitution can be at least partly attributed to the Endorois struggle which brought into sharp relief the inability of the existing trust-based legal framework to offer them protection from a predatory state and powerful corporations for whom game parks for tourism, followed by prospecting for valuable natural resources in the form of enzymes from Lake Bogoria and mining for valuable ruby deposits was prioritised over the livelihood of the Endorois. Indigenous peoples' own engagement with the constitutional review process called into question that very framework for land in Kenya: the Ogiek and the Sengwer people made a joint submission to the Constitution of Kenya Review Commission in 2005 explicitly mentioning the failure of the domestic courts to respond adequately to their longstanding struggle. I return to the struggles of indigenous peoples in Chapter 7.

Openness to wider political struggles was one of the great strengths of Kenya's constitutional review process. Specifically, a conjoined constitutional and land reform movement in the 2002–10 period allowed both spheres of change to gain strength and momentum from one another. But it must be admitted that that twinning also limited the scope and effectiveness of the land movement in significant ways. First, the constitution-making process was fragmented across a range of different sectoral issues which had to be significantly pushed onto the reform agenda, with mixed results. Whilst this multi-interest and multi-sectoral approach (Macharia and Ghai 2017) was a strength of the Constitution of Kenya Review Commission's approach, and arose out of its participatory constitution-making methodology, it also meant that a variety of different sectors battled for attention. At stake were control of the executive powers of the presidency (summed up in demands to 'end the dictatorship' (Mutua 2008: 200)), the achievement of devolution and the drafting of a constitutional schema that empowered local communities in the overly centralised state, and the guarantee of civil and political rights. Harbeson sums up the aims as follows:

> The central feature of the new Kenya constitution is the shrinking of executive power, which was untrammeled from colonial times through the first decades of independence. It accomplishes this by entrenching a rich panoply of individual rights, institutionalizing a more independent judiciary, providing for an electoral commission more insulated from executive interference, and perhaps most significant, devolving substantial governmental responsibility from the central government to forty-seven county governments, bypassing provincial administrations which are to be abolished. The constitution adds a second house of Parliament, the Senate, with responsibility for protecting the interests of the counties at the national level. (2013: 17)

Change in the land domain was only one amongst many that were sought. It was a difficult task to ensure it received due attention in the cacophony of claims on the new Constitution. Second, because there was also significant 'divergence' on social and cultural matters, including women's rights, reproduction, sexuality and religious laws (the part to be played by Kadhi or religious courts) (Mutua 2008: 185), a powerful conservative tradition exerted influence over the entirety of the constitutional process. Constitutional reform was marked by divisions and fragmentations that required significant compromises.

Third, alongside differences, there were other divisions. Chief amongst these was class, a mode of analysis of Kenyan state, society and indeed constitutional reform which has not received its full due (Leys 1975). The need to steer a course between different and diverging class interests deeply marked the constitution-making process. Indeed, Berman et al. (2009: 480) caution against an overly romantic interpretation of civil society in this period, arguing that although members of civil society often paid a high personal price for their activism and endured both detention and violence directed against them, 'the motives of civil society opposition in Kenya were mixed and often contradictory due to its complex linkages with the regime and political class' (see also Bosire and Lynch 2014 for a discussion of civil society fractures in the context of Kenya's Truth, Justice and Reconciliation process). Berman et al. cite with approval Murunga and Nasong'o's (2006: 15) argument that analysis of 'civil society as an unmitigated bastion of liberty, agent of political change, and midwife of regime transformation is ... flawed, given the reproduction of corrupt and authoritarian tendencies within civil society'.

An elite with longstanding stakes in a stable property regime sought to dampen or at least control the extent of reform. It sought to hold onto both concentrated power in the President and the access this arrangement provided to valuable patronage resources in the form of land. As they perceived the dangers to private property rights that might be posed by reform, the private sector sought to play a more prominent role. For example, the Kenya Landowners Association was formed in 2007 in order to lobby for the withdrawal of the Draft National Land Policy and retention of the status quo' (see Ayieko 2009). Similarly, the Kenya Landowners Federation condemned the Draft National Land Policy (see KLF 2007) as 'introducing numerous radical, untested, undemocratic and in some cases Marxist concepts'.

It fell to a vocal middle-class civil society movement made up of professionals (and dominated by lawyers and academics) to translate the demands of citizens into constitutional demands. Standing between the President and Wanjiku, the ubiquitous everywoman of Kenyan life, was a civil society movement determined to keep land wrongs in the political spotlight. They did this by mobilising the many land wrongs archived in official reports and popular knowledge (as discussed in Chapter 3) to present Kenyan land history as an exemplar. By the history of land, they suggested, we can know what a predatory executive is capable of. Writing a new normative framework governing the state's relations to society must necessarily encompass reducing executive control of land. This had a number of implications. First, land reform was folded into political reform. Second, the prescribed cure for an overly centralised state – the creation of strong new institutions – was taken also to apply to the land domain. As I show in Chapter 2, this put the rule of law at the centre of twinned reform processes, ensuring land reform was equated with land law reform. Wider claims – to agrarian reform including redistribution – was not on the agenda. As Mutua has shown, even parties associated with a more reformist agenda did not embrace radical land reform. Instead they 'hewed to a cautious liberal democratic model, endorsed open market reforms, and shied away from agrarian, radical centre left or leftist politics' (2008: 146).

On this reading, the achievement of the Land and Environment chapter of the Constitution was fragmentary, partial and the result of significant compromise. The preeminent aim of the constitutional review process was to end 'executive despotism' (Mutua 2008: 58) and the centralisation of power. Land reform was subordinate to that, to be achieved if possible whilst addressing constitutional change and where prescribed changes found a fit in both domains, but not the sole and certainly not the dominant focus of change.

Composition and role of civil society

In his account of land and the constitutional reform movement, Harbeson has perceptively argued: 'While many of Kenya's achievements since 2008 have been accomplished with international assistance (or because of international pressure), the principal driver of [land] reforms has been the energy and decades-long persistence of Kenyan civil society' (Harbeson 2012: 15). Unlike other substantive spheres, the nature and tone of the land reform movement has been determined significantly by those individuals who have driven it in Kenya by their vigilance and tenacity. Land issues, aside from those pertaining to private land (as systematically recorded for example in regular issues of the World Bank's *Doing Business* reports), received little international attention. The international community found little to say over the many years of the Kenyatta and Moi presidencies when public land was being systematically 'pilfered' (Klopp 2000). Rather, Kenyan citizens organised themselves into civil society groupings and registered as NGOs. Many of these individuals had long engaged in opposition politics and in the struggle to end an autocratic state. They were also active on specific sectoral issues, such as the struggle for human rights or the fight for land reform. Examples include the Kenya Human Rights Commission and the Kenya Land Alliance respectively.

The conjoining of the land and constitutional movements described above can be ascribed to the overlap of the main actors in both the constitutional and the land domains. Members of civil society crossed and re-crossed the boundaries between these movements or sought to show how one could not be meaningful without the other. What was the nature of the civil society so widely held to be responsible for political change in Kenya? As I have hinted above, this is an especially important question in relation to land because as Klopp (2000, 2012) has surely been right to argue, much of the struggle for justice in land matters was indigenous to Kenya and of little interest to the international community. Waged by ordinary citizens and members of civil society, opposition to land grabbing for example has been part of a wider dissatisfaction with the elite's attempt to hold onto power and to control wealth and natural resources both as a route to personal enrichment and, after 1992, as a way to fund electoral competition in a new era of multiparty diversity. The international community was indifferent to the abuse of public land. Describing Kenya's 'land-grabbing mania', Klopp (2000: 8) shows that even as the irregular and illegal allocation of public land reached its height in the 1990s, it was an 'under-scrutinized case of deepening corruption'. Klopp argues that whilst 'greater international scrutiny of some forms of corruption' dogged the Moi Government 'public land, highly accessible and less encumbered by international conditionalities than private property' became an increasingly 'attractive patronage asset' (ibid.). 'Detecting a difference in the international reaction to land grabbing compared to other forms of corruption' the Moi regime was emboldened in its land grabbing. The result of this in Kenya was important. For Klopp (ibid.: 15), although land grabbing 'provoked a mild international reaction' it in fact 'generated much greater and more widespread mobilization in Kenyan society than other corruption scandals'.

If in the land domain the struggle has been one waged by ordinary citizens and driven by activist NGOs, rather than demanded or dominated by the international community (Harbeson 2012), we should not overdraw the degree of separation between the local and the international. Tracing the shortcomings of civil society in this period, wa Gīthīnji and Holmquist (2012: 63) argue that there were 'three main local constituencies active in the reform process – reformers among the political elite, civil society, and donors'. They each faced difficulties in building broad national movements for change. Contrary to the portrayal of NGO autonomy in representing national constituencies presented by Harbeson (2012) and Klopp (2000), wa Gīthīnji and Holmquist (2012: 63) argue that because Kenyan civil society was significantly dependent upon donor funding, 'in subtle ways it became as responsible to donors and their perspectives and demands (as well as the demands of donor funding cycles) as it was to the demands of Kenyans'. wa Gīthīnji and Holmquist (2012: 63) enumerate the structural problems facing civil society that led to their dependence on external donors: their lack of an 'organized membership base apart from popularly based religious institutions', a worsening economy and a structural-adjustment-induced shrinking of the state, leading 'many educated Kenyans to turn to the creation of often externally funded civil society organizations as effective self-employment mechanisms', and the existence of a mix of both 'well-run professional organizations but also many less effective "brief case" NGOs'.

It is also important that Kenyan civil society through this period was organised around 'urban-based elitist organisations' that 'lacked a popular base' (Mutua 2008: 164). The civil society that advocated for democratic reform and for constitutional change beginning in the 1990s had been in place since the 1970s. It had significant roots in academic institutions, notably Nairobi University. Students and academics nurtured a nascent civil society movement when, through the 1970s and 1980s, political opposition was banned and any criticisms or protest carried real risks of a violent state response and imprisonment (Gikandi and Wachanga 2018; Kamencu 2013; see also Amutabi 2002; Klopp and Orina 2002). A monopoly on state power by KANU suppressed dissent through opposition parties, trade unions and the media. By the 1990s, when political space began to open up, what had been an underground civil society movement was able quickly to give expression to its demands. In a varied civil society with many sectoral demands, this long period of underground gestation had allowed time for significant convergence to emerge. As Mutua notes,

> civil society organisations, the single most important actors in the struggle for constitutional reform, had the clearest and the most steadfast vision of a democratic constitution. Over the years, they had forged a national consciousness on such a document. The general areas of convergence were known because of that struggle: the democratization of the executive, the reform of the judiciary, a full bill of rights, affirmative action for women and marginalised groups, devolution, and economic and land reforms. (Mutua 2008: 163)

In the 1990s, members of civil society began to make more visible their work to insert themselves between a despotic state and the people. Having had to stay in the wings through the 1970s and 1980s, NGOs and those who spearheaded them were able slowly to move centre stage and to bring the spotlight to bear on the political agenda they had been distilling and perfecting for the past two decades. Constitution debates offered them a concrete way to do this. Their most important promise was of a people-led constitutional review process, informed by the wishes of the people and driven by their expressed needs. In this way, the reform movement would break with the earlier dispensation. Before independence and after it, consultation with the people had been lacking. That would need to change.

In the land arena this would mean that 'the role of experts in the Constitution-making process has been radically transformed, to include listening to the people, and translating their views into constitutional terms' (Chief Justice Mutunga in Supreme Court Advisory Opinion:

para. 319). Civil society in Kenya had been driven first and foremost by a deep 'scepticism ... of state power' (Mutua 2008: 167). Now they had an opportunity to sketch out a path to constitutionalism (Okoth-Ogendo 1993b) As Mutua argues:

> Political debates in Kenya had, over the decade of the 1990s, zeroed in on the essential features of [constitutionalism]. There was broad agreement amongst civil society ... that popular sovereignty as a principle was the floor and therefore incontestable ... the essential features of the system sought by reform advocates in Kenya were accountability of the state through a series of techniques, institutions, processes, and mechanisms, the most important of which was periodic, regular, and genuinely competitive elections; a tangible scheme of checks and balances, with real and effective separation of powers; an independent judiciary to safeguard the rule of law, and a guarantee of individual rights, enshrined in a bill of rights. (2008: 167)

The land reform movement, folded into and a fundamental part of the wider constitutional pressure for change, did not in some regards make their demands in circumstances of their own choosing. This limited the sorts of demands that could be admitted into the process. In Chapter 1 I suggested that the circumstances under which Kenya's property regime came to be called into question can usefully be contrasted with South Africa's. In van der Walt's (2009) analysis, the end of apartheid there occasioned a sudden break with the previous dispensation and enabled the calling into question of the very basis of the property regime. In Kenya, the experience has rather been one of a slow grinding to a halt of property institutions and rules. There has not been a radical break. My interpretation finds echoes in Mutua's analysis of the wider constitutional review process. He offers a similar reading in his discussion of Kenya's constitutional conference, arguing that whereas '[n]ational conferences elsewhere on the continent were spontaneous, unscripted revolutionary situations through which *ancien regimes* were written out', in Kenya 'the constitutional conference was a staid affair calculated and scripted by the departing KANU regime' (Mutua 2008: 143).

This lack of a radical or revolutionary moment explains the important ways in which Kenya's land debate was circumscribed. The constitutional provisions written into the final document are aspirations and guiding principles. They are an attempt to vocalise national values. They visualise a better future rather than demand immediate change. This is especially apparent in the provisions on social and economic rights with their language of progressive realisation. According to Kramon and Posner (2011: 96): 'In order to address the issue of socioeconomic inequality, the constitution recognizes an extensive set of rights, including such "second-generation" rights as healthcare, food, education, and housing. These provisions are, however, largely aspirational'.

Land as a constitutional category

In this section, I seek to retrieve the history of constitutional provisions on land and to show how they fared during what was an elongated process of constitution making from 2000 onwards. This act of retrieval is important because it provides a historical account of legal provisions over land and how they entered the Constitution, showing that they were the outcome of ideological debate and struggle. The narrative is not straightforward. A teleological account of the achievements of Kenya's constitutional provisions on land is not possible. Rather, I show in this section that it took concerted effort, a long-running struggle and many years to ensure that demands for land reform found their way into the Constitution and took concrete form in that document.

When the disputed December 2007 elections gave rise to widespread and deadly violence, serious steps had to be taken to calm the political waters. In order to do this, a Kenya National Dialogue and Reconciliation process (KNDR) began in early 2008 with the government and the opposition signing an agreement to end the political violence. In this fraught and sensitive process, the African Union's Panel of Eminent African Personalities led by Kofi Annan acted as mediator. In settlement, the parties agreed to form a coalition government. It was also agreed that they would undertake major reforms in key sectors in order to guarantee the rule of law and respect for human rights. In their assessment of the National Dialogue and Reconciliation process, Kanyinga and Long (2012) argue that the intervention of Kofi Annan and his colleagues gave important impetus to the reform movement, effectively kick-starting a stalled constitutional review process. For them, 'strong pressure from below for constitutional reform ... exists, in general, above and beyond partisan and ethnic divides' (2012: 36). The post-election violence of this period created 'strong pressures from below [which] may have helped to realign political incentives in important ways. This, as well as a situation of crisis and institutional features arising from the mediation process, combined to spur reform.'

In its report, KNDR set out key issues that lay at the heart of Kenya's political troubles as manifested in the 2007–08 violence and which had to be addressed in order to bring about long-term peace. These included addressing long-standing issues, amongst which was land reform. The report acknowledged that land has been a major source of conflict and of tension between different ethnic groups. 'These conflicts arise from perceptions by many Kenyans that the current land ownership system is unjust' (para. 83). In order to address this, the mediators set out the steps that should be taken to address land problems in Kenya. In so doing, they set out in writing the contours of the reform that the new constitution would come to address in its provisions. To formulate them, the team reached back in time to the Ndung'u report and its findings and to the demands of civil society through the 1990s. It demanded that land reforms take place and detailed the nature of these reforms. The report included recommendations for constitutional review, policy development and legislative development. What was needed was a process to address fundamental issues of land tenure and land use. A new land policy would reflect the linkages between land use, environmental conservation, forestry and water resources. The Draft National Land Policy on which land NGOs had been working should be published, and new land legislation enacted. To accompany these policy and legal changes, institutional change should also be set in train, including more transparent and decentralised land information systems such as registries backed up by geographic information system data (GIS) both at the level of the Ministry of Lands and at local level. It was also recommended that a National Land Use Master Plan be formulated which would pay particular attention to environmental considerations. It was recommended that a land-use transformation unit be created at the Ministry of Lands which would be charged with implementing the land reform programmes to be set out in the National Land Policy. A Land Dispute Tribunal Act should be enacted. In addition, land management should be devolved to local level so that more sustainable land rights regimes could be enacted.

It had long been a concern of those active in the struggle for land reform that Kenya had not formulated a national land policy since independence. Land laws had proliferated and become incompatible and complex. Land management and administration were breaking down. Land was becoming more concentrated in the hands of a few powerful individuals and families. By the 1990s, environmental degradation, urban sprawl, insecure tenure and land grabbing were visibly worsening (Hirst and Lamba 1994). Civil society took upon itself the task of organising against land grabbing, drawing the public's attention to the most egregious examples and actively finding mechanisms for citizen engagement against illegal dealings in land. Leading examples of this were the work of the Green Belt movement under the leadership of Wangari Maathai and the formation of the Firimbi (whistleblowing) initiative which sought to activate citizens to report on land grabbing. The success of these movements in working together against the grabbing of the urban Karura Forest in Nairobi is perhaps the best-known example of citizen activism on land (Manji 2017b). Together, a number of civil society groups called for the revocation of illegal allocations of land on the outskirts of the forest (Klopp 2000). When the leading organisation in the land arena, the Kenya Land Alliance, was formed in 1999, it was a sign of growing momentum for change in the land sector. The Kenya Land Alliance was formed specifically to lobby and do advocacy work on a possible framework for the National Land Policy. Sensing the opportunity provided by the 2002 elections which inaugurated the Kibaki Government, the KLA persuaded the Ministry of Land to press the government to formulate a land policy (RIPOCA 2010).

When it was finally published in 2009 after considerable legal pressure had been brought to bear, the National Land Policy had been long in the drafting and, much like the later constitutional process itself, had an elongated life course. This process had begun many years before but now, as the momentum for change in the land sector built up, civil society focused its considerable energy on completing the drafting of the National Land Policy. Once again, the context for this is important. The Ndung'u Commission, explored in Chapter 2, had carried out its work. The illegal and irregular allocation of land that it investigated was widely known. The commission's work was widely publicised, the press took a detailed interest in it and ordinary citizens heard on an almost daily basis about the commission's findings, giving official confirmation of what Kenya's citizens had long known, and validating their suspicions that widespread land corruption was underway to the benefit of a small elite with considerable political power.

Because the work of the Ndung'u Commission, and efforts to write a guiding document in the form of a national land policy ran in parallel, they became intricately connected in the minds of citizens and in the aims of those seeking to influence land and constitutional policies. They shared the same temporality, feeding into and strengthening each other. According to Africog, there was a risk when the Ndung'u report was published in 2009 that the government would simply fail to implement its many recommendations and instead use the inquiry, as it had many earlier ones, as a means to 'circumvent justice' (Africog 2009: 6. But one of the positive effects of the Ndung'u Commission of Inquiry was that it quickly became

> the reference point for a symbolic stand that previous impunity in public land dealings is no longer acceptable. In this regard, the Report, and even the half-hearted attempts to implement it, have generated a sense of caution in dealings with public land. This has arguably, to some extent, curbed the previously unbridled tendency for wrongdoing in relation to public land. (Africog 2009: 30)

In this way, the Ndung'u report played an important role in setting the contours of a nascent national land policy debate. It made it difficult for the government to ignore arguments that land governance and political governance were intricately connected. Nonetheless, the government did attempt to stall the publication of both the Ndung'u report (Southall 2009) and the National Land Policy. On the latter, the intervention of the post-election National Dialogue and Reconciliation process was important in forcing the government to act. According to the KNDR report:

> Although the Draft National Land Policy was completed in May 2007 it awaits Cabinet discussion and adoption. There has also been intense lobbying by largescale land owners against the draft policy. The main point of contention has been the reduction of the lease period from 999 years to 99 years ... an aspect that might have contributed to the delay in adopting the policy. Politicians and other powerful individuals have also been accused of contributing to the delay in adopting the policy because they reportedly fear the reallocation of land they own or irregularly acquired. (2009, pp. 20–21)

From the private sector came vocal opposition to the Draft National Land Policy. The thrust of the criticisms directed at the draft are summarised in the views of the Kenya Landowners Federation that 'principles of land redistribution, restitution and resettlement with absolute disregard to sanctity of title and first registration suggest that the policy, if not driven, was drafted by minority lands rights groups.' (see KLF 2007) The Federation was made up of large agriculturalists such as tea and coffee farmers and maize growers as well as ranchers, most of whom were based in the Rift Valley and Central Province. Alleging that the policy was drafted with funding by 'non-Kenyans', the group claimed that it was weighed in favour of minority concerns (such as those of communities and 'gender') and had a 'focus on poverty reduction almost exclusively at the cost of wealth creation' and was 'fundamentally injurious to the future of Kenya'. Claiming that the draft was partisan, the Federation argued that the policy constituted 'an unbridled assault on all landowner's constitutional right', that it would reduce the value of property titles, disrupt the mortgage market and lead to chaos in land administration:

> if implemented, the provisions set out in this Draft National Land Policy will at a single stroke weaken the economic foundations of agri-cultural and commercial development in Kenya and thus undermine the accumulation of wealth by its citizenry. It will lead to capital flight and disinvestment, and it will create, accentuate and perpetuate both rural and urban poverty. (KLF 2007)

The main objections of these groupings were that the draft policy would remove security of tenure for commercial and agricultural users and interfere with the rights of registered title holders. They warned that this would damage investor confidence in Kenya. They expressed concern that the policy draft sought to increase the powers of compul-sory acquisition by the state and introduced no requirement of compen-sation.

Chapter 18 of the Final Report of the Constitution of Kenya Review Commission provides a detailed account of the mandate of the Review Commission, its findings and its recommendations. This report itself constitutes and supplements the official land archive explored in Chapter 3. It provides an analysis of the 'land question in Kenya' and sets out that it was mandated by the Constitution of Kenya Review Act to examine and review the place of property and land rights, including private, Government and trust land, in both the constitutional framework and in the laws of Kenya, and that it was further required to recommend improvements to secure the fullest enjoyment of land and other property rights. Subsequently, Chapter Seven of the Bomas Draft was devoted to land and property. The delegates found common cause with the Ndung'u report, recommending the establishment of a National Land Commission as a guarantor of above politics land relations (Boone et al. 2019: 216). When however the Harmonised Draft Constitution was being discussed, there was considerable opposition to this proposal in the Kalenjin areas of the Rift Valley where the National Land Commission was viewed with suspicion:

> When they talk about national land commissions, we begin to get defensive. The same people want to take away land. It's always the big Nairobi guys who come and divide land and take away land, and we think they're looking at our empty lands when they talk of settling the landless. That's why in the pastoralist areas most people are opposed to this constitution as they think it's a legal way of getting land, of taking away what you have. (Lynch 2008: 560)

Given the struggles described above, it has been an article of faith amongst Kenyan land activists and civil society that the insertion of the Land and Environment chapter in the new Constitution was a considerable achievement. It was taken to be a concrete outcome after many years of struggle for recognition by the land sector. It is undoubtedly the case that the insertion of a detailed chapter dedicated to land rights was an important marker of the status of land issues in the country's wider politics. The chapter makes a number of important declarations. Chief amongst this is arguably that land in Kenya belongs to all people, as direct a way as possible to counter claims of autochthony (having originated in a given place) and ethnic belonging. In addition, provisions that laid out that principle of equity should guide land use were seen as important declarations against land concentration by the elite.

Harbeson (2012) has traced the ways in which the provisions of the National Land Policy entered the Constitution. He shows that the National Land Policy forwarded around fifty legislative mandates to Parliament. Of these about twenty-five were written into the Constitution. Harbeson identifies the most important provisions to find their way into the Constitution as those prescribing maximum and minimum private landholding sizes, those that set out how land can be transferred from one category to another (that is, between private, public and community land), those that govern how dispositions of public land are required to be done, and finally those that set out protections for the land interests of dependents and spouses. Harbeson also sets out the land mandates which were accepted by Parliament but did not come to be enshrined in constitutional provisions. These included a direct provision on addressing landlessness, a public purpose requirement for any investments in land, the creation of greater access to land through leasehold routes, new legislation to govern compulsory land acquisition, regulatory powers given to planning authorities to ensure that land is used in the public interest, and the creation of leasehold mechanisms as a way to access land (ibid.)

Whilst acknowledging that giving constitutional force to land issues was a key achievement, it is nonetheless important to recognise the limits of the Land and Environment chapter. Because the constitutional process was driven predominantly by an impetus for democratisation, reform of the democratic order and embedding of the rule of law, other wider demands did not find their way into the constitutional text. As Mutua recognises, the Constitution 'did not envisage any programmes for land and agrarian reform, which were necessary to address the problems of landlessness, land redistribution, and equity in land ownership' (2008: 174). Rather, such a liberal constitution contains broad principles and aspirations for change. In this regard, Alden Wily is surely right that 'the constitutional treatment of property rights is a barometer of the intended nature of the agrarian state' (2018c: 84). In her extensive exploration of constitutional provisions on private property and on compulsory acquisition by the state, she argues that although much focus is on how land laws stipulate the rules governing these areas, as much importance should be attached to how constitutional principles treat them. This is because such principles are more readily known to citizens when contained in constitutions and also because when they are enshrined in a constitution they become more difficult to revise. Alden Wily also shows that there is no African constitution that does not explicitly recognise the right to private property in land, with only the constitution of Guinea Bissau offering no protection for this form of property (2018a). This recognition of private property comes logically from the fact that radical title is vested in the state and so 'property is defined as a right to occupy and use part of that state' (ibid.: 85; see also Okoth-Ogendo 1975). Very few states go further by imposing positive obligations on the state for example in relation to the right to adequate housing, with only Kenya, Morocco, Mozambique and South Africa providing for this in their constitutions (Alden Wily 2018a). Crucially, these positive obligations do not extend to any 'prescription against landlessness' although, as discussed above, Chapter 5 of the Constitution of Kenya does set out that land should be held equitably (ibid.). In Kenya, the provisions guaranteeing private property rights clearly demonstrate the liberal bent of the Constitution. Although Kenya drew extensively on the South African Constitution in its drafting, it did not copy South Africa in setting out rules for compulsory acquisition of land in the Constitution, leaving this to be stipulated instead in land laws. In South Africa, the Constitution provides that it will be lawful for the state compulsorily to acquire property if it is for a public purpose and 'the nation's commitment to land reform and to reforms to bring about equitable access to all South Africa's natural resources is a stated purpose' (ibid.: 87). In Kenya, the constitution did not lay this groundwork for agrarian reform.

Constitutions and constitutionalism

In this section, I refer to 'constitutionalism' rather than simply to 'the Constitution'. I do so to draw attention to the existing and continuing gulf between these terms in the land domain as in many other domains in Kenya. For Ghai, the distinction is critical. He describes how by constitutions we refer to 'a set of rules and institutions' that should govern a country, and by constitutionalism we mean 'an ideology based on certain values, procedures and practices' (Ghai 2014: 119). Beyond the text, what is envisaged by the term constitutionalism as Ghai attempts to elucidate it in the face of what he sees as its overuse and under-specification, is the question of how best to confront enormous – and often overwhelming – state power against the rights of citizens, and so compel the state not to infringe these rights (2014). But as Ghai points out, new constitutions in the transformative mould, as South Africa and Kenya are widely taken to have inaugurated, also require not just restraint by the state but also positive action to further social justice by taking actions for its citizens. The inclusion of socio-economic rights and of equality provisions envisages a different kind of state, one engaged in activism in service of the people (Ghai 2014; Harrington 2014; Harrington and O'Hare 2014). But, as Ghai also reminds us, responsibility for constitutionalism lies not just with the constitutional text but in other spheres such as the judiciary, professions and civic associations (Ghai 2017).

In a detailed essay considering the reception and understanding of Okoth-Ogendo's seminal paper, 'Constitutions without Constitutionalism: Reflections on an African Political Paradox' (1993b), Ghai (2017) compares and contrasts analyses of African constitutionalism by Okoth-Ogendo and Shivji and sets these alongside his own reflections on the theme. Okoth-Ogendo was concerned with showing how independence constitutions were subverted by introducing amendments or replacements that worked to continue the colonial constitutional method. This created constitutional orders as being on a continuum. This could range from the *coup d'état* – in effect an abrogation of the constitution – to a disregard for constitutional processes and conventions. Shivji (1991) too wrote of the post-independence wave of constitutional amendments or suspension as manifesting 'a resurgence of the colonial legal order' (Ghai 2017: 158).

Okoth-Ogendo pointed to what he saw as the legal order's coercive tendencies. Shivji, from a quite different political perspective but nonetheless in agreement with this aspect of Okoth-Ogendo's interpretation (Ghai 2017), described as 'despotic', a 'legal order inconsistent with constitutionalism' (ibid.: 158). For Shivji (1991), the post-independence period of the developmental state saw the embedding of an authoritarian neo-colonial state. According to Ghai (2017), relations between the state and the economy made the state patrimonial rather than Weberian legal-rational. The form of domination exercised in a patrimonial state is rooted in personal rule.

In Ghai's view, Okoth-Ogendo (1993b) did not explicitly set out his understanding of constitutionalism (and in consequence the essay, although widely cited, has been largely misapprehended and the thrust of the 'political paradox' at its heart poorly understood). Ghai (2017) explains that we can infer Okoth-Ogendo's thoughts on constitutionalism from a careful reading of his critique of the history of post-independence constitutional change. In relation to administrative law, for example, Okoth-Ogendo shared a common perspective with McAuslan (2003), in distrusting administrative discretion and preferring strong administrative law as a means to protect citizens against unlawful decisions and acts by state officials.

For Ghai, constitutionalism was not just undesirable to African governments, it wholly interfered with the 'kind of economy' that they wished to construct. In this economy, a leading role would be played by politicians and bureaucrats in alliance, facilitated by 'the discretionary powers of the state over the economy' (2017: 160). Ghai makes the following distinction:

> The 'entrepreneurs' in Europe were the private sector who wanted a reliable legal framework for their plans and contracts, while in Africa the 'entrepreneurs' were those who used the state mechanisms which they did not want fettered or questioned, and preferably not accountable to a legal regime. (Ibid.)

Personal power is central to the form of domination enjoyed by the patrimonial state. Here, administration is based not a legal framework developed through deliberation but instead is based on the exercise of power and the assertion of the untrammelled discretion of the ruler.

Evocatively likening this exercise of domination to a ruler's domestic power (see Musila 2018), Ghai notes that

> the bureaucracy is an extension of his household ... there is no clear separation between the private and the public spheres of the ruler. He is above the law, as are his officials ... petitions to him for ... generosity substitute for legal writs. The ideological superstructure of such domination is the goodness, generosity, and concern of the ruler for his people. (Ibid.)

The consequences of Ghai's model which we might label 'personal rule patrimonialism' is that rules have a particular 'status and role'. They play a secondary part in the economy. Instead, the economy is an 'administered economy' which is fundamentally incompatible with rule-of-law norms. For Ghai, 'it is the character of the state and the nature of the process of accumulation ... that undermine constitutionalism' (2017: 155).

The account of irregular and illegal dealing in land provided in Chapter 3 invites us to reflect on the nature of African land bureaucracies. The constitutional provisions discussed above as well as the land law reforms passed in 2012 and discussed in the next chapter, were attempts to confront malfunctioning and misdirected bureaucratic power over land. For Okoth-Ogendo (1993b), African states derived their power from 'the structure and powers of the bureaucracy' rather than from a constitutional mandate (Ghai 2017: 155). From the colonial period, bureaucracies acquired increasing powers and exercised these 'without the rule of law and impartiality' (ibid.). According to Ghai, this has meant that the bureaucracy has steadily 'established a relationship with the political class to plunder the resources of the state'. Ghai emphasises Okoth-Ogendo's analysis that the bureaucracy did more than simply 'accede to colonial administrative power' as set out in Ghai and McAuslan and explored in Chapter 2. In reality the role of the bureaucracy was expanded as it was given a key role in managing the economy.

Conclusion

In this chapter, I have shown that land-related civil society was one of a range of sectoral interests that made up a wider opposition movement struggling for constitutional change after 1990. If the wider task was to 'write a new contract between state and society' (Mutua 2008: 141), land reform was presented as a fundamental element of a new 'normative framework for state reformation' (ibid.: 203) Those committed to seeing a comprehensive and achievable programme of land reform had to calibrate their claims in the wider context of the constitutional review process. The priority of the movement for constitutional change was to end power personalised in the President. To 'constitutional engineers' (ibid.: 266), the concentration of powers over land in the hands of the President was presented as an exemplar. Kenyan land history showed what could happen when despotic power was exercised by an unaccountable executive, when power was overly centralised and when resources were treated with impunity. Kenya had effectively become 'the President's plantation' (Ngugi wa Thiong'o quoted in Ndirangu Wachanga 2018: 17), they argued, and that had implications for our understanding both for land (skewed ownership, landlessness and inequitable access) and political power (an imperial presidency with commanding control over resources). A political transition therefore necessitated a land transition: a new architecture of land governance would be a fundamental achievement in the building of a new, accountable state.

In his writing on land and constitutionalism in South Africa, Klug raises difficult questions about the limited achievements of the post-apartheid years and asks 'whether constitutionalism in the post-apartheid context is as transformative as is claimed ... or if adherence to constitutionalism ... has not, in fact, precluded the degree of change necessary to build a sustainable society' (Klug 2018: 473). In Kenya, struggling for a 'formulaic liberal constitution' (Mutua 2008: 168), the focus of the constitutional movement was on 'the normative identity of the state' (ibid.: 173). Land activists made common cause with this struggle by showing the ways in which the state had acted as 'predator' (ibid.) over land. In the fight to end state despotism, the creation of strong institutions was front and centre. The solution to personalised power over land, to abuse of discretion, to widespread irregular and illegal looting, and to subversions of the law was to strengthen the administrative law undergirding land relations. Strong, accountable institutions staffed by rule-bound individuals would guarantee better land management and administration. Essentially an exercise in doing public and administrative law better, there was an unarticulated assumption that structural and institutional changes would trickle down and so bring about material change in the economy and in society.

On this reading, longstanding land problems were never treated to their own solutions. Agrarian reform, redistribution, challenges to the sanctity of private property were never on the agenda. Instead, land reform was folded into constitutional reform – the solutions indicated in the constitutional arena were assumed to be also indicated for the land arena. Most notable of these were robust institutions. This is the context in which the architecture of land governance that I explore in the next chapter was constructed.

5

The New Institutional Framework
for Land Governance

The existing institutional framework for land administration and management is highly centralized, complex, and exceedingly bureaucratic. As a result, it is prone to corruption and has not been able to provide efficient services. In addition, it does not adequately involve the public in decision making with respect to land administration and management and is thus unaccountable. (Sessional Paper No. 3 of 2009, National Land Policy)

Introduction

In this chapter, I consider the main constitutional and legislative provisions which lay out the architecture of land governance in Kenya. I argue that three major and interrelated forms of restructuring were attempted in the period after the ratification of the 2010 Constitution. These were: to anchor land law in clear public law values, emphasising the role of good administration and first creating and then increasing the powers and status of institutions that might control the Executive's interference in the land domain; to decentralise or deconcentrate (Boone et al. 2019) land administration and management; and finally, to embed land law reform in wider efforts at devolution. I explore each of these three interrelated aspects in this chapter in order to show the complexity and ambition of what was being attempted.

The concern of the previous chapter was with the political and constitutional context from which Kenya's present suite of land laws emanated. As I have shown, getting the institutional arrangements for land governance right was a major preoccupation of the constitutional review process. The period 2012 to 2016 was one of legislative plenitude as new land laws were passed and amended. This was the culmination of many years of pressure for reform during which institutional change was held out as a solution to Kenya's land problems. As the extract from the National Land Policy provided above shows, the ways in which land had been administered and managed was seen as too bureaucratic and untransparent, too removed from citizens, prone to manipulation and corruption and serving only the powerful. The new land policy laid out that a reformed system of land administration must be more accountable. By bringing land institutions closer to the people and involving the public in decision making, administration would be done in a more accountable manner. In the background was the corrupt, inefficient and by now entirely discredited Land Ministry, whose central role in the land wrongs described in Chapter 3 made its continuation as a central institution of land management untenable. There was an overwhelming need finally to disperse or devolve power over the administration of land to new institutions untouched by this land history. At base, what was being suggested was that Kenyan land matters must at long last be reformed so as to locate them in a clear public and administrative law framework.

Land law as administrative law

In their text *Public Law and Political Change in Kenya* (1970), Ghai and McAuslan's chapter on land is, significantly, entitled 'The Development of Agrarian Administration'. In it, the authors show in detail how 'the incoming colonial authorities used the law to obtain full government control over land' (ibid.: 79). In doing so, they forged a detailed 'system of agrarian law administration' which was inherited by the independence government and continued fundamentally to shape land relations. The aim of their chapter was to explore the political and economic consequences of the inherited system of law and administration in land and so to place these problems in historical context. Ghai and McAuslan provide a number of important examples of the role played by law in the colonial period. They show that law played a deeply coercive role in African reserves. In contrast to European agrarian development, which was founded on cooperation between producers and administrators who saw their role as one of facilitating and supporting European producers, in African reserves coercion was used to get work done that the colonial authorities had decided was necessary, for example to tackle soil erosion. Ghai and McAuslan cite the continued use of by-laws to shape and direct land usage in the reserves as an example of the administrative laws that undergirded the bifurcated agricultural system I described in Chapter 2, consisting of European land and African reserves. Rather than pass national legislation on land usage, the colonial authorities formulated a rich body of rules and by-laws. For instance, for new settlements of conservation projects, new rules would be promulgated specifying the responsibilities of occupiers and the sanctions for non-compliance. Each native settlement area therefore had its own rules, resulting in an extensive but deeply fragmented body of administrative law. Ghai and McAuslan provide the example of the Native Lands (Kimulot Land Utilization) Rules which laid out the powers of the District Commissioner to require fencing to be developed, and animal husbandry to be carried out to his approval, on pain of cancellation of an occupier's license or forcible eviction. In the Olenguruone settlement area, rules set out how animal stock was to be treated and also that 'conviction and imprisonment for an offence involving moral turpitude could lead to loss of the occupation permit needed to be allowed to live in the settlement' (1970: 111). Residential segregation, animal husbandry, and agricultural productivity were all determined by detailed administrative rules and Ordinances. The form of law was here as important as its substance (ibid.: 124): in this period, we see colonial control exercised through the incremental development of a dense and detailed body of administrative law.

Ghai and McAuslan argue that although Kenya's first independence Constitution introduced in 1962, was meant to encapsulate liberal democratic values and to be founded on constitutionalism, defined as 'the limitation of the powers of government, the assurance of the rights of the citizens' (1970: 513), the experience of colonialism had been far from these values. Instead, colonial society for the majority of the population had been overwhelmingly autocratic and 'took the form of an authoritarian administrative structure' (ibid.: 514). The gulf between the experience of administrative rules and the values asserted in the Constitution meant that it had little if any legitimacy and quickly became an irrelevance. Instead of 'greater standards of objectivity in administration', the purpose of administrative institutions quickly became subverted. Controlled by Ministers, they were used to accumulate power and to build patronage networks in the land domain, for example by rewarding supporters with land.

For McAuslan, the history of Kenya's legal framework for land – and in particular the dominant role of administrative rules in governing land in most of the country – underscored the need to recognise that the study of land law is in fact the study of public law, a perspective he subsequently carried into his groundbreaking work on United Kingdom planning law (see Loughlin 2017), on curriculum reform in legal education (ibid.), in his reconceptualisation of public law (McEldowney 2017) and in his contributions to land law reform and debates on legislative drafting (Manji 2017b). An administrative law orientation deeply informed his work as a legal consultant: as well as writing widely on land law reform, he worked as an adviser on land law reform in forty-three countries (see Manji 2015). It was in the context of considering different approaches to and philosophies of legislative drafting that McAuslan elaborated on his idea of land law as administrative law (see 2003: 255). Contrasting South African statutes with proposals about how new land laws might be drafted in Tanzania following the work of the Presidential Commission of Inquiry which reported in 1992, McAuslan argued that powers must be spelled out in as much detail as possible, as a way to constrain officials' actions. He acknowledges here that detailed laws were used to create and sustain apartheid and that the same approach was subsequently used to try to dismantle it (see also Klug 2000).

In McAuslan's view, the evidence of administrative abuse presented to the Tanzanian Commission of Inquiry served to confirm that 'officials armed with powers and subject to few or no constraints, cannot be relied upon to behave reasonably' (2003: 255). In this, his approach was at odds with that advocated by the chairperson of the Tanzanian Commission itself who argued that the Bill's drafting as carried out by McAuslan in his role as consultant created an overly bureaucratic structure in which there are even more opportunities for the abuse of official power than previously (Shivji and Kapinga 1997). (I have explored these differences in legal methodological approaches elsewhere: see Manji 1998; 2006.) McAuslan argued that a challenge to unreasonable actions by officials is more feasible where a detailed statute setting out their powers can be relied upon. Moreover, a more detailed piece of legislation makes it less problematic to challenge administrative action in the courts. Because judges would in these circumstances be asked to interpret statute, the more detailed the legislation, the less likely that the judiciary would be accused of 'interfering in policy', 'a charge which becomes more plausible where statutes are very broad and 'general principles' of administrative law are used to overturn an administrative decision' (McAuslan 2003: 255). In addition, McAuslan argued, where title to land is vested in the President, the state or its organs, land law 'ceases to be a matter of private law but becomes part of public law; it is in fact administrative law' (ibid.)

To return to Kenya, we can see that the National Land Policy and Chapter 5 of the Constitution – and then the translation of these principles into concrete laws from 2012 onwards – was in fact an exercise in constructing a robust framework of 'applied administrative law' (McAuslan 2003: 256). After decades of land corruption and mismanagement, it was hoped that by stipulating the manner and form of officials' powers over land, new land laws would end the post-independence era of mismanagement and maladministration which had manifestly failed to govern land in the public interest and which had led to the extensive irregular and illegal dealing in land documented in the Ndung'u report.

In fact, this administrative law approach to land can be traced to the first significant land inquiry in the post-independence era, that is, the Presidential Commission of Inquiry into the Land Law System of Kenya (the 'Njonjo Commission') which reported in 2002. As indicated in Chapter 3, the Commission was explicitly mandated to review the country's policy and legal framework for land. Unlike the later Ndung'u report which inquired into longstanding land grievances such as land grabbing, the remit of the Njonjo Commission was rather narrow and technocratic. Its narrow mandate was to explore policy and legal options for reform. The comprehensive report produced by the Njonjo Commission very firmly brought land law within the purview of constitutional, public and administrative law. The report explicitly recognised that how land is regulated and how control of land is exercised forms the basis of the exercise of administrative and political power. For this reason, it argued that land required protection in both legislation and in the Constitution. In doing this, the Commission laid important groundwork. By emphasising that land matters could be regulated as matters of public and administrative land rather than simply of private law, the Commission was making important links The report recognised that the legal status of land cannot be ascertained only by reference to private law but that land law raises critical questions about the scope of the public exercise of administrative law. Recognising that land rights can only be asserted and then provided through 'the mobilization of institutional mechanisms and personnel', the report notes that 'these are processes which, in Kenya, are run as part and parcel of public administration' (Republic of Kenya 2002).

The Commission's recommendations were therefore explicitly located within an administrative law framework. Significantly, it noted that what was needed was a reconsideration of the tenure regime as a whole. It recommended new land categories of public land, common land and private land. Critically, the Commission's major contribution was to recommended that radical title to land be vested in an independent land body. This independent national land institution, it was suggested, should be known as the Kenya National Land Authority to govern private land, as well as a body to be called the District Land Authority which would be entrusted with common land. In the Commission's vision of a reformed legal framework for land, a National Land Authority would be responsible for categorising land under different tenure regimes, mapping and recording all customary land rights, verifying land titles and preparing a comprehensive register. The National Land Authority would also be responsible for setting up a network of decentralised land registries. Because radical title would be vested in this body, it would no longer be the responsibility of the powerful and centralised control of the Commissioner of Lands, a key recommendation which would indirectly reduce presidential access to land which had long been exerted through the Commissioner of Lands.

The influence of the Njonjo Commission recommendations on the National Land Policy published in 2009 can clearly be discerned (see Proceedings of National Civil Society Conference 2004). What was envisaged was a more explicit and a more robust administrative law framework to govern land. Radical title, already kinetic in the colonial era as I described in Chapter 1, would be removed from the President and be vested instead an independent body, a National Land Commission, that would be able to withstand pressure from the Executive when administering and managing land.

The devolution experiment

Kenya has had a long history of demands for decentralisation which have ebbed and flowed since 1961 (Anderson 2005a). Hornsby has described 'a thread of conflict between centralisation and decentralisation' running through Kenyan history (2013: 805) and has argued that the choice of a centralised constitution in which an executive president has a key role, or a decentralised constitution with dispersed powers has been a conflict between different understandings of land politics and land ownership. Supporters of a 'willing-seller/willing-buyer' model of land allocation advocated a strong centralised system in which anyone could buy land and live anywhere in the country. It was driven by the private property model of land relations I explored in Chapter 1. Broadly speaking, ideas of decentralisation were on the other hand more likely to be founded on ideas of land as collectively held in trust by communities, and resisted its acquisition by settlers from outside the community.

The demand for devolution, quieted by an authoritarian presidency and a strong central state since independence, gained impetus after multiparty elections were held in 1992. The constitutional review process was dominated by the question of devolution. The Constitution of Kenya Reform Commission found: 'There is a widespread wish for people to take charge of their own lives. They want to use community institutions for land management and other local affairs; they want power closer to where they live' (CKRC 2005b: 290) In Mutua's analysis this was to be expected: 'Structures of government are usually the most contested sections of any constitution-making process because they are about the distribution of power and control of resources' (2008: 188).

As a result, much of the Constitution is concerned with the 'transfer of authority to subnational entities' (Mutua 2008: 189), 'a complex, ambitious and transformational governance project' (Bassett 2017: 547). In Kenya's new two-tier system of government forty-seven new county governments would have legislative powers through county assemblies. Executive powers would be exercised by a Governor working with an appointed cabinet (Waddilove 2019). This would allow the people to take part in governance, promoting a central tenet of the Constitution on participation of the people, and enabling them to take part in decision making. What was envisaged was a radical restructuring of land governance. Decentralization, and the democratized control of land would bring the rule of law into the land domain (Boone et al. 2019).

Land reform and constitutional change had become intricately connected, such that as the constitutional review process got underway it would have been difficult to envisage one without the other. Confronting an authoritarian presidency also meant confronting the politics of land, including different understandings of land ownership and rights. The same analysis can be applied to the twinning of land reform and devolution. At heart, demands for devolution have also been a way of expressing differing conceptions of land. Those who favoured a strong imperial presidency sitting astride a centralised state also favoured private property and the right of individuals to own land and live anywhere in the country. As past and present beneficiaries of the willing-seller/willing-buyer model, their approach to land was rooted in a liberal individualist model of the self-fashioning 'economic man' beloved of neo-liberal economists (de Soto 2000; Bhandar 2017; Manji 2006; Nyamu-Musembi 2007). In contrast, the struggle for devolution was understood by its advocates as a way to assert community rights and priorities of self-government and ontological freedom. The practical consequence of these intertwined political demands was the simultaneous effort to introduce new land laws and to initiate a vast and complex new system of government in the form of devolution.

The scramble for new land laws

In the previous chapter I showed that a radical and ambitious new architecture of land governance was envisaged as a key aim of land reform. I traced this back as far as the 2002 Njonjo report when demands first began to be voiced in authoritative, official reports for substantive land reform. The process of constructing the new institutions of land governance has been described by Harbeson (2012) as a process of transforming constitutional principles into workable laws. This enactment of policy principles into concrete legal proposals began to occur after the new Constitution was promulgated in August 2010. The impetus for this came from the Constitution itself. Article 68(a) provided that Parliament shall revise, consolidate, and rationalise existing land laws, and Article 68(c) set out the areas for future legislation, including legislation to prescribe minimum and maximum private land holding; to regulate the manner in which land may be converted from one category to another; to 'protect, conserve and provide access to all public land'; to protect the dependents of deceased persons with interest in any land, including spouses in actual occupation; and to provide 'for any other matter necessary' to effect the land and environment policies of the Constitution.

The fifth schedule to Article 261(1), which was included to specify the timeframe within which certain key pieces of legislation must be enacted, required that land legislation must be enacted by Parliament within eighteen months of the promulgation of the Constitution. As a consequence of this provision, the outer time limit for enacting legislation relating to land was set at 27 February 2012. As I show below, this tight timeframe (McAuslan 2013) appeared firmly to require the enactment of new land laws within two years of the Constitution's passing, on pain of the dissolution of Parliament by the Attorney General. The work of drafting new land bills began in the course of 2011. This resulted in a series of new land bills coming before Parliament in February 2012. Below I describe the less-than-ideal way in which this significant bundle of land law proposals was handled. The new bills were characterised by poor drafting, by the wholesale replication of entirely irrelevant provisions from elsewhere (Tanzania's 1998 Land Act was a particular source of copied provisions) and a rush to meet the constitutional deadline for the new laws which precluded any semblance of debate and, most importantly – given the emphasis laid on this value in the two-year old Constitution – hindered participation by the people.

A recap of the rushed process of enacting Kenya's new land laws in 2012 is worthwhile because it was an early indication of fundamental weaknesses in both the content of the laws and in the process of law making. The Land Bill, the Land Registration Bill, and the National Land Commission Bill were given their first and second readings before the Kenyan National Assembly on 15 and 22 February 2012. In the run-up to these readings, academics, commentators and members of civil society sought to study the proposed new legislation. As former chairperson of the Constitution of Kenya Review Commission and founder of the new Katiba (Constitution) Institute, Yash Pal Ghai brought together a group of experts on land matters to attempt to engage with a process of land law making. I was part of this group. Our common impression was that the swift pace of drafting the new land laws was precluding meaningful discussion, whether by accident or design. Those of us wishing to attend consultative hearings struggled to find and read drafts of the bills. Documents were available for download from various websites, such as that of the Ministry of Lands and the Commission for the Implementation of the Constitution, but it was seldom clear to us if these were the latest and most reliable versions of the bills. The draft bills were finally released by the government printer on 22 February, the day that the Committee on Land and Natural Resources held its first consultative hearings with members of the public. Most of the groups and individuals who attended the session held in Nairobi on that day, including members of the Law Society of Kenya, the Kenya Human Rights Commission, the Kenya Institution of Surveyors, the Kenya Private Sector Alliance, and the Land Sector Non-State Actors Alliance, commented that they had not had the benefit of reading the newly published draft bills. Neither, indeed, had members of the committee themselves, as they openly admitted.

This first consultative meeting immediately raised concerns. The main weakness of the bills included incoherent drafting; widespread borrowing of the provisions of the land laws of other African countries without due attention to their relevance or suitability for Kenya; the failure to identify the misconduct that the land laws needed to address; inconsistencies between the National Land Policy and the Constitution; and the failure to specify in detail the functions of devolved land administration bodies. A number of the groups who attended publicly stated that in their view the drafts of the bills failed to enact the Land and Environment chapter of the Constitution. A number of groups went so far as to point out that as they stood, the bills would fail the test of constitutionality (see Opiyo 2012). This was a powerful claim to make, especially as it came in the wake of an audit by the Commission for the Implementation of the Constitution reporting that many of the new laws approved since the promulgation of the Constitution did not pass this test (Republic of Kenya 2012a). The Katiba Institute Land Research Consortium told the Committee on Land and Natural Resources that, in drafting the bills, the Ministry of Lands had not been faithful to the National Land Policy 2009, nor to the Constitution of Kenya (Ghai 2012). Despite these glaring shortcomings, the Commission for the Implementation of the Constitution, whose role it was to be vigilant in relation to the constitutionality of legislative proposals, issued a statement that the bills 'to the largest extent possible, conform to the Constitution' (Republic of Kenya 2012a).

Because of the inadequacy of the drafts, a number of groups recommended that the bills be withdrawn altogether. The recommendation was that more time be given for the revision, consolidation and rationalisation of the laws. This suggestion was resisted by the Minister of Lands, James Orengo, and the Chair of the Land Committee, Mutava Musyimi, on the grounds that the constitutional deadlines could not be breached. However, on 9 March 2012, the National Assembly voted by the needed two-thirds majority to delay the final vote on the constitutionally mandated legislation by a further sixty days. The delay was supported by the Constitution Implementation Oversight Committee, the Legal Affairs Committee, and the Land Committee. According to the chairperson of the latter committee (quoted in Ghai 2012), the extra sixty days would allow wider consultation on the draft bills and promote the participatory processes required by the Constitution. The new deadline for enactment of the laws was now set at 23 April 2012.

With this extra time, members of the Land Committee, having split into small groups, toured Kenya's forty-seven counties to discuss the proposed legislation with citizens. Civil society groups organised to try to inform the public about the new laws and generate debate. In order to ensure that members of the public received adequate information about the proposed legislation, short 'question and answer' pamphlets were drafted in English and Kiswahili by many groups and distributed around the country. Some civil society groups also briefed the media. Others placed large spreads in the daily newspapers seeking to inform the public about the implications of the proposed land laws.

At the public hearings in Nairobi on 22 February there had been a notable degree of consensus about the weaknesses of the bills, but despite the scale of the technical work that was called for, the Minister for Lands, James Orengo, told the press on March 4 that the bills had been reconsidered and reworked (Opiyo 2012) although it was clear to most observers that they could not have been thoroughly redrafted in that time. A number of groups had submitted detailed material to the Land and Environment Committee in the form of memoranda, notes, scorecards and clause-by-clause commentaries. In its submission, the Katiba Institute's land research group made detailed recommendations on the bills, and in the Foreword written by Yash Pal Ghai, sought to make a broader point about 'the enactment of laws to implement constitutional values and objectives':

> The practice so far has been to issue bills without any useful explanation of what policies are being implemented or how. The people are confronted with lengthy legal texts, for the most part badly drafted, often copied from laws of other countries, often with internal inconsistencies or inconsistencies with other legislation. This is particularly the case with land bills ... It is impossible for most Kenyans (including lawyers, other experts, ministers and parliamentarians) to understand the content of the bills (especially since, unlike the constitution, the drafting style is complex, convoluted, old fashioned). This effectively prevents the participation of the people in law making required by the constitution. (Kituo cha Sheria et al. 2012: n.p.)

The proposed amendments to the land bills to be presented in Parliament became available on 16 April, and it was immediately apparent that what was proposed was not the revision and redrafting widely called for but consisted rather of brief amendments to the three pieces of legislation. The bills had largely been unaltered. The most important changes that had been recommended, and over which there was little or no disagreement amongst various groups commenting on the land bills – such as the need explicitly to detail the role and powers of the proposed National Land Commission in relation to the Ministry of Lands – had been left unaddressed. Nonetheless, the three bills reached the committee stage in Parliament shortly thereafter and were approved on 26 April 2012.

The resulting land laws were the result of a deeply flawed process of law making. The Constitution's specific timeframe for the enactment of new legislation was used in order to rush or foreshorten debate. It is difficult to say to what extent this was a deliberate strategy and to what extent it came about by accident. What is clear is that by invoking this deadline, space for detailed consideration of the proposals was limited. Those who argued for strict adherence to the constitutional deadline maintained that a failure to do so would risk the dissolution of Parliament by the Attorney General. Those who did not think adherence to the timeframe was necessary countered that the land bills were an important set of laws and that it was unlikely that Parliament would be dissolved for taking time to consider the proposed laws in detail (see Ghai 2012).

McAuslan (2013) argued that the time specifications set out in the Constitution were entirely unrealistic. Eighteen months in which to formulate, debate, and enact the legislation was an untenable basis on which to start addressing longstanding land problems, as experiences in Tanzania, Uganda and Mozambique had shown. McAuslan noted that this was a failure of the drafters of the Constitution. The idea of including deadlines for the enactment of legislation was that this would prevent legislative drift, as has occurred in other jurisdictions after the promulgation of new constitutions. In Kenya, however, the process of identifying time specifications for legislation mandated by the Constitution was ad hoc and far from comprehensive. Some legislation that was required was not included in the fifth schedule and the lists provided there are to some extent arbitrary. Why, for example, was it necessary to distinguish between legislation on community land, which was mandated to be completed within five years, and general land legislation, which had to be enacted within eighteen months? Or indeed between general legislation on land and the legislation on urban areas and cities (Article 184), for which one year was specified?

Because the deadlines led to rushed legislation and to a lack of participation and debate, it can be argued that they in fact assisted in the defeat of important principles of the Constitution. Although the Commission for the Implementation of the Constitution claimed, contrary to the views of many, that the land legislation passed the test of constitutionality, the process of debating the new land laws manifestly did not conform with the spirit of the Constitution with its emphasis on participation in law making. Civil society groups lobbying for land reform, in their anxiety to keep up the momentum on land issues and to ensure that the promised land reform was forthcoming, may not have given enough consideration to the effect of the tight constitutional deadline of eighteen months. The consequence has been confused, contradictory and rushed legislation.

Why has there been such a disjuncture between the 2009 National Land Policy and the Constitution on the one hand, and the new land laws on the other? Why have the undoubted gains embedded in these two documents not resulted in concrete land laws of the sort expected? The achievement of the National Land Policy and the land chapter of the Constitution can be credited to civil society activists, who have long worked to expose and define Kenya's land problems. As Harbeson recognises, it is in large part due to such efforts that the 2010 Constitution went beyond guaranteeing respect for basic civil and political rights to ensure that 'socioeconomic and cultural requirements and roles within the Kenyan state be constitutionally recognized and upheld' (2012: 16). Given the centrality of civil society to the land debate in Kenya, at least some of the explanation for the failure to translate these achievements into concrete laws must be sought in this sphere. In fact, many land-related civil society groups seemed unwilling to challenge the retreat into a technical legal approach, which marked the 2012 period. A constant refrain heard during the public meetings of the Land Committee was that the laws were highly technical and complex. This claim, as well as the imposed time limits, seemed to be deployed as strategies to foreshorten debate and to limit citizens' participation. This is not to deny that the land laws in Kenya as elsewhere are complex, but rather to show how objections to more open participation were framed in technical legal terms. McAuslan (2003: 251) has noted this tendency elsewhere:

> To move from policy formulation to drafting laws is not, as some people assume, to move from a debate on policy to one on legal technicalities: the move changes the context of the debate but it remains, none the less, a policy debate ... The broad general policies set out in, for example, the Tanzanian government's NLP [National Land Policy] or the Namibian government's Land Reform: To Promote Equity and Fairness (1994) can be readily agreed by (almost) everyone. Who, after all, could be against equity and fairness? However, when these ideas are turned into precise powers, duties, limitations, restrictions, procedures, when it becomes clear who is to benefit and who is to lose out, then objections begin to be voiced. These are not, of course, objections on 'policy grounds' but on technical legal grounds; a particular clause 'wouldn't work'; a certain provision is 'unnecessary'; another goes too far or is 'impracticable'.

The response of civil society groups involved in land matters was not to challenge the claim that the technical nature of the proposed laws precluded participation, but rather to accept and to some extent reinforce this approach.

Rather than playing a role in showing that the process of drafting is itself a highly political and contested matter and one that merited attention and debate, civil society seemed to 'back-off' from the land question. Although they became involved when the bills appeared, their failure to make a visible and concerted contribution at the earliest stages, such as when drafting began in 2011, meant that they lost significant momentum. It is clear that not all the blame can be placed at their door – the process of legal drafting was hardly transparent and accessible. But after the significant achievements to which they can lay claim and which I describe in the previous chapter, there was a failure to see through reforms in the land domain which have had significant consequences since 2012.

As I have shown in previous chapters, distrust of bureaucratic power over land is widespread amongst citizens, and the extent of land grabbing had long been either known or shrewdly suspected (see Klopp 2001; Southall 2005). The allocation of public land has long been exercised by successive presidents and their land commissioners in pursuit of political patronage and personal accumulation. It is in this context that the new land laws were widely seen as an opportunity to redress Kenya's grossly skewed structure of land management and end predatory land practices by the state. But the achievement of this aim would have required civil society to wrest control of the debate from bureaucrats, to see the process of discussing proposed new land laws as a political and not simply a technical exercise, to resist the rush to legislate, and to make real the Constitution's promise of participation by the people in major policy changes. In this regard, the Supreme Court has subsequently reflected explicitly on the meaning of participation in land matters (I discuss this in detail in Chapter 6). Chief Justice and President of the Court Willy Mutunga cited the South African Constitutional Court in considering specifically the question what role the public should have in law making. In *Doctors for Life International v. Speaker of the National Assembly and Others* the Court urged public involvement in law making which is a species of participatory democracy. It held:

> The participation by the public on a continuous basis provides vitality to the functioning of representative democracy. It encourages citizens of the country to be actively involved in public affairs, identify themselves with the institutions of government and become familiar with the laws as they are made. It enhances the civic dignity of those who participate by enabling their voices to be heard and taken account of. It promotes a spirit of democratic and pluralistic accommodation calculated to produce laws that are likely to be widely accepted and effective in practice. It strengthens the legitimacy of legislation in the eyes of the people. Finally, because of its open and public character it acts as a counterweight to secret lobbying and influence peddling. Participatory democracy is of special importance to those who are relatively disempowered in a country like ours where great disparities of wealth and influence exist. (Paras 115, 116)

At the level of process, it is clear that the debate surrounding new land laws failed to engage citizens in any meaningful way. It was conducted largely out of public view, in closed workshops and consultative meetings that remained inaccessible to the public and almost entirely neglected by the media. What little public consultation took place occurred in the final moments of the process when the Land Committee toured the country to consult the public and when, arguably, very little substantive change to the draft bills could be achieved. This is not especially novel: lack of consultation has dogged most African countries that have passed new land laws in the last two decades (Manji 1998). What is different in the case of Kenya is that the country has embedded the principles of participation and procedural fairness in its 2010 Constitution, and citizens' hopes in this regard – both generally and in relation to land issues – were high.

Despite what Harbeson (2012: 15) called the 'intensely redistributive potential ... in Kenya's land regime' as envisaged by the National Land Policy and the Constitution, the new legislation is not redistributive in either its intention or its effect. Here we can distinguish between *deep* redistributive reform – in relation to land, an aim of such change might have been to call into question the nature and foundations of land ownership and control – and *shallow* redistributive reform – which is concerned solely with institutional change and with questions of administrative capacity, and which aims to wrest control over land from a centralised and corrupt state. In their intention, Kenya's new land laws are redistributive in the latter rather than the former sense: they challenge bureaucratic power rather than the structure of land holding. In this regard, it is notable that the Supreme Court in a key judgment on the relationship between the Ministry of Lands and the National Land Commission (which I discuss in detail in the next chapter) drew an incorrect historical analogy between the Land Commission in Ireland and Kenya's new National Land Commission (see paras 302–4). The Irish Land Commission, established by the Land Law (Ireland) Act in 1881 was redistributive in both intention and effect: its purpose was to redistribute farmland from landlord to tenant. By 1920 it had redistributed 13.5 million acres (see Lucey 2011). Unintentionally, the Court has provided us with a useful counterpoint to the new Kenyan Land Commission. The Kenyan National Land Commission whose format was first envisaged by the Njonjo Commission and labelled the Land Authority, was envisaged from the start as a body concerned with management and administration of land, never with redistribution, the purpose for which the Land Commission in Ireland was set up. Insofar as controlling Kenya's infamously predatory land bureaucracy might lead to better land outcomes for citizens such as greater consultation before land awarded to foreign investors, opportunities to challenge acquisition of public or community land and greater transparency at land registries, it is possible that the legislation does offer some means to challenge bad administrative practices and so perhaps retain citizens' access to land. But the new laws do not address longstanding grievances about Kenya's grossly unequal land distribution. As I show in the next chapter, however, even the limited task of challenging centralised bureaucratic power through the new body of the National Land Commission has not been accomplished.

There is global context for the approach taken to reform in Kenya. The preference for institutional over redistributive change must be understood as having a global normative power. Just as the pursuit of political reconstruction through constitutional change in Kenya can be located within the wider context of the rise of 'world constitutionalism' (Ackerman 1997), so we must seek to understand approaches to land reform globally. If the 1990s saw a rise in 'faith in the judicial branch of government' and 'an emphasis on the rule of law as being an essential component ... of state reconstruction' (Klug 2000: 1), these tendencies were also manifest in the land sector in specific ways. Here, the 1990s witnessed 'a global intellectual climate', which 'in effect encouraged or pushed countries into seeing that land law reform ... was, if not essential, then certainly something that was an appropriate way forward to developing a better system of land management' (McAuslan 2013: 60). In Tanzania, for example, the land law reforms of the late 1990s closely linked formalisation of tenure with the promotion of the rule of law (Manji 2006). In the process, however, the emphasis on the reform of land *law* foreclosed debates about redistribution. Debates over land reform in Kenya can similarly be said to have taken place within these strictly proscribed parameters. With an intellectual formation that predisposes them to embrace ideals of the rule of law and administrative justice over substantive redistribution, civil society groups proved ineffective in revealing the political import of the final stages of land law reform. The land debate in Kenya has been about the redistribution of bureaucratic control over land, as well as transparency of decision making, rather than the redistribution of land *qua* land. Ironically, as I show in the next chapter, the incoherent land laws that have resulted have in fact further perpetuated Kenya's long-running land problems.

New land institutions

Because one of the main objectives of the new legislation passed in 2012 was to divest the Land Ministry of some of its functions and so reduce its powers, a major reconstruction of the architecture of land governance and management had to take place through the new laws. For the first time, the Land Ministry would no longer be the only body to hold important information about land, by managing land registries for example. The sole charge it had long enjoyed over the allocation and management of public land would come to an end. Crucially, decisions about the revocation of land titles where land had been found to be illegally acquired and powers over resettlement of land would now no longer lie with the Ministry. The idea was to create for the new institutions of land governance 'a visible presence away from traditional centres of power and administration' and effectively to 'deconcentrate' land administration (Boone et al. 2019: 9). This would be achieved by creating the National Land Commission. That body would have a deconcentrated (ibid.) presence in the newly created counties because it would be represented in each by County Land Management Boards (CLMBs). This was seen as a way to address the long-expressed complaint that access to land services had become concentrated in Nairobi and was not accessible to the vast majority of Kenyans, as the National Land Policy (2009) described. This demand entered the Constitution in the form of Article 6(3) which required that the National Land Commission ensure that reasonable access was possible to its services in all parts of the country. The resulting land law provision was Section 18 of the National Land Commission Act which established County Land Management Boards. The National Land Commission would be responsible for appointing and staffing these. Their members (between seven and nine in number) would be appointed by the National Land Commission subject to approval by the County Assemblies. In addition, in each county the Governor was given the power to appoint one member from the county lands ministry. In addition, Section 16 of the National Land Commission Act 2012 set up county offices and committees in an effort to bring services of land administration and management closer to the people. In order to promote constructive relationships between the levels, this was supplemented by a provision in Section 17 that services were to be provided in close consultation with the National and County governments. Assessing this new architecture, Boone et al. (2016: 9) have argued that 'deconcentration thus intersects with devolution, imposing an element of local democratic control over the CLMBs'.

The National Land Commission needs to be understood as nestled within a wider constitutional architecture. It was one of a number of independent commissions stipulated by the Constitution. In total, Chapter 15 of the Constitution of Kenya 2010 sets out ten new commissions to be created. They are the Kenya National Human Rights and Equality Commission; the National Land Commission; the Independent Electoral and Boundaries Commission; the Parliamentary Service Commission; the Judicial Service Commission; the Commission on Revenue Allocation; the Public Service Commission; the Salaries and Remuneration Commission; the Teachers Service Commission; and the National Police Service Commission. The Constitution sought to present the broad principles which would govern these commissions. These include setting out at Article 249(1) that the object of the commissions is to 'protect the sovereignty of the people, secure the observance by all State organs of democratic values and principles; and promote constitutionalism'. The Constitution did not provide detail as to the role of each but allows that legislation could be passed to do this. Article 252(1)(d) provides that the commissions 'may perform any functions and exercise any powers prescribed by legislation, in addition to the functions and powers conferred by this Constitution'.

The other important body created by the new land laws was a Land and Environment Court. The lack of a specialist forum for hearing disputes relating to land has been a concern for many years. The Njonjo report which I discussed in Chapter 3 had recommended that mechanisms for dispute resolution be introduced. The Environment and Land Court has its origins in the Constitution and in particular in Article 162(2)(b) which requires Parliament to pass a law to establish a superior court with the status of the High Court for the purpose of hearing and determining disputes relating to the environment and the use and occupation of and title to land. By Article 162(3) Parliament was required to determine the jurisdiction of the court and specify its functions. The Environment and Land Court Act was passed in 2011. Section 13 provides that the Court has original and appellate jurisdiction to hear and determine all disputes in accordance with Article 162(2)(b) of the Constitution. The court can hear cases relating to environmental planning and protection, climate issues, land use planning, title, tenure, boundaries, rates, rents, valuations, mining, minerals and other natural resources. In addition, it can hear disputes involving compulsory acquisition of land and those involving land administration and management. Its jurisdiction covers all categories of land (public, private and community land). The court is further entrusted with cases relating to violations of rights or fundamental freedom in connection with a clean and healthy environment (under Articles 42, 69 and 70 of the Constitution) (Odote 2013).

Ouma (2019) has traced the history of demands for a Land and Environment Court. As far back as the Commission of Inquiry into the Land Law System of Kenya (2002) (known as the Njonjo Commission and discussed in Chapter 3) it was recognised that land dispute mechanisms were failing to work adequately and were marked by a range of problems including delays, political interference and uncertainty over roles and functions which had resulted in confusion and often in conflict (Ouma 2019; Republic of Kenya 2002). In its turn, the National Land Policy (2009) cited the importance of putting in place resolution mechanisms for land-related disputes. Ouma (2019) also shows that in the course of the constitution-making process, citizens articulated their concerns that disputes were not being handled in suitable ways, demanding more efficient and simpler mechanisms. Ouma's study shows that jurisdictional uncertainty has characterised the early years of the Land and Environment Court. Just as the National Land Commission and the Land Ministry have disagreed over their respective roles and powers, so the Land and Environmental Court's early years have been marked by jurisdictional wrangles with other courts.

Recentralisation

Three years after the new land laws were passed, in August 2015, the government introduced a new Land Law (Amendments) Bill, the aim of which was to revise the Land Act, the Land Registration Act and the National Land Commission Act 2012. It was immediately apparent that the objective of the draft bill was to remove key functions from the National Land Commission and instead to vest them in the Cabinet Secretary for land. This was 'a bold attempt at recentralisation of land functions' (Bassett 2017). Most importantly, Section 39 of the Land Law (Amendments) Act 2016 repealed one of the main areas of devolved land administration which the 2012 laws had created. The County Land Management Boards set up by the National Land Commission Act 2012 were abolished.

This was effectively a dismantling of the complex new architecture of land governance that Kenya sought to put in place as a result of land law reforms in 2012. New tenure regimes, classifications of land and reformulation of institutions were all introduced by the trio of new land laws in 2012 that traced their roots to the National Land Policy 2009 and to the 2010 Constitution. This was a major reform of the legal framework governing land: in all, seven land laws were repealed and a trio of land laws passed in 2012. The National Land Policy extracted at the start of this chapter insists that reform of the architecture of land governance was critical because 'the existing institutional frame-work for land administration and management is highly centralized, complex, and exceedingly bureaucratic'. The account I have provided in this chapter sets out how an alternative approach was sought. But it also calls into question whether meaningful change has indeed been achieved. Today, Kenya's institutional structure for the administration and management of land remains complex and bureaucratic. It has been recentralised to a worrying degree. It has shown itself, like the previous dispensation, to be prone to corruption and unable to provide efficient services. It is questionable whether today's structures 'adequately involve the public in decision making with respect to land administration and management' or is any more accountable than the system it sought to replace.

How to assess Kenya's land law reform experience? I have argued in previous chapters that the emphasis on law reform has trumped other wider considerations of equity and justice. In this regard, my concerns echo those expressed by Klug (2018) when he asked whether the South African Constitution might have in fact hindered meaningful reform of racially skewed and historically enduring property relations. My concerns are similar: have we resorted to law as a way to avoid more difficult discussions of what it means to distribute land more fairly? But more immediately for the purposes of this chapter, I would wish to make a narrower point. Even on a bare doctrinal assessment, that is to say, an assessment of law making to change the legal dispensation on land, the Kenyan example raises a number of concerning issues. Poor legal capacity to draft robust and clear laws marked the start of the process in 2011–12. This was followed by a hiatus of four years from 2012 to 2016 in which the country's new land institutions were barely able to function due to uncertainty over their roles and responsibilities. (I elaborate on this in Chapter 6.) By 2016, the government had prepared for introduction to Parliament a set of land law amendments that to all intents and purposes ended the devolution experiment in land. Although in the event the Land Law (Amendment) Act 2016 did not go as far the preceding bills (described as the Omnibus Bill) had threatened, the changes brought about by the amendments did curtail the wide and deep decentralisation of land management and administration that the Constitution and its undergirding policy documents (the National Land Policy) had envisaged. Ghai and Cottrell (2015: 27) have argued in their account of the making of the 2010 Constitution: 'The Kenyan process provides a textbook example of how the democratic will can be, at least temporarily, frustrated, by governmental recalcitrance and obstruction, corruption and manipulation'. The same might be said of the land law reform process. A determined recentralising state intent on holding on to land not just as a patronage resource but also an indicator of administrative power and dominance had, within four years, amended land law to remove key decentralised powers over land registries: land management by the County Land Management Boards.

The short life of the Country Land Management Boards points us to one further issue. Ginsburg et al. (2009), in their consideration of ways in which to assess the success or otherwise of constitutional change, have forged the term 'constitutional endurance'. In his review of how long a series of constitutions around the globe have 'lived', Coldham (1978a) argued that this is one metric through which it is possible to assess their success. Extended to the land law arena, this mode of analysis enables us to assess land law reform similarly. The short life of the County Land Management Boards suggests a certain volatility in the land law domain. That, so quickly after their enactment, the series of 2012 laws should come before Parliament for review demonstrates that the gains of legal change can soon be lost. Just as with the Constitution, so with land law reform. If the impetus for change was to confront head-on an imperial presidency and an over-weaning executive, the experience of attempting land law reform has shown just how difficult a task that could be.

Conclusion

I argued in Chapter 3 that in the years leading up to the review of the constitution, citizens had found ways to talk about land matters that amounted to labour to create an accumulated archive of land knowledge. I drew on Musila (2017) to suggest that counter-hegemonic strategies of rumours and story-telling about land were a way for citizens to participate in knowledge making about politics and society. Before the space opened up for formal participatory democracy, first in the form of civic education in advance of the constitution-making process and then as drafts of the constitution were debated and put up at referenda, ordinary Kenyans did not rest on their laurels in relation to land. It formed the subject of conversations in the home and on the street (Klopp 2013). When the time came to pass new land laws as required by the Constitution, the formal and technical nature of the task was used to trump a more ubiquitous peoples' narrative on land. Viewed in the long arc of Kenyan land politics, the process of drafting, deliberating on and passing new land laws in 2012 was as far from participatory as it is possible to get. Indeed, students of law making may in the future be referred to that time as a rich case study in how not to make law.

6

Land Governance Before the Supreme Court

The making of Kenya's Constitution of 2010 is a story of ordinary citizens striving to overthrow, and succeeding in overthrowing the existing social order, and then defining a new social, economic, political, and cultural order for themselves. (Chief Justice and President Willy Mutunga Supreme Court Advisory Opinion No. 2 of 2015: para. 320)

Introduction

In this chapter, I discuss in further detail the politics of the National Land Commission. In particular, I explore what happened when this politics was played out in a court of law. I showed in Chapters 4 and 5 how institutional change in the land arena was a key aim of the new Constitution when it was inaugurated in 2010. It was hoped that a new architecture of land governance would ameliorate Kenya's longstanding land problems. A set of new land laws was enacted in 2012. Amongst other things, these laws set up a new National Land Commission. Envisaged as an independent constitutional commission, it was anticipated that this body would stand apart from existing institutions which were closely associated with facilitating a multitude of wrongs, including corruption and the irregular and illegal use of land as a patronage resource as detailed in Chapter 3. The path to the creation of the National Land Commission was by no means easy. Although there was powerful advocacy for it at the start of the constitutional review process it also encountered its opponents. At one point, the proposal to create this Commission was deleted from constitutional drafts. Reinstated at a later stage after concerted work by civil society groups, it was hoped that creating a strong land commission undergirded by constitutional guarantees of its independence would mark the beginning of a new land order for Kenya (Mwathane 2018a). It would put into effect Chapter 5 of the Constitution which emphasised the importance of land being 'held, used and managed in a manner that is equitable, efficient, productive and sustainable'; and it would be guided by the principles of land policy inscribed in the new Constitution and by its national values, including those of participation, consultation and transparency, all of which had entered the Constitution after concerted debate and struggle.

In spite of these aspirations, what we have witnessed in the short life of the National Land Commission has been concerted resistance to the changes it might have brought about. As Boone (2014) has argued, Kenya's land tenure regime is 'statist in intention and effect' (quoted in Bassett 2017: 539). The aim of the land law reforms was to challenge this dispensation. But the National Government has fought hard to retain its control over the key land functions, including land registration. There has been a powerful centralising effort by a state determined not to lose control of management of and access to land, including regional and central land registries. The then Ministry of Lands, Housing and Urban Development was the prime actor in this struggle for control. An incumbent institution with vast experience, it has worked hard to keep the new National Land Commission in check.

By 2014, with much of the business of land administration at a standstill, the Supreme Court was asked to provide an advisory opinion on what should be the relationship between the two bodies in light of the Constitution and the relevant land laws. Advisory opinions are a judicial mechanism that enable the Supreme Court to provide 'authoritative and impartial interpretation of the Constitution' (s.3 Supreme Court Act 2011) (see Gathii 2016; Lumumba and Franceschi 2010). They are discretionary and are provided only rarely. Resorting to the court for its guidance was a clear indication that the two bodies with responsibilities on land had reached a stalemate. For the first time, the country's highest court was being asked to rule on a key question: what are the responsibilities and duties of the institutions envisaged by Kenya's new legal framework for land governance? The court was being requested to resolve questions about the scope of administrative power and duties over land. This judicialisation of land politics marked a critical moment in Kenya's reform process.

The specific question before the court was: what are the Land Commission's functions and powers and what are those of the Ministry of Land? By exploring how the courts dealt with themes of land history, constitutional values and institutional architecture we can see how important the National Land Commission was to the changes envisaged by the transformative period inaugurated by the enactment of the National Land Policy in 2009. In this new constitutional dispensation, constitutional change and land law reform went hand in hand. But through a close analysis of the Supreme Court's Advisory Opinion, we also see how great is the challenge not just of building but of bringing to life a transformative land governance architecture.

I argue that despite its keen sense of the history of land in Kenya and its stated commitment to constitutional transformation, including the role of the Land Commission in this, the court did not provide the direct and forthright judicial support the Commission needed at this critical stage of its infancy. The Supreme Court is charged by legislation with being a guardian of the Constitution and its values. Section 3 of the Supreme Court Act 2011 provides that the objectives of the court include to 'assert the supremacy of the Constitution and the sovereignty of the people of Kenya' and 'develop rich jurisprudence that respects Kenya's history and traditions and facilitates its social, economic and political growth' and to 'enable important constitutional and other legal matters, especially matters on transition to the new Constitution [to] be determined with due regard to the circumstances, history and cultures of the people'. The Supreme Court's ruling in this matter is extremely detailed (it runs to sixty-two pages). It is perhaps one of the best rehearsals of Kenya's land history and of the connections between land reform and constitutional transformations currently in existence. It therefore presents an important opportunity to understand how the principles set out in Chapter 5 of the Constitution (the Land and Environment chapter) have fared in the difficult translation from aspiration to concrete laws and everyday practice (Harbeson 2012).

The status and importance of the judgment is undeniable. Issued by the country's highest court, it is a rare ruling on matters of constitutional law and land law and their interaction. Never before has the Supreme Court had an opportunity to elaborate on this. In addition, the Supreme Court explicitly noted the advisory jurisdiction it exercises, stating that its opinion is binding: it does not take the form merely of advice but is akin to a judgment (para. 316). Although the National Land Commission itself has received scholarly attention (Boone et al. 2019; Lumumba and Franceschi 2010; Lumumba and Klopp 2017; Mulevu 2014), there has been no detailed analysis of the landmark Advisory Opinion on the National Land Commission (but cf. Bassett 2017 for a brief discussion). This chapter seeks to provide a detailed and accessible legal analysis of the Advisory Opinion and to assess its impact. I conclude that, whilst the Supreme Court showed extensive knowledge of Kenya's land history and of its constitutional history and paid particular attention to the transformative potential of a new land governance architecture, its ruling failed to provide the new Land Commission with the support it required. One might say that the Supreme Court's historical analysis is powerful but its jurisprudence disappointing. I argue that the court adopted an attitude of deference to the political arena and shied away from setting out clear and robust guidance on how the new body should operate both in its own right and in relation to the Land Ministry.

This chapter is structured as follows. In the next section, I explore the strained early years of the Land Commission and show that it had a difficult start to its work. This background explains why by 2014 it had become necessary to refer matters to the Supreme Court. Unable to work together and uncertain about their roles, the Land Commission and the Land Ministry had become deadlocked and many land functions had almost entirely ceased. In the succeeding section, I analyse the Supreme Court's judgment in detail. I show how the parties sought to project their positions and how they defended their respective roles in the land domain. Following this, I provide an analysis of how the court dealt with these issues. The penultimate section provides an assessment of the judgment's enduring effects, and the concluding section argues that an opportunity was missed to steer land politics along the path of constitutionalism.

Land administration under strain

As shown in Chapter 5, getting the institutional arrangements for land governance right was a major preoccupation of the constitutional review process. The new land laws passed in 2012 were the culmination of many years of pressure for reform during which institutional change was held out as a solution to Kenya's land problems. Bringing about that institutional change was the thrust of these laws: their aim was to decentre the corrupt, inefficient and discredited Land Ministry and disperse or devolve power over the administration of land to new institutions untouched by this land history. But to paraphrase McAuslan's wry comment on land reform in Uganda, the new laws had created a situation where the Land Commission 'had lost an empire but had not yet found a role' (McAuslan 2003: 331) By 2014, the strained relationship between the two bodies charged with overseeing the management and administration of land, the National Land Commission and the Land Ministry, was widely known. Reform in the land arena showed evidence of being stalled. Everyday but critical land functions, such as land registration, had stopped being carried out as the two bodies wrangled over responsibilities and powers. There was widespread public dissatisfaction with this state of affairs. It became apparent that the courts would have to be asked to mediate between the Ministry of Lands and the National Land Commission and to rule on their respective roles.

With hindsight, signs that the National Land Commission would be systematically hindered and opposed began to show as soon as the 2012 law was enacted. Parliament approved the names of the nine members of the Commission in 2012 but it took an intervention by the High Court in 2013 to compel the President to gazette the names of the members of the Commission to enable the Commission to be set up. This was an early clue that significant hurdles would be put in the way of the new land body. Starved of an independent budget, the Commission struggled to breathe life into its functions. There were public skirmishes as to staffing. Some new recruitment took place but many of the new staff of the Commission were transferred from the Ministry. This was a staffing process envisaged by the National Land Commission Bill in 2012. It was one against which a number of civil society groups working in the land area strongly advocated. The Katiba Consortium on Land led by Yash Pal Ghai of which I was a part pointed out that the proposal to transfer staff went against the spirit of independent commissions and risked importing into a new body the corruption and mismanagement with which the Ministry had long been associated (see Kituo cha Sheria 2012; Manji 2014). In our submission to the National Assembly Land and Environment Committee on 22 February 2012, we noted that, even with the staff vetting procedures provided for in the Bill, the transfer of staff from the Ministry to the Commission would create the perception that the land corruption with which the Ministry was associated would simply continue. These objections were ignored and the National Land Commission Act 2012 provided for staff transfers (s. 31). It was no surprise thereafter that threats to recall Ministry staff serving at the National Land Commission had by 2013 become a key way for the Ministry to exert its control over the new body.

Uncertainty over the National Land Commission's responsibilities marked the period between 2012 and 2014. A frustrated National Land Commission continued to be co-housed with the Land Ministry and made little headway in carving out a role for itself (Bassett 2017; Lumumba and Klopp 2017). Between 2012 and 2014, the two bodies tussled for authority. Without clear parameters regarding their respective roles, the Ministry of Land fought back hard against any loss of its powers. As well as starving the independent National Land Commission of funds and staff, there were fierce skirmishes over functions. These related to two main areas: which body is entrusted with the performance of land registration functions and which body has power to deal in public land? In relation to registration, the National Land Commission argued that it required access to land registries in order to do any meaningful work on one of its key functions, the consideration of historical land injustices. In relation to the issue of powers to allocate public land, it argued that it had been granted the power to administer and manage public land. The Ministry retorted that the function of the Commission was simply advisory and that its role was only to make recommendations to the Ministry, rather than directly to carry out these functions. As well as resisting the decentralisation of land governance and the loss of significant powers, the Ministry of Land under the leadership of Cabinet Secretary Charity Ngilu was also widely perceived to have a material stake in winning on this particular issue. In this period, the allocation of public land as a patronage resource, as a source of significant personal wealth, and as a means to win political allies was continuing apace. As I showed in Chapter 2, control over public land has been a key touchstone for political power in Kenya. The Ministry could not contemplate being marginalised in this arena. I elaborate on this point below.

By the end of 2013, the business of land administration was almost entirely at a standstill. A newspaper account gives a flavour of the problems:

> It is notable that from the last quarter of 2013 to the first quarter of 2014, no new grants/titles were issued following ... wrangles. The market was seriously affected as it meant that of subdivisions, change of users, amalgamations, extension of leases, grants from new allotments, were severely crippled, which in turn frustrated numerous transactions. For example, the sale of land slowed down in cases where vendors needed to subdivide the land, registration of leases for multiple dwelling properties was hampered as the change of user could not be completed, banks declined to finance developers whose lease terms on their title were about to expire as they could not obtain an extension of lease, among other issues. (*Daily Nation* 28 January 2016)

The judicialisation of land politics through the lower courts was well under way by 2012. A number of cases had started to come before the High Court in which the powers of the National Land Commission had been at issue. For example, in 2013 the Land and Environment section of the High Court at Malindi was asked to rule on the correct procedures for the alienation of public land. In its determination, the court held that although this responsibility formerly belonged to the Commissioner of Lands, the passing of the 2012 Land Commission Act now meant that the management of public land and its alienation or allocation was a role of the National Land Commission. Despite this favourable outcome, the Commission found itself continuing to be stymied in its work and, by 2014, it had resolved to apply to the Supreme Court for guidance.

The Supreme Court's Advisory Opinion

The first stage of the landmark Supreme Court case took place in 2014 when it had to consider whether it had jurisdiction to hear a case relating to the National Land Commission and its status relative to the Land Ministry or whether that issue should be heard by the High Court where a Constitutional Petition on the matter (No. 219 of 2014) had already been lodged. The Attorney General and the Lands Ministry had objected that the Supreme Court did not have the jurisdiction to hear the case because that discretionary jurisdiction is only to be exercised rarely and the matters were in fact properly within the remit of the High Court. Rejecting these arguments, the Supreme Court decided it would exercise its discretionary jurisdiction to hear the case but, in a signal that the relationship between the parties was already fraught, required that prior to the conduct of any hearing, the National Land Commission and the Ministry of Lands should, during a ninety-day period, seek constructive engagement with each other aimed at 'reconciliation and a harmonious division of responsibility' (para. 3). It was necessary for the parties to engage one another in good faith, and to seek mutual understanding. Should this endeavour fail, the Supreme Court laid down that the question it would consider was a narrow one. Simply:

> What is the proper relationship between the mandate of the National Land Commission, on the one hand, and the Ministry of Land, Housing and Urban Development, on the other hand – in the context of Chapter Five of the Constitution; the principles of governance (Article 10 of the Constitution); and the relevant legislation? (Para. 4(iv))

When the parties failed to make progress on these instructions, the Supreme Court sat to hear the case. The parties to the case were the National Land Commission as applicants with a number of interested parties joined. These were the Attorney General, the Ministry of Land, Housing and Urban Development, the Institution of Land Surveyors of Kenya, the Land, Development and Governance Institute, the Commission for the Implementation of the Constitution, and the Law Society. Kituo cha Sheria and Katiba Institute applied to act as *amici curiae* (friends of the court as provided by Article 22(3)(c)).

In its Advisory Opinion, the Supreme Court sought to mediate on the relationship and responsibilities of the new National Land Commission in relation to the Lands Ministry. The Court recognised the import of the question before it, stating in its judgment that 'at the heart of the controversy raised by the Reference, is the proper constitutional and statutory boundaries between the powers and functions of the National Land Commission on the one hand, and the Ministry on the other' (para. 2(c)). In this sense, the Advisory Opinion is more than simply the court's intervention to set out the architecture of Kenya's land institution. This is because the judgment provided an opportunity for the court to review fundamental questions about the guiding principles of land policy and land law.

The immediate question facing the court was: in what sort of relationship are the Ministry and the Land Commission to be bound? Counsel for the Commission rehearsed the constitutional background to the creation of Kenya's independent commissions and argued that the Land Commission was in effect a fourth arm of government. Counsel for the Ministry retorted that Kenya in fact has a tripartite separation of powers model (I return to this issue below). This question of fundamental constitutional importance absorbed much of the discussion in the case. What is to be the status of this new, land-related Commission and, by extension, the status of other constitutionally mandated commissions? It is important to remember that the National Land Commission is one of a number of independent commissions stipulated by the Constitution. In total, Chapter 15 of the Constitution of Kenya 2010 sets out ten new commissions to be created. They are the Kenya National Human Rights and Equality Commission; the National Land Commission; the Independent Electoral and Boundaries Commission; the Parliamentary Service Commission; the Judicial Service Commission; the Commission on Revenue Allocation; the Public Service Commission; the Salaries and Remuneration Commission; the Teachers Service Commission; and the National Police Service Commission. In an important sense, the case before the Supreme Court's judgment was seen as also providing commentary of the status and future of these independent commissions.

Counsel for the Land Commission sought to place the present case in the historical context of land relations in Kenya. Citing 'the troubled history associated with access to, and ownership of land in this country' (para. 6) he reminded the court of the series of reports that documented this troubled past in the land domain, invoking what in Chapter 2, I describe as Kenya's land archive made up of official reports such as the Ndung'u report. Reminding the court of the constitutional dispensation which the country sought to leave behind when it enacted the Constitution in 2010, Counsel recalled how under laws repealed by the 2012 land laws, the President had had power over the allocation of land. As I showed in Chapter 3, this enabled the President to order the Commissioner of Lands to allocate land and led to widespread and well-known malpractices which were much resented by Kenyans. Counsel reminded the court of the role these reports had played in bringing about the drafting and enactment of the Land and Environment chapter of the Constitution. This was an important point for Counsel to raise: it sought to place the present issues in the wider context of the struggle for land and justice in Kenya, reminding the court of the wider constitutional transformation of which the restructuring of land relations and governance was a part.

The National Land Commission also sought to argue that it was now the body in charge of public land. It argued that although this responsibility had previously been vested in the Commissioner of Lands, it was now the Land Commission that was charged with the management, alienation and allocation of public land (see paras 8, 10, 21 of the Advisory Opinion). The new body argued that the Commissioner of Lands had had his administrative functions removed by the new laws and that the new Land Commission's mandate in relation to public land is a constitutional one. Because neither the National Government nor the County Government could carry out this function, logic dictated that they were unable to withdraw it from the Commission (para. 10). Rather, the Commission carries out this function 'as an agent of the public' (para. 16). Crucially, this meant that the Land Ministry now retained only a policy role in regard to public land (para. 21). Citing Section 5(2)(a) of the National Land Commission Act which allows the Commission to alienate public land 'on behalf of' and with the consent of the National and County governments, Counsel for the Commission argued that this was explicitly about its relationship with devolved structures of national- and county-level governments. This provision, it argued, was not intended to require the Commission to seek such approval from the executive when alienating public land (para. 15). In relation to recent efforts by the President to provide a role for a Cabinet Minister for Lands through Presidential Executive Order No. 2 of 2013 (Executive Order), Counsel submitted that this was in breach of Chapter 5 of the Constitution (para. 17).

Similarly, the Commission sought to persuade the court that responsibilities for land registration were now also passed to it and that any department doing that work under the Ministry must now fall under the control of the Land Commission (para. 12). It was argued that 'the registration process, at every stage, ought to be controlled by the National Land Commission' (para. 9). It argued that in order to ensure the Commission could carry out this work, it should be responsible for the appointment of key staff such as a Director of Physical Planning and Survey and that such staff would have to be made accountable to the Commission as a member of its staff rather than to the Ministry. In the view of Counsel for the Commission, 'to do otherwise, would subject the National Land Commission to possible sabotage of its constitutional mandate' (para. 9). Indeed, Counsel went further to argue that it would be a violation of the Constitution (specifically Article 62) and of the 2010 National Land Commission Act (specifically s. 5) for the Ministry to exercise any functions relating to the management and administration of land (para. 11). The Commission argued that Land Registrars play an important role in land administration and management and that if the Commission are to carry out any of its envisaged land registration functions (for example in relation to unregistered trust land or unregistered community land or in relation to alienating public land) then the Land Registrars must be answerable to it. Counsel argued that the Land Commission 'cannot effectively undertake its constitutional mandate, without having control over the Registrars' (para. 13).

The issue of access to and control of land registries had been an important one in the everyday life of both the new and the old land body and a key area in which the guidance of the court was now sought. For its part, the Commission argued that because Land Registrars play a central role in land administration and management, they were a necessary part of the work that it was constitutionally charged with doing.

It argued that, in order to carry out and registration functions such as ensuring the registration of currently unregistered trust land or safeguarding community land or public land, the Land Registrars must be responsible to the Land Commission. The Ministry retorted that it was not possible for the Commission to carry out land registration functions because it would be impossible to run parallel registries, one for public land, the other for private land. Launching an argument based on logic, it argued that Kenya's land classification system could not be divided up and that only one body, the Ministry, should have registration powers and responsibilities.

In a bid to ensure that it would be guaranteed financial independence from the Land Ministry, the Commission argued before the court that Section 28 of the Land Act 2012 provides that the Commission is 'mandated to receive any rent, royalties and payments reserved under any lease or licence' and that it must only account to either the National Government or the County Government for these funds (para. 18). The new body was entitled to retain money raised in the exercise of its functions. Counsel also raised the question of tax collection powers and the function of assessing taxes. He argued that Article 209 of the Constitution makes it clear that the Commission's role is that of collector so that it would in effect be replacing the Ministry in this function. But the Commission also argued that tax assessing and collecting functions cannot be separated and that both related functions now lie with the Commission (paras 22, 25).

A major preoccupation of the Advisory Opinion is how best to guarantee the independence of the National Land Commission. This question was framed before the court as: is the Land Commission to be understood as a 'fourth arm of government' (guaranteeing its independence) or does it function in an agency relationship with the Ministry of Lands (which subsumes it more clearly under the executive)? Whilst this issue went to the heart of the Commission's ability to function in the future – with its advocates strongly arguing that its independence from the executive must be fiercely guarded – the argument rested on how the Constitution itself is to be understood. For the Commission, Counsel argued that it would be wrong to see the new body as being part of Executive arm of government. This is because the Constitution is not built along the lines of a traditional model of separation of powers. Instead, precisely because such a body was created in order to 'address situations where ordinary Government departments may fail the neutrality test' as evidenced by Kenyan history in 'the mischief of irregular allocation of public land, and corruption in land matters' (para. 85), what must have been envisaged in creating an independent commission for land alongside the other constitutional commissions was a body able to exercise freedom from the executive, particularly through its guaranteed financial independence. It was argued that although the Commission must report to Parliament and to the President on an annual basis and submit its finances for audit to the Auditor General, its neutrality was otherwise constitutionally protected. Counsel argued that in this regard it can be contrasted with the Ministry of Lands 'which has a mandate determined by the President' (para. 88).

The Ministry vigorously disputed this interpretation. It argued that the National Land Commission is not akin to other constitutional commissions. Unlike other commissions, the Land Commission is in fact to be understood as standing in an agency relationship to the Ministry. This means that it has a duty to work with and to consult the Ministry. Under this model, the Ministry asserted, it was the 'principal' (para. 45) to which the National Land Commission stood explicitly in a subordinate role. Counsel argued that this would not infringe Article 249 of the Constitution which sets out the objects, authority and funding of the commissions and independent offices envisaged by the Constitution. Rather, it was argued, these objects would still be applicable to the Commission under the structure of an agency relationship.

The Advisory Opinion also contains a brief discussion of the mandate of the Commission in relation to historical land injustices. The Ministry did not seek to strip this function of the Commission and the role that the new body would play in this regard was recognised by the judgment. It can be described as having been conceded by the Land Ministry. In making a wider argument about the powers of the Commission as regards private land, over which the Ministry forcefully argued the Commission does not have power, Counsel submitted that the new body's mandate has a 'public orientation' (para. 46). This is evidenced by the fact that it has been given functions relating to the classification of land which it must carry out on behalf of National and County governments. Counsel for the Ministry used this argument to show that such a publicly oriented mandate must preclude the Commission having any responsibilities over private land. This was a major concern for the Ministry and in seeking to constrain the Commission's mandate in this regard, it appeared willing to concede that as 'an adviser, overseer, and a watchdog of the public interest' it must have a responsibility to recommend the correction of historical injustices in relation to public land. But in return and logically, it was argued by the Ministry, this must mean that the new body had no role in relation to private land. The Commission, it was recognised by the Advisory Opinion, has a constitutional mandate 'to initiate investigations, on its own initiative or on a complaint, into present or historical land injustices, and recommend appropriate redress' (Advisory Opinion: para. 359). I discuss the origins and importance of the debate over historical land injustices in Chapter 7.

The creation of the *amicus curiae* or friend of the court role by the 2010 Constitution enabled two parties to be added to the Advisory Opinion hearings in the case. Their detailed submissions provide important insights into key issues: their arguments sought to remind the court of the constitutional history of the case and the national values it implicated. Yash Pal Ghai has argued that this important role provides scope for the court to include in a case representation from those who seek to protect the Constitution and ensure it is not 'violated or derogated from'. Ghai points out that '[a]n amicus argues on law not on facts' (Ghai preface to Kekering and Mabazira 2017). It is worth exploring the interventions of the friends of the court in the Land Commission case because their independent stance as envisaged by the Constitution enabled them to provide nuanced alternative perspectives on the issues before the court. The different lens with which the *amicus curiae* are able to view the questions before the courts is neatly summed up in the argument of Counsel on behalf of the Katiba Institute who asserted that, in trying to work out the relative roles of the Commission and the Ministry or indeed any other arm of government, what is important is not to get side-lined by a preoccupation with these two bodies but to recall that the constitutional background to the Land Commission and its roots in Kenya's constitutional history mean that what is necessary is to pay attention to the relationship 'between the National Land Commission and the people of Kenya' (para. 77).

This was an attempt by the *amicus curiae* to sketch a genealogy for Kenya's land laws. It was a reminder to the court that the Land and Environment chapter of the Constitution had at its foundation the National Land Policy and that in turn, the National Land Commission Act 2012 must be interpreted in that light. The court was likewise reminded that the principles set out in Article 60, relating to land governance and management in Kenya, had their origins in constitutional debates and, concretely, in drafts of the Constitution in their various iterations. In tracing this genealogy, Counsel reminded the court that these ideas and principles had their roots in 'what the people told the Constitution of Kenya Review Commission in relation to land' (para. 77). In its report, the Commission 'had called for the establishment of an independent Commission, to administer and manage land in Kenya, and the decision to institute a land commission is to be viewed in that context' (para. 83). This plea for historical awareness is echoed in Chief Justice Willy Mutunga's concurring opinion in which he argues that a key national value underpinning the creation of the Commission was that of participation.

Having tried to establish a genealogy for the National Land Commission and thereby root it jurisprudentially in Kenya's history of constitutional demands, the *amicus curiae* went on to use this as a basis on which to construct an argument for the National Land Commission's independence. The argument rested on a consideration of the separation of powers argument made by the Ministry. Counsel disagreed with this way of viewing Kenya's constitutional model: it argued that the Constitution of Kenya was not created along these lines. Instead, the Land Commission's independence was guaranteed by the fact that it constituted, like other independent commissions, a fourth arm of government. Counsel reminded the court how other independent commissions around the world are constituted and enabled to function, and for what purposes. He drew an analogy with human rights commissions which it was argued are those best known around the world. He argued that key elements of these commission's workings are internationally agreed, such as the stipulation that they be financially independent. The court was reminded that:

> Commissions are intended to address situations where ordinary Government departments may fail the neutrality test, as they act upon certain sensitive matters, such as corruption, or elections. And in the case of Kenya ... the mischief of irregular allocation of Public land, and corruption in land matters, have been a disturbing reality ... this led to the creation of an independent National Land Commission, with the necessary provision for financial independence. (Para. 77)

Sufficient financial support was key to the proper functioning of any independent Commission, as was the unbiased appointment and security of tenure of its commissioners. Counsel argued that commissions are nonetheless accountable because they are required to report annually to Parliament and to the President and to submit themselves to audits of their accounts. Counsel also drew an important distinction between the Land Commission, which is constitutionally protected, and the Ministry of Lands whose mandate is set by the President (para. 78).

The *amicus curiae* also pointed out that although the term, 'land administration and management' is used repeatedly in both constitutional and statutory provisions, the exact meaning and scope of the term has not been elaborated anywhere. Going to the heart of the problem facing the court, Counsel urged that the court itself 'provide the necessary definition' (para. 79). Relying on Section 8 of the Land Act which Counsel submitted provides that the new Commission is responsible for the 'management of land', it should be responsible for identifying parcels of public land, managing data on land and playing a role in land-use planning. The *amicus curiae* stressed that the Land Act envisaged an expansive role for the Commission which is empowered to keep a register of private land converted to public land, as well as community land converted to private or public land.

In their ruling, the court rejected the argument made by the *amicus curiae* Counsel that the Commission stands as a fourth arm of government and that in this way its independence is best guaranteed. According to the judgment, the Land Commission is 'required to function in a collaborative and consultative constitutional and legal setting' and in its view this suggests that the best legal framework within which to envisage the relationship between them is that of 'checks and balances'. The court argued that this way of understanding the relationship between the two bodies is preferable to one that sees the Commission as a fourth arm of government. The court argued that this is not envisaged by Article 1(3) which states that that the people's sovereign power devolves to the Executive, the Legislature, and the judiciary and independent tribunals. Showing its strong preference for a practical and pragmatic solution rather than a judgment strongly rooted in principle, the court argued that the only model that enables the collaborative work that must be done by the National Land Commission and Ministry is one based on checks and balances (para. 301). The court described the fourth arm of government model as one which isolated the Commission and was thus undesirable.

On the relationship between the two bodies, the court urged cooperation and held that the Commission and the Ministry were complementary and must work in consultation. They declined to provide detail as to how the relationship should work as requested by the *amicus curiae*. The court held that what was needed was a pragmatic approach that would require the parties to come to agreements over their work. Nonetheless that schema that the court held out placed the Land Commission in a decidedly subordinate role. Most critically, the court ruled that the Land Commission has no power to register titles and in so doing drew a series of distinctions the effect of which is to reinforce a hierarchy between the Land Ministry and the Land Commission. Analysing the Land Registration Act, the court held that the process of registration is in fact undertaken by various agencies. It may begin with the Land Commission but it ends with the registrar playing a role in issuing title deeds. It particular, the court pointed out that Section 6(6) provides that 'the land registration units shall be established at County level and at such other levels to ensure reasonable access to land administration and registration services'. In the court's reasoning, the existence of a further layer of devolved bodies below the Land Commission was used to justify the powers of a body above it in the form of the Ministry.

The court found that the Land Registration Act envisages a separation the role of 'land administration' from that of 'registration'. The court accepted that land administration is a wider term and could be argued to include registration, but argued that a definition alone cannot confer a power and that only a substantial provision could have done this. The Land Registration Act does not provide that provision, it ruled, and so it cannot be held that the Commission has any power to register title. The court argued instead that the roles of the Land Commission can be found in its own governing statute (the National Land Commission Act) and in the Land Act. The court enumerated these as follows: allocation of land; disposing of public land; leasing; and effecting change of user. According to the court however these roles can only be regarded as 'preparatory steps towards registering a title'. 'Neither of the two statutes gives the National Land Commission the function of *registration of title*, in express terms' (para. 292, emphasis original).

The court then undertakes what it sees as a logical explanation of the roles that the Land Commission is excluded from performing. According to the court's reasoning, because registration involves all categories of land and it cannot have been envisaged by legislators that the role of registration would be fragmented between two bodies, it must be right to find that the task of registering land titles in fact lies with the National Government. Only the Ministry has the authority to do this on behalf of the government. The court therefore concludes: 'National Land Commission has a mandate in respect of various processes leading to the registration of land, but neither the Constitution nor statute law confers upon it the power to register titles in land. The task of registering land title lies with the National Government, and the Ministry has the authority to issue land title on behalf of the said Government' (para. 308). This is because land title

> by its singularity as the mark of entitlement to landed property, is the ultimate expression of a vital property right ... On that account, the sole national repository to issue, and to guarantee the validity and integrity of title, is the central State machinery, as a player on the international plane, acting through the Executive organ. (para. 309)

The Advisory Opinion ends with a recommendation that all the land laws be reviewed by the Attorney General and the Law Reform Commission.

Analysis

Throughout the Advisory Opinion, the Court is manifestly aware of its critical role as constitutional interpreter. Relying on a case in which it was called upon to adjudicate on the actions of the Speaker of the National Assembly in failing to refer a legislative matter to the Senate or upper house, the court reiterated its view that:

> Each matter that comes before the Court must be seized upon as an opportunity to provide high-yielding interpretive guidance on the Constitution; and this must be done in a manner that advances its purposes, gives effect to its intents, and illuminates its contents. (Supreme Court Advisory Opinion No. 2 of 2013: para. 98)

But despite setting itself this interpretive task, in practice the court resisted the opportunity in its National Land Commission advisory to

advance the purpose of the Constitution and to interpret statute in light
of this wider constitutional context (known as the purposive approach).
Instead, it declared itself hindered by poorly drafted legislation. Given
the account provided in Chapter 5 of the failings of the legislature in
relation to the drafting of the 2012 land laws, this is disappointing.
The stance of the court only aggravated an existing problem. The court
held that because specific provisions did not provide powers to the
Commission (in relation to its registration functions) and these could
not be read off from definitions of the body's role, no such functions
could be ascribed to the Commission. I would argue that that position
contradicts the Court's own elaboration of its interpretive constitutional duties as set out in the Advisory Opinion. Had the court failed to
elaborate on and understand the deep roots of Kenya's land history and
its intricate connections with constitutional struggle, this might have
been understandable. But the judgment is in many regards an exemplar
of a historically sensitive jurisprudence. Its conclusions are all the more
puzzling for this reason.

The Advisory Opinion, despite its close attention to history, is curi-
ously power blind. It fails to recognise that cooperation can only take
place where the parties are matched in terms of power and status.
The National Land Commission, newly created and since its inception
starved of funds and a meaningful role, needed the court to assist in
developing its shield of independence and its fledgling status. The court
held back, treating the Ministry of Land and the National Land Commission as equals who might negotiate some equilibrium if urged to do so,
and failing to recognise the overwhelming advantages possessed by an
incumbent institution, a longstanding and experienced Land Ministry.

Particularly in relation to titling responsibilities, the court in the
Advisory Opinion fails to grasp how the case presented a unique
jurisprudential opportunity. Faced with key questions of land law,
administration and management, the court might have developed in
its judgment reasoning that had the effect of 'locking in' a public law
perspective on land issues (see Chapter 5 for a discussion of the need to
understand land law as a matter of public (as contrasted with private)
law). If the court had emphasised in its interpretation of the terms
'management and administration' that what was being asked of it was
an interpretation of public functions, essentially administrative law,
this would have enabled it to provide robust and detailed guidance on
the powers and responsibilities of institutions and individuals in the
land arena. Instead, the court relied rather too much on a view of the
case as predominantly based on land law and specifically private law.
This is evidenced by its reading of the function of registration of title.
Its reasoning here was that the legislature cannot have envisaged a
fragmentation of the role of land title issuance between the Ministry
and the Land Commission. That would be bad for the market and lead to

uncertainty. This emphasis by the court on the need to avoid fragmentation in a key area of land dealings shows a private law interpretive inclination. The court prioritises a private law view of land as a tradeable asset. It fails to see that the task of breathing life into terms such as 'land management' and 'land administration' is essentially an elaboration of public law. Such a stance might have led the court to reason differently. Its own alertness to constitutional and land history should have led it to that point. Aware of the mischief which a new dispensation in land management and administration was developed to address, the court should instead have provided jurisprudential backing for a strongly protected constitutional commission rooted in administrative law.

Instead, the Advisory Opinion falls short of issuing specific detail of how to resolve the impasse between the Land Ministry and the Commission which had come to characterise the years since the new land laws had been enacted. The judgment leaves this for the two bodies to work out. Given the strains of the past few years and the impasse at which they found themselves on the eve of the Advisory Opinion, it is hard to see how this order could be an effective one. Despite the elaboration of constitutional history and principles which it provides, the Advisory Opinion is disappointing in this regard. It refrains from setting out a coherent and prescriptive answer to the questions before it. It explicitly refuses to do so, arguing that the role of an advisory opinion is to consider pragmatic and constructive ways to promote cooperation and consultation between two institutions. It declines to set out the exact relationship to be enjoyed by the two state organs as the *amicus curiae* asked of it. In doing so, I suggest that it fails its own test. The judgment provides everything needed for a historically informed jurisprudence. The court knows why there is a need to guarantee the independence of the National Land Commission. But it falls short of concretely building a sturdy and enduring architecture with detailed and carefully elaborated roles specifically set out. Instead, the court recommends that the entire statutory framework governing land in Kenya be referred for review to the Attorney General and the Law Reform Commission.

The outcome of the judgment is that the role of the Land Commission is truncated. The roles remaining to it are the conduct of research on land issues and on natural resources; initiating inquiries into historical land grievances and recommending redress; and promoting traditional methods of resolving land conflict. The mandate of the Commission is succinctly summed up by the court as 'a brains-trust mandate in relation to land grievances, with functions that are in nature consultative, advisory, and safeguard-oriented' (para. 310). Thinker, but not doer, the resultant Land Commission is a far cry from that envisaged by the Constitution and the National Land Policy.

Aftermath

Whilst the Supreme Court was considering the Land Commission advisory, a set of land law amendments were introduced which did in fact reduce the powers and responsibilities of the National Land Commission. The Land Law (Amendments) Bill 2016 (known widely at the time as 'the Omnibus legislation') was introduced. The Bill was introduced by the ruling Jubilee party and had the clear aim of challenging the powers vested in the National Land Commission and unpicking the devolved architecture that gave the counties powers over land as discussed in Chapter 5. The effect of the new law when it came into force in October 2016 was to remove powers over land registries from the National Land Commission. Instead, the work of maintaining land registries was firmly returned to the Land Ministry with both the Land Commission and the counties retaining only the right to access these records.

Most importantly, by the new law and an amendment to the National Land Commission Act 2012, the County Land Management Boards were abolished. As I showed in Chapter 5, these boards were a critical element of the devolution of land governance experiment on which Kenya had embarked. A major element of the land devolution architecture which was envisaged by the National Land Policy and the Constitution, and which had as long ago as the Njonjo recommendations been seen as a key way to challenge the over-centralisation of land governance, was effectively removed. In the recentralisation battle, the abolition of the County Land Management Boards was a major victory for those seeking to put the brakes on reform.

Conclusion

The Advisory Opinion is a landmark intervention by Kenya's highest court in land matters. It was an opportunity to determine the contours and workings of Kenya's land institutions. I show that, throughout the case, counsel and judges were attentive to the constitutional import of the case before them and sought to develop a historically nuanced jurisprudence of land governance by reference to the history of land reform. This was evident for example in the arguments of Counsel for the National Land Commission who urged that the National Land Commission Act, the Land Act and the Land Registration Act of 2012 are 'normative derivatives of the Constitution' (para. 23). Throughout the case, the intricate connections between reforming land governance and reforming Kenya's constitutional framework were repeatedly invoked. In his concurring judgment in the Advisory Opinion, the then Chief Justice and President of the Supreme Court Willy Mutunga was at pains to point out that the story of constitutional change in Kenya must be understood as one in which the people chose a new social order and rejected the previous dispensation in which the elite made law and wrote constitutions in their own interests. The Chief Justice sought in particular to explore the constitutional values underpinning land management and administration. He argued persuasively that participation was a key value of the National Land Policy and that this had permeated the Land and Environment chapter of the Constitution (see Chapter 5 paras 319–56).

As I showed in Chapter 5, the land law reform of 2009 onwards can be read as a reassertion of the role of public and administrative law in the land arena. As McAuslan (2003: 255) argued, where title to land is vested in the President, the state or its organs, 'land law ceases to be a matter of private law but becomes part of public law; it is in fact administrative law'. Seen in this light, Chapter 5 of the Constitution and its translation into concrete laws in 2012 was an attempt to reassert the role of 'applied administrative law' (McAuslan 2003: 256). By stipulating the manner and form of officials' powers over land, it looked to law to end the longstanding practices of corruption built on administrative discretion that had led to irregular and illegal dealing in land.

The National Land Commission Advisory Opinion is a rare occasion on which questions of land politics and land administration have been aired in Kenya's highest court. In this chapter I have shown that an intervention by the Supreme Court became necessary in order to clarify ambiguities in the new laws passed in 2012, that is the Land Act, the Land Registration Act and the National Land Commission Act. As I showed in Chapter 5, these laws failed to set out the specific duties and responsibilities of those charged with managing and administering land. Although these new land laws were required by the 2010 Constitution of Kenya which provides that Parliament would revise, consolidate and rationalise existing land laws, the process of developing these new laws was far from adequate. I have shown how the laws were passed in haste and with minimal consultation with experts or the public. One important outcome of this imperfect process was that the National Land Commission Act 2012 failed to elaborate the role of this new independent commission, whose establishment was intended to remove centralised control from a corrupt and dysfunctional Ministry of Lands. The legislation was poorly drafted and did not specify the duties of land administration with sufficient clarity. The vague provisions requiring the two bodies to work in consultation and cooperation were inadequate.

In this chapter, I have used the Supreme Court's Advisory Opinion to elaborate on the wider themes that I am concerned with in this book: constitutional change, the role of law and the possibilities of land justice through more equitable land governance. Although the outcome of the Advisory Opinion is well known, there has been no detailed analysis of the court's approach and the jurisprudence it developed in its Advisory Opinion. I have remedied that shortcoming in our knowledge of Kenyan law and jurisprudence by providing a close reading of the Advisory Opinion and exploring its key themes. I show that the wrangle over the National Land Commission is a wrangle over constitutional history and the country's constitutional future. The story I have told is one of enduring unequal power between these two institutions, one old and one new. I have argued that the case before the Supreme Court was an opportunity to present a detailed jurisprudential working out of the precise meaning and role of the new bodies created by the Constitution and to give life to the broad-brush principles set out by the Constitution and, reaching further back (as I show in Chapter 5) to the National Land Policy, constitutional drafts and the Njonjo recommendations.

The failure to protect the National Land Commission has had a concrete impact. In the period after the Advisory Opinion was issued, the Commission became mired in controversy (Mwathane 2018a). Allegations of impropriety and of corruption have become commonplace. Its credibility has been called into question since the loss of data on compensation payments for land which it was holding on an internal computer. Indeed, it has been embroiled in land compensation scandals. Serious doubts have been cast over the integrity of some commissioners. As the Commission has become distrusted, it has lost its status as an independent guardian of the Constitution in the land arena and has become associated instead with the sorts of land wrongs for which the Land Ministry is infamous. There is of course no way of knowing what a more forthright defence of the Commission by the courts might have achieved. Would it have prevented the steep decline in trust and the widespread malpractice which has since occurred? At the very least, we can speculate that had the court thrown its weight behind this new body, spelling out explicitly how it is a critical independent commission undergirded by constitutional values and required to be transparent, accountable and participatory, the fate of the Land Commission might have been different. Instead, like the Ministry before it, it seems to have lost the trust of citizens as its commissioners fail to uphold constitutionalism and ignore the aspirations with which it was created.

7

Rethinking Historical Land Injustices

The settler and the native are old acquaintances. In fact, the settler is right when he speaks of knowing 'them' well. For it is the settler who has brought the native into existence and who perpetuates his existence. The settler owes the fact of his existence, that is to say his property, to the colonial system. (Fanon 2001: 28)

In legal scholarship, law's time has too often been assumed rather than problematized. (Mawani 2014: 69)

Introduction

In this chapter, I offer a critique of current approaches to the concept of historical land injustices. Whilst Kenya provides the starting point, my analysis can be extended to other African and non-African countries trying to address historical wrongs connected with land, especially those of indigenous peoples. Before tracing the provenance of the term in a range of legal and policy documents, this chapter opens by exploring what must surely be an exemplary case of colonial and post-colonial injustice relating to land, dispossession and the loss of a way of life (Roux 2009). I discuss the colonial legal struggles of the Maasai and suggest that the ontological and material harms of settler colonialism were inherited and deepened by the post-colonial Kenyan state. Having shown how the term historical land injustices emerged as critical terms in contemporary politics and law, I go on to offer a critique of our current understanding of this idea. I argue that we need to be attentive to its complex temporalities and inter-temporalities. I suggest that past and present cannot be neatly sealed off from each other, and that historical land wrongs bleed into and shape the present-day economy.

The Maasai and the colonial encounter

There are a number of reasons why the Maasai are explored here as an exemplary instance of historical land injustices and its conceptualisations. Most obviously, the two treaties signed between the Maasai and the British colonial authorities in 1904 and 1911 constituted the earliest concrete taking of land or colonial expropriation in Kenya (Ngugi 2002). A century later, in 2004, the question of the legality of the Anglo-Maasai treaties was still under discussion (Kantai 2007). This is a case of a longstanding land-related injustice grounded in contested law (specifically, the status of the 'Maasai treaties'). It was still a live issue as the constitutional review process got underway (ibid.) and there is perhaps no better example of a land injustice which lives on vividly in (sections of) the popular imagination and in the popular archive.

In the present day, the Maasai live in Narok, Kajiado and Trans Mara in the southern part of present-day Kenya. Whereas in pre-colonial times they lived on both side of the Rift Valley escarpment, an area that measured 600 miles in length and 200 miles in width which they used as fertile grazing grounds, with the advent of colonialism the Maasai steadily lost territory (Gathii 2007; Kantai 2007; Ngugi 2002). In 1904 and again 1911, at the point of a gun (Hughes 2006), they were moved from land that was discovered to be 'eminently suitable for settlers' (Ghai and McAuslan 1970: 20). Ngugi (2002: 329) notes perceptively that the consequences of this were more than simply the loss of territory. 'Since land relationships are an incident of the total culture of a people, and the culture is, in turn, shaped by the peoples' way of life, which is influenced by the ecological conditions of the areas they occupy' what the moving of the Maasai (Hughes 2006) denoted was the destruction of a way of life (Okoth-Ogendo 1979; Roux 2009).

In *Ol le Njogo and others v. A-G of the EAP* (1914), the Maasai challenged the legal basis of their removal from their ancestral lands. In 1904, senior members of the Maasai had agreed to vacate land and to be regrouped in two areas. The agreement stipulated that Europeans would not be allowed to take up land in these newly created settlements. That agreement was to subsist for seven years. Recognising the value of the land being thus occupied by the Maasai, settlers began immediately to press for access to it and for increased 'white reservation of the land' (Hughes 2006: 28) and, in 1911, a further violent moving of the Maasai was carried out. In the 1914 case, brought on behalf of some of those who had been made to move in 1911, the plaintiff argued that the 1904 agreement had been breached, that it was a civil agreement which was still subsisting in 2011 and that the 1911 agreement was not made with Maasai capable of binding the whole tribe. In addition, damages in tort were sought for confiscation of cattle during the move (Ghai and McAuslan 1970; and see the account given in Hughes 2006).

In response, the Crown argued that the courts had no jurisdiction because the 1904 and 1911 agreements were not contracts. They were treaties. What had occurred in the taking of the cattle which was an alleged tort was in fact an act of state. Neither of these matters could be ruled upon in a municipal court. Both at first instance and later in the East African Court of Appeal these arguments were successful. In essence, the argument that was constructed was that the Maasai were a sovereign entity. This meant that they were capable of entering into a treaty and crucially, of surrendering the land in this way. The Maasai's 'vestigial sovereignty' (Ghai and McAuslan 1970: 21) retained by them after the country had been taken over, enabled them to make a treaty. How did the court come to the conclusion that the Maasai retained a 'residual sovereignty' (ibid.: 1970: 22)? It argued that radical title to their territory was vested in them and remained so. The argument, Ghai and McAuslan point out, was circular: 'To the question: can the Masai make a treaty? The answer was: yes, because they retain an element of sovereignty. And to the question: what element of sovereignty do the Masai retain? The answer was, the treaty-making element' (ibid.: 22). Happily for the colonial regime, it was found that the agreements were not civil contracts and no remedy could be afforded by a municipal court for wrongs that might have been done in the removal of the Maasai from their land. The absurdity of this position is summed up by Ghai and McAuslan in their observation that it amounted to ruling that 'the Masai retained sufficient sovereignty to make a treaty but not to make a civil contract about land' (ibid.). The case was in keeping with a line of findings that showed that the courts were unwilling to 'allow challenges to the legal base of colonialism' (1970: 24). Ngugi (2002), commenting on the treaties, notes that 'the British constructed the Maasai as a sovereign group to facilitate carving off land from them'. In his consideration of the case, Gathii (2007) has also pointed to the paradoxes inherent in the court's treatment of the 1904 and 1911 treaties. In a protectorate declared in 1895, the Maasai nevertheless had to be accorded sufficient sovereignty to sign away their land. In the acerbic assessment of Ghai and McAuslan (ibid.: 25), the import of the judgment was that 'a British protected person is protected against everyone except the British'.

In the post-independence era, the Maasai 'were denied the political space in which to revive their claim to the "lost lands"' (Kantai 2007: 109). The Maasai 'unnervingly on the move and impervious to the benefits of the constraints of civilization' in the colonial period, were held now to be resistant to 'modernization and development' (Ngugi 2002). If the colonial-era project was aimed at ending their pastoralism and imposing fixity of residence the better to tax them, in the post-colonial period, the 'tyranny of property' (Atieno-Odhiambo 2002: 225), traced in Chapter 1 this volume, continued the mission to civilise the Maasai by ending their 'conservative and primitive' pastoral way of life and bringing to them the benefits of sedentary individual tenure.

With the inauguration of the National Rainbow Coalition in 2002, it was hoped that promises to confront historical wrongs would enable the Maasai to draw attention to their longstanding land claims once again (Kantai 2007). For Kantai (ibid.: 109) the failure of this hope confirms 'the deeply rooted conservative structures of Kenyan politics'. Kantai traces the re-emergence of Maasai land claims to the recognition by what was called the Maa Forum ('a group of Maasai professionals lawyers, journalists and NGO activists') that the expiry of leases signed in Laikipia where thirty-seven settler families occupied the land were imminent and that it followed that 'the two million acres that consti- tute the former Northern Maasai Reserve should revert to the Maasai people'. Kantai powerfully recounts the role of land rumours in this period:

> there had been rumours that the Laikipia sellers were worried about the expiry of the leases; with a new government in place, there were no guarantees that their interests would be protected. Stories abounded of panic selling, secret missions by settler lobby groups to the Minister of Lands. I was never able to confirm any of them. (2007: 111)

Kantai critiques the terms in which the campaign was framed in ways that are suggestive for the discussion I develop below regarding the intertwining of historical and present-day land claims. For Kantai (2007: 114) the 'strategy to target white-owned ranches as an entry point into a wider land restitution debate' had important effects. It enabled the Maasai campaign to emphasise the colonial and historical context when they presented a petition demanding the return of Laikipia land and fair compensation. For Kantai the petition was strongly rooted in the colonial context and astutely avoided the politics of post-independence 'ethnic cliientalism' (ibid.). In this way, 'the Maasai had racialised the Laikipia claims without ethnicising them'. In his analysis of the public understanding of the campaign and in particular the approach of the Kenyan press to it, Kantai shows that the campaign was framed as 'a drama of land dispossession and British colonial injustice' whilst avoiding the ongoing land dispossessions of the Moi and Kenyatta eras: 'by casting the Maasai story as a drama whose implications did not necessarily threaten the course of contemporary Kenyan politics, the media was taking its audience on a museum tour' (ibid.). In its presenta- tion to international audiences, the campaign enabled connection to be made between the reinvigorated Maasai land claims and growing fears surrounding the contemporaneous Zimbabwean land invasions, as the Maasai were presented as armed and dangerous and willing to attack white settlers in their homes, a depiction Kantai (2007: 115) describes as their being 'Mau-Maued'.

As well as a powerful account of present-day attempts to confront historical land injustices by those who have inherited dispossession, Kantai (2007) makes the important connection between past and present, putting the failure of the new government after 2002 to take seriously the land claims of the Maasai down to their imbrication in the current structures of land and the economy. For Kantai, the state could not resolve longstanding historical wrongs in the land domain because they have an 'active interest in perpetuating them' (2007: 115): 'The nationalist elites profited hugely from retaining the colonial order. The State became a vehicle for their accumulation, land – especially Maasai land – a tool to support their ethnic patronage system.' We can thus assess the Maasai experience of colonial expropriation and post-colonial domination as a continuum. This suggests that we should treat the end of colonial rule not as a rupture but as continuing and deepening structures of domination (Wolfe 2006).

Bhandar (2018), developing a theoretical framework that owes much to the work of Cheryl Harris' 'Whiteness as Property' (1993), explicitly reaches beyond this to argue that 'racial subjects and modern property laws are produced through one another in the colonial context' (2018: 8). Bhandar argues that ownership and control of property was not just dependent on race in settler colonies: race 'was and remains subtended by property logics' that determine whose ways of holding and valuing land is worthy of legal recognition and protection. Bhandar explores notions of improvement as central to this racial subjectivity, citing Ranajit Guha's (1996) history of property in Bengal as a reminder of England's long history as improving landlord. Similarly, in his essay on property and empire, McAuslan (2013) explored how ideologies of improvement were developed first in Ireland. He shows how this outlook on property then spread through colonial conquest all over the world. It is captured in the justification, indeed injunction, provided by Sir John Davies, the English Attorney General for Ireland in the late 16th and early 17th centuries, in a letter to the Earl of Salisbury in 1610, to the effect that the king was 'not only entitled by law' but 'bound in conscience' to seize land and enact the formal replacement of Irish land law by the English common law in order to 'reduce his people from barbarism to civility'. This because, in the words of Sir John Davies, 'if [the natives] were suffered to possess the whole country ... they would never, to the end of the world, build houses, make townships or villages, or manure or improve the land as it ought to be' (cited in Meiksins Wood 2003).

These authors have in common a concern with settler colonialism as an ontological project. Bhandar's (2018) focus on racial regimes of property leads her to important insights on the intimacy of colonialism. Citing Fanon's observation that 'the settler and the native are old acquaintances', Bhandar stresses the psycho-affective dimensions of racial property regimes. For her, property law must be understood as 'a form of colonial domination' (2018: 5). The experiences of indigenous peoples, as explored above, lend themselves to a similar analysis. Ngugi has argued that the domination of the Maasai was taken to be necessary as part of a modernising, improving and civilising impetus. The Maasai case provides an excellent example of 'the instrumentality of the law as a device aimed at modernist development' (Ngugi 2002: 300) as Ghai and McAuslan showed in their 1970 text in relation to agrarian policy asserted through administrative rules. For Ngugi, decolonising in its modernisation garb was also domineering of certain parts of the state, so that decolonisation had an important dangerous aspect that must be recognised. In this modernisation model, a powerful binary was at play that constructed the indigenousness as opposed to modernity (Ngugi 2002: 327) 'in a linear historical progressivist fashion'. Deprecated by a racial colonial land regime that refused to acknowledge communal relations to land (Okoth-Ogendo 1975), in the post-colonial era the state's domination of indigenous peoples was a continuation of this racial regime of ownership (Bhandar 2018). Attitudes to the Maasai and to indigenous communities that deprecate a perceived lack of modernity in respect of land thus have a long provenance.

The emergence of a term

The Maasai example provides just one instance of 'involuntary land losses' (Alden Wily 2018b: 662) and the 'illegal taking of land' (Sing'oei 2011: 519) in the colonial period and under Kenya's post-independence administrations. The term that has come to be used for these losses and the domineering practices that have underpinned them is 'historical land injustices'. Early uses of the term can be traced to the Njonjo report discussed in Chapter 3, when it arose as part of the Inquiry's attempt to press for recognition of longstanding grievances relating to land. At that stage, it would not have been straightforward to provide a definition of the term: it was used to express a sometimes nebulous sense that grievances on and about land had affected a given community or territory. It was often used as citizens strained to find a vocabulary in which to construct a popular archive on land. If it emerged alongside the publication official reports on land and other human rights issues it was also in tension with them, often expressing what Musila (2017: 692) has described as 'different epistemic framings' of land stories by the marginalised and the powerless.

Since these early usages, the term has firmly taken hold in Kenya's constitutional and political lexicon. It was used during the elongated process of constitutional review, not least through civil society activism. For example, the Kenya Human Rights Commission published a report entitled 'Redress for historical land injustices in Kenya' (KHRC n.d.: 2). The 2008 Kenya National Dialogue and Reconciliation (KNDR) process lent real impetus to discussions of land wrongs and historical land injustices by recognising and expressing in official documents how land clashes had been an integral part of political and ethnic mobilisation in the 1990s, for example in the Rift Valley. In its agenda item 4, KNDR explicitly asserted that 'poverty, the inequitable distribution of resources and perceptions of historical injustices and exclusion on the part of the Kenyan society constituted the underlying causes of tensions, stability and cycle of violence' (KNDR 2008). The discussions surrounding dialogue and reconciliation enabled Kenya to hold the mirror up to itself and to confront the root causes of the systemic and cyclical violence that had characterised elections. Recognising how land clashes had been used as tools of political mobilisation throughout the 1990s in the Rift Valley, as well as other forms of grievance such as those that had long festered at the coast, the KNDR process specifically confronted these issues when formulating its agenda. In doing this, it was seeking to revive attention to the issues contained in the draft constitution which had been rejected at the 2005 referendum. This explicitly required historical land injustices to be addressed as a result of the Constitution of Kenya Review Commission's receipt of ample evidence to show this was urgently being called for by citizens. Much later, the Truth, Justice and Reconciliation Commission report (Republic of Kenya 2013) provided perhaps the best illustration of the links being made between land issues and claims to justice. The term 'historical land injustices' is used throughout the report, although it does not appear in the legislation creating the TJRC. Nonetheless, the term had by this time 'entered the Kenyan lexicon in the context of activism and agitation for constitutional reform and the establishment of transitional justice mechanisms aimed at addressing past human rights violations' (TJRC 2013).

Most concretely, in Article 67, the 2010 Constitution directs the National Land Commission 'to initiate investigations, on its own initiative or on a complaint, into present or historical land injustices, and recommend appropriate redress'. The first legislative attempt to give content to the term 'historical land injustice' came in the National Land Commission Act (Republic of Kenya 2012), which provides the broad contours of a historical land injustice definition in Section 15(2). This stipulates that a historical land injustice means

> a grievance which – (a) was occasioned by a violation of right in land on the basis of any law, policy, declaration, administrative practice, treaty or agreement; (b) which resulted in displacement from their habitual place of residence; (c) which occurred between 15th June 1895 when Kenya became a protectorate under the British East African Protectorate and 27th August 2010 when the Constitution of Kenya was promulgated.

Section 15(1) of the National Land Commission Act provides that 'pursuant to Article 67(3) of the Constitution, the Commission shall receive, admit and investigate all historical land injustice complaints and recommend appropriate redress'. Section 15(3) provides the criteria by which a historical land claim may be 'admitted, registered and processed' by the Commission. It requires that it must be verifiable that the act complained of resulted in displacement of the claimant or other form of historical land injustice. It requires that the claim has not or is not capable of being addressed through the ordinary court system on the basis that the claim contradicts a law that was in force at the time when the injustice began or has not been barred by the Statute of Limitation. The claim must be made within five years of the Act being passed and the claimant must have been either a proprietor or an occupant of the land upon which the claim is based.

Section 15(4) sets out the heads under which a claim alleging historical land injustice is permissible. To be allowable as a historical land injustice claim, the complaint must have been occasioned by either colonial occupation; the independence struggle; a pre-independence treaty or agreement between a community and the government; development-induced displacement for which no adequate compensation or other form of remedy was provided, including conversion of non-public land into public land; inequitable land adjudication process or resettlement scheme; politically motivated or conflict based eviction; corruption or other form of illegality; natural disaster; or, finally, any other cause approved by the Commission.

It took the National Land Commission until 2014 to establish the Task Force to draft the law governing the investigation of historical land injustices. This was eventually achieved in 2016, by amending the National Land Commission Act under the Land Laws (Amendment) Act. The Chairperson of the National Land Commission published the National Land Commission (Investigation of Historical Land Injustices) Regulations 2017 (Legal Notice No. 258 of 2017). These regulations set out the procedures to be followed in lodging a claim and also govern how investigations will be carried out, hearings held and cases decided. Under these procedures, a person may lodge a claim stating description of the property, the period when the injustice occurred, particulars of the respondent, witnesses, previous recovery attempt and suggested remedy.

Intertemporal land injustices

There is scarcely a region of Kenya that has not suffered from historical land injustice, whether by displacement to make way for European settlers or to create game reserves, through evictions for mining concessions or from forests, because of unjust allocations under settlement schemes, or by displacement as a result of politically motivated clashes or irregular and illegal land allocation processes. If this chapter has taken the Maasai case as an exemplar of land claims stretching back into the colonial period over which unresolved questions and claims still hang today, they are by no means an isolated example. For their part, the Endorois people claims that they are indigenous to Lake Bogoria in Central Baringo, Rift Valley Province. Between 1973 and 1986, the community claim, they were forcibly moved from the area to make way for a game reserve. The Endorois also failed through the Kenyan courts. Korir Sing'oei, who was Lead Counsel in the Endorois case before the African Commission, reads their struggle as one characterised by asymmetries of power between a dominated and excluded people and powerful and unchallengeable corporate interests. In a detailed assessment of the judicial struggle of the Endorois, Sing'oei (2011: 519) argues that their 'pastoral cultural configuration' came up against a developmental state intent on the promotion of the market and on attracting tourism and extractive industries in energy and mining. Their forced eviction led to the loss of livelihoods and disconnected them from cultural and spiritual spaces and temporalities. Forced by an overbearing, modernising and corrupt state to give up their way of life and their livelihoods, which Sing'oei (ibid.) describes as 'the illegal taking of Endorois land' they sought to claim their rights through the domestic High Court in Nakuru in *William Ngasia and Others* v. *Baringo County Council and Others* in 2000. The court rejected their claims in a poorly argued judgment which Sing'oei notes failed to engage with the broader issues they had attempted to raise: the court simply dismissed the Endorois arguments perfunctorily with the scant argument that 'the law did not allow individuals to benefit from such a resource simply because they happen to be born close to the natural resource' (2011: 520). Thereafter, the Endorois looked to assert their claim through international judicial mechanisms. In *Centre for Minority Rights Development (CEMIRIDE) and Minority Rights Group International (MRG) (on behalf of the Endorois) v. Kenya* in 2010, the African Commission on Human and Peoples' Rights found that the Endorois had suffered violations of their rights to freedom of religion, property, health, culture, religion and natural resources under the African Convention on Human and Peoples' Rights. In a landmark judgment, the Commission recommended restitution of the traditional lands of the Endorois and recognition of their ownership rights as well as the payment of compensation to them for the harm occasioned by the process of displacement. The Kenyan Government has been markedly reluctant to implement the decision.

The historical land injustices experienced by hunter-gatherer communities such as the Ogiek and the Sengwer and their marginalisation by the state continues to rankle in the present day. The marginalisation and dispossession of hunter-gatherers began in the colonial era when colonial administrators in Kenya actively encouraged the assimilation of hunter-gatherers into larger tribes, a policy that continued after independence. So, whilst the Kenyan Government recognised forty-two tribes in Kenya in 2018, it categorised hunter-gatherers as 'other', or simply counted them together with neighbouring peoples (Ohenjo 2018). Losing their land to commercial logging and prohibited from their customary practices such as hunting, they also suffered a lack of access to basic services such as healthcare (ibid.). At the point when a new constitution was being drafted, communities such as the Ogiek lobbied for hunter-gatherers to be specifically classified as a community but failed to achieve this. They continued to lobby for political representation such as reserved seats but made little headway. They were repeatedly threatened with eviction from their lands, a vital water catchment area, and in 2016 such a violent eviction did in fact take place, dispossessing approximately 1,000 Ogiek and with considerable use of force. Following repeated attempts to use the domestic courts to secure their claims to the Mau Forest, the decision was made to approach the African Court of Human and Peoples' Rights. In 2017, the court ruled in favour of the Ogiek and against their forced evictions in the Mau Forest. As with the Endorois, the implementation of the decision has proved immensely difficult.

Returning to the observation that land has been the cause of simmering discontent regularly breaking as violent conflict throughout Kenya's colonial and post-colonial history (Ogot 1976; Okoth-Ogendo 1975), these instances of land injustice demonstrate the multi-faceted, intertwined and complex ways in which land dispossessions have taken place. Although the ontological and psycho-affective impacts of these dispossessions (Bhandar 2018) cannot be captured by any one description or term, the label historical land injustices has come to be used as a kind of shorthand for a range of land wrongs. The term historical land injustice has entered policy and legal arenas whilst also having multiple meanings in popular archives, the everyday language and the daily politics of those struggling over land. It has become a firm feature of Kenya's political and legal lexicon. But the slow pace of material change for indigenous communities such as the Endorois, Ogiek and Sengwer, and the marked reluctance of the Kenyan state to implement findings in their favour, requires us to consider historical and present-day land claims in a broader context and in particular to explore their connection with the wider political economy. Assessing the Ndung'u report on illegal and irregular land allocations under both Presidents Kenyatta and Moi, I characterised Kenya as a 'grabbed state' (Manji 2014). Since that time, analysts have alluded more vividly to 'state capture' (Maina 2019), articulating in forthright terms the intricate links between state power and economic power.

Drawing on the discussion of the Maasai case offered above, we can see how deeply the present-day economy is rooted in the racial exclusivity of the colonial period being continued after the end of the colonial period, with dispossession on a massive scale as racial exclusivity in access to land transmogrified into what Shivji (2009) has described as an ethnicised land question. As I showed in Chapters 1 and 2, Kenya's land question cannot be understood apart from its status as a settler economy in which the hegemony exercised by the colonial state underpinned dispossession of land on a massive scale. When the 'enclave(s) of super-exploitation and racial privilege' (ibid.: 78) thus created were Kenyanised so that land ownership was no longer racialised, the fundamental relations of production and accumulation did not change. When 'racial privileges were replaced by ethnic preferences underwritten by the neo-colonial State' (ibid.) a deeply conservative structure was bequeathed to Kenyan politics (Kantai 2007). Radical change became impossible in a neo-colonial state with an ethnicised land question.

Understanding the continuities in the perpetuation of land injustices and exposing its colonial racial roots is critical, and not only in Kenya. We can achieve this by avoiding a model of historical land injustices founded on exceptionalism. Instead, we must recognise that there is nothing past about historical land injustice. This requires us to complicate law's linear temporality. We must recognise that in the present day, our political economy is deeply imbricated with land wrongs. Land injustices are sedimented in the political economy. By this I mean that the 'normal' economy is founded on what Harvey has labelled 'accumulation by dispossession' (as discussed in Chapter 1). It is not possible to isolate present and past historical land injustices and it is not possible to understand Kenya's political economy absent an understanding of how the normal and the supposedly abnormal (corruption, land grabbing) are co-dependent. Refusing a neat temporal account of land injustices also requires us to refuse an account of historical land injustices that seals it off from properly functioning politics and economics. A useful starting point for the argument I wish to make here is the distinction made in the National Land Commission Act 2012 between historical land injustices and what it labels 'present land injustices'. This distinction invites us to reflect on temporalities of justice. Conceptually, can we really distinguish between past (historical) and present land injustices? The purpose of the legal cut off point contained in the Act and which appeared in the subsequent Investigation of Historical Land Injustices Regulations in 2017 is of course instrumental: it enables legal claims to be made. The process of applying for a claim to be considered and for a remedy to be set out requires this. However, the law's efforts to contain the idea of land injustices through this neat temporal distinction should not prevent us from thinking more broadly about the consequences of land injustices. I suggest that the temporality of land-related injustices cannot be neatly contained in categories such as historical land injustices (defined by the regulations as those dating from colonial times up to the promulgation of the new Constitution) and present land injustices (those that occurred since the new Constitution).

Here we can draw on Wolfe (2006) to suggest that historical land injustices are structures not events. A nuanced and responsive analysis of land injustices in Kenya and the struggle against them needs to take seriously the structural consequences of land wrongs rather than treat them as an event taking place within a given timeframe (or even leaking beyond this timeframe into the present). Such an approach would allow us to see more clearly how land injustices have led to regimes of ownership that are deeply rooted in the present-day political economy and are difficult to separate from it. Indeed, it is impossible to envisage the present-day economic structure of Kenya without roots deep in the regimes of land ownership that were facilitated first by a settler political economy and then, post-independence, by an elite that reserved for itself access to and ownership of land on a massive scale. Land wrongs in Kenya do not admit of the neat temporal categorisations that law and policy set out. Instead, the proceeds of land wrongs circulate and recirculate in the wider economy, shape the very structure of the country's political economy and feed back into the land sector. On this reading, the reports of commissions of inquiry such as the Ndung'u report and the report of the Truth, Justice and Reconciliation Commission are not land reports alone but important archives of the entire political economy and of who owns and controls what. It is no wonder then that a redaction of the TJRC report by those whom it exposed was critical to them (Slye 2018). Their role not just as political actors but as key economic players would be made glaringly obvious by the publication of an unedited report.

Recognising that accumulation by dispossession has characterised Kenya since before independence implies that we must rethink our assumptions about how property rules function. Returning to van der Walt's (2009: 22) suggestion that it is when property rules are called into questions by a revolutionary break that we are afforded opportunities to look anew at such relations and to consider property from the 'unfamiliar vantage point of the margins', the discussions in this book suggest a modification of his thesis in important regards. In relation to South Africa, van der Walt's injunction to study 'property from the margins' (ibid.) was constructed on an assumption that South Africa underwent a moment of profound political change and of transformative changes in property law. Economic and political developments – as well as the work of critical legal scholars and constitutional theorists in the intervening years – have suggested that this is not the case. The end of apartheid did not constitute a radical break. The structures of racial inequality, dispossession and discrimination were left intact.

Modiri (2018), challenging the very designation 'post-apartheid', has queried assumptions of change, calling into question whether radical reforms of property and constitutional law did in fact take place in South Africa. It is important to recall that the most radical proposal on the table in the negotiated settlement – a wealth tax to be levied on those whites who benefited from accumulated wealth as a result of 'racial regimes of property' – never in fact came into being (Klug 2018). Far from bringing 'system-challenging change' (van der Walt cited in Bhandar 2018: 185), the South African 2019 election has shown that there is much yet to understand about the extent of the post-apartheid settlement. The Economic Freedom Fighters under Malema have argued that neither constitutional reform nor property reform has been sufficiently radical. For Modiri, 'the negotiated settlement that delivered constitutional democracy in South Africa' was 'a finale in which the fundamental economic structures of society would remain largely uncontested' (2018: 248). He goes further to argue that the Constitution 'works to consolidate and preserve particular arrangements and relations of power and knowledge'. Understood in this way, the constitution itself is implicated in the continuation of colonial-apartheid power relations, value systems and subjectivities. How else could we explain why 'the advent of constitutional democracy in South Africa has left white supremacy and coloniality largely undisturbed?' (ibid.: 305).

South Africa's debate about the protection of private property and the different interest at stake in the debate are instructive for Kenya. Klug (2000) has shown in his detailed account of the negotiations on whether to adopt or to avoid constitutional protection for private property how those seeking 'the legal entrenchment of apartheid's spoils' (2000: 127) came up against those who had hoped to see fulfilled the 1955 Freedom Charter's aim of land nationalisation which held that 'national wealth of our country ... shall be restored to the people'; Klug 2000: 124; see also Ackerman 2019) Whilst Klug notes that 'the recognition of different forms of tenure de-centred private land ownership and provided a basis for the recognition of communal and other forms of land tenure' (2000: 127), it nonetheless remains true that there were no 'affirmative action-type policies' (ibid.). The corollary of the view that a miraculous constitution brought about a radical break with the past is the great emphasis in analyses of South Africa on litigation and the judiciary as sites of democratic social change. In this sphere, a number of scholars have argued that the jurisprudence of the courts has been liberal, reformist and gradualist. As a result, in the words of Justice Sachs in *Port Elizabeth Municipality*, for some, 'dispossession' remained 'nine-tenths of the law' (para. 9).

Fraser (2007) writing about South African land reform, draws on Gregory (2004) to describe as the 'colonial present' situations in which social relations based on inequality, violence and dispossession endure even when at first glance change (in the form of the end of colonialism or the start of land reform) is underway. Saul (2012, cited in Kepe and Hall 2018) refers to 'false decolonisation' and adopts the term 'recolonisation' to describe where redistributive work has not taken place. These perspectives are richly suggestive for analyses of Kenya which, as Mutua (2008) has suggested, has been badly let down by its ruling elite since independence. Fraser's (2007) formulation of a 'colonial present' echoes Shivji's (2009) critiques of the limits of the post-colonial developmental state which were summed up in his question 'where is Uhuru [freedom]?' Taking seriously the continuities between the colonial past and the recolonising practices of the present enables us to connect historical and present land injustices. Intricately connected, the land injustices of the past enable and deepen those of the present, structuring the economy, determining who owns what, and deeply affecting class formation. Although a neat temporal break is inscribed in law and policy by the distinction between past and present land wrongs, this is conceptually inaccurate. If we are to think meaningfully about Kenya's 'colonial present' (Fraser 2007; Gregory 2004), we need to keep in mind the structures of dispossession created by and since colonialism. These structures endure so long as redistributive work has not taken place, as Saul (2012) has suggested. It is to the possibilities of such redistributive work that I now turn.

The Kenya Land Alliance and the Kenya Human Rights Commission (1994) have called for a national land restitution law to provide the architecture and institutional context Kenya needs in order seriously to address longstanding land grievances. A number of commentators have pointed out that Kenya lacks a legal framework providing for restitution, despite calls by civil society and others for this change. Critically, powerful interventions by the international community have raised this possibility. Karanja (2010) has located calls for land restitution in the context of wider transitional justice debates, arguing that both the Kenya National Dialogue and Reconciliation process and the Truth Justice and Reconciliation Commission have called for Kenyans to be afforded opportunities for legal redress of historical land injustices by restitution. However, the legal framework for restitution remains weak (Syagga 2015). Although such a law may not be achievable any time soon, the reason for discussing it here is to unsettle the elite consensus on land in Kenya, rooted as it is in a neo-liberal model undergirded by liberal legalism. Instead, I want to attempt to trace in brief what other possibilities we might imagine. My intention in so doing is 'prefigurative'. Feminist and other scholars have coined the term prefigurative to try to press claims in imaginative and creative ways even as they confront the reality that their demands are a long way from being 'on the table' (Cooper 2019). I elaborate on this in Chapter 8.

Roux (2009), reflecting on South Africa's Restitution of Land Rights Act (22 of 1994) has written that, despite a well-intentioned framework for land restitution, it has largely failed to address the moral harms caused during the forced removals of the apartheid period. Acknowledging that the scheme enacted in South Africa was the outcome of a 'constrained policy choice' (ibid.: 153), Roux writes that the compromise that was reached was that 'the restitution of land rights would not detract from the new legal order's overarching commitment to the protection of property rights'. Roux goes further in explaining why a restitution framework was not just allowable but necessary to protect existing entrenched property rights: 'land restitution was central to that commitment in so far as the legitimisation of the post-apartheid property rights order was seen as a necessary condition for the constitutional protection of private property rights' (2009: 155).

Roux reminds us that land redistribution was also promised during the negotiations:

> What was envisaged in South Africa was ... formation-based rectification up to the point at which the historical record runs out, and category-based rectification for unjust transfers that occurred before this point ... land restitution [was] conceived as an attempt to do individual justice to those who could prove that their rights in land were lost as a result of a particular kind of unjust transfer after 1913, and land redistribution, at least initially, as a welfare scheme for those who were unable to relate their demand for land to an unjust transfer of the specified type'. (2009: 156–7)

For Roux (ibid.: 160), the land restitution scheme 'was conceived, in very legalistic terms, as being about the reversal of a particular set of unjust transfers, rather than the need to redress the deeper social and psychological impacts of apartheid land law'. According to Walker et al. (2003: 10): 'There has been a lack of attention by the state to the symbolic, cultural and psychological elements of restitution ... only minimal attention has been given to the non-material issues around memory, public recognition and identity that inform many claimants'. In Kenya, the situation has perhaps been the reverse. In 2015, President Uhuru Kenyatta made a general apology to Kenyans but avoided making specific apologies as recommended in the TJRC report (see Maliti 2015). Discussions of the possibilities offered by restitution laws have not made significant headway.

Alden Wily (2018b) has argued convincingly that the new Community Land Act 2016 may provide a good framework for the restitution of lost communal land even though the legislation, unlike the National Land Commission Act, does not mention historical land injustices. This is important because the mechanisms available through the Community Land Act 2016 may give concrete form to longstanding work to ensure that law and policy recognise the importance of communal land claims. As far back as the National Land Policy, activists in the land arena were keen to ensure that the policy document explicitly noted the history of trust and former government land. In the event, the document committed the government to 'resolving the problem of illegally acquired trust land' and demanded the 'reversion of former Government land along the Coastal region to community land after planning and alienation of land for public usage' (see Republic of Kenya 2009c: para. 66(d)(ii), (iv)). Assessing the sorts of outcomes that might be expected as a result of submission on communal land-related histor-ical injustices to the National Land Commission, Alden Wily (2018c) has argued that, because it provides for the recognition of collective title, it might be a useful construct through which it will be possible to work to transfer land to community ownership. This might most likely be where the claimed lands are presently defined as unallocated or unoccupied public land. However, Alden Wily provides the caveat that, thus far, the Kenyan state's approach to restitution suggests that even where it is feasible to restore lands to community ownership, the strong preference is to carry out eviction of the complainants and provide compensation for this. Roux (2009: 159) showed that in South Africa similarly, compensation became the main way in which urban claims were settled, with 'the compensation burden in respect of rural land claims growing exponentially each year'. Alden Wily's analysis strongly shows that where suitable mechanisms have been developed to carry out restitution and so restore property to communities, there is no excuse for failing to do so. In her view it is not the lack of a legal mechanism but in fact political resistance to the idea of restitution that prevents action.

At the heart of the term historical land injustice is an attempt to capture something of the truth of what has taken place in relation to a given place, territory or parcel of land. What is being sought is a way to express that there has been an unjustly acquired interest in land. As Alden Wily has suggested in her analysis explored above, there are certainly legal mechanisms available for dealing with these injustices relating to communal land. What is likely to be missing is political will to do so. The constitutional settlement arrived at by 2010 was the result of significant compromises (Mutua 2008). In common with South Africa (Klug 2018), Kenya embedded a provision protecting private property in the Constitution. On one reading, the existence of a constitutional guarantee of this sort alongside a provision compelling the investi-gation and resolution of historical land injustices is a contradiction, a good example of Harbeson's observation that the Constitution makes 'possibly conflicting promises to itself' (Harbeson 2012: 29). Only by adopting the narrowest construal of historical land injustices is this contradiction able to be overlooked: lawyers' historical land injustices

over people's historical land injustices. The current deeply conservative structure of Kenyan politics (Kantai 2007; Musila 2009) shields
those who have unjustly acquired land from demands for redistribution
and restoration except in the most glaring of cases. It treats historical
land injustices as events not structures (Wolfe 2016) and forces only
a narrow reading of how land and other resources, including political,
economic and reputational capital, is unjustly acquired.

What do we foreclose by settling on one definition of historical
land injustices and not another? By enabling a legalistic and narrow
conception of historical land injustice to predominate, we have failed
to develop a conception of land wrongs that recognises how land and
other economic injustices are intertwined. Efforts to conceptualise
historical land injustices seek to compartmentalise them and discon-
nect them from their wider social and economic context. Unjust gains
recirculate in the economy entering business and commercial spheres
and are inseparable from it (Harrington and Manji 2013). Here there is
much to be learned from the South African debate on property (Modiri
2018) and indeed on debates on the history of slave wealth in the United
Kingdom which seeks to uncover the effects of unjust enrichment: in
Kenya, our analyses would surely be different if, as well as focusing on
those who suffered land wrongs, we kept in view the multitude of ways
in which individuals and institutions benefited by being able unjustly
to enrich themselves thorough the forced taking of land (Slye 2018).

A shortcoming of most of the legal and policy approaches to historical land injustices traced above is that they represent these wrongs
as separated from the regular work of the economy. In contrast, it is
important to recognise the close and pervasive links between the
injustices described above and the regular functioning of the economy.
Just as the Ndung'u report, explored in Chapter 3, suggests that there
are in fact close and pervasive links between land corruption and the
regular economy (Harrington and Manji 2013), so we need to be alert
to how historical land wrongs and the present-day political economy
interact. The Mutua Commission distinguished itself from most others
by directly making the link between land wrongs and the economy,
specifically economic collapse, arguing that land

> is an economic asset, and the killing or forcible eviction of the lawful
> owners from their lands constitutes both economic crimes and human
> rights violations. Similarly, the looting of the public purse and the
> stealing of public monies in bank accounts at home or abroad has
> translated into a collapsed infrastructure and economic decomposi-
> tion. (TJRC 2003: 8)

The report elaborates on this as follows:

> economic crimes, due to their complexity, are very difficult to inves-
> tigate. Yet, the Task Force believes that a truth commission should

investigate a selected set of economic crimes that directly lead to the violations of economic, social and cultural rights ... The failure by a contractor for the production and provision of clean and safe drinking water because of fraud or theft of public funds resulting in ill health or deaths ought to be the subject of an investigation by a truth commission. The same should be true for the grabbing of public land to displace a school, a community cultural center, or other public amenities ... In other words, a truth commission should address a selected set of economic crimes that have a direct bearing on the enjoyment of economic, social and cultural rights. (Ibid.: 56)

Far from being unproductive waste which results in economic sterility, land injustices underlie regimes of land ownership across the country. On this reading, historical land injustices are not 'aberrant and deviant' phenomenon that can be sharply distinguished from normal business practice (Rocha et al. 2011: 159). Forced taking and violent dispossession is not incidental to the economy but is fundamental to it (Luxemburg 1913/2003: 432–33). It has concentrated capital in the hands of a few and creating a class of property-less wage labourers (Marx 1867/1976: 873). Attempts to delineate the workings of 'state capture' (Maina 2019) are seeking to show how grand corruption represents an accumulation strategy (Iyayi 1986) Aspects of primitive accumulation are evident in the historical land injustices explored above. Forced, unlawful and irregular appropriation of land has transferred capital to a privileged few. On the other hand, the unavailability of land for subsistence farming or petty commodity production creates an expanding class of wage labourers who have no option but to work for the owners of agri-businesses or tourist facilities (see Bush et al. 2011: 191).

Archives of historical land injustice

There has been a lawyer's approach to historical land injustices just as, as Roux (2009) argued, there was a lawyer's approach to land restitution in South Africa. Designed and driven by lawyers, the legal framework for land restitution in South Africa failed to grasp the pychological and social harms done by apartheid, but framed land wrongs as unjust taking that could be reversed. Roux describes the attitude of lawyers as a simplistic one that viewed apartheid as a legal scheme and which therefore assumed it could simply be 'unlegislated' (ibid.: 160) Central to claims of historical land injustice of the sort explored above is an assertion of the ontological and pycho-affective harms done by such land wrongs but which the bare legal language of the provisions set out above cannot capture. Ngugi wa Thiong'o has described these pycho-affective harms as amounting to a 'dismemberment':

> They are enactments of the central character of colonial practice in general and Europe's contact with Africa in particular since the beginning of capitalist modernity and bourgeois ascendency. This contact is characterized by dismemberment. An act of absolute social engineering, the continent's dismemberment was simultaneously the foundation, fuel, and consequence of Europe's capitalist modernity. (wa Thiong'o 2009: 5)

This imposes an evidential burden beyond the empirical and factual claim to a given territory. To claim historical land injustices have been committed is also to claim that ontological and spiritual harm have been caused by dispossession. But the conversion of a peoples' archive of land wrongs into the language of law and of the law courts has been a major challenge to groups such as the Ogiek, Sengwer or Endorois. They have been met not just with legal but with ontological scepticism and suspicion. In her analysis of the 2010 ruling of the African Commission of Human and Peoples' Rights on the Endorois, Lynch has written that the case 'encouraged adoption of a new identity "as indigenous" to market injustices in an international judicial context' (Lynch 2013: 27). For Lynch (ibid.: 28), the appeal of 'being indigenous' is 'a means to mobilize resources and moral, political, and legal advantage on a global stage'. My assessment of the indigenous people's situation and strategy is quite different. Given the poverty and marginalisation they have endured since their removal from Lake Bogoria, a state of affairs widely acknowledged to be intolerable, this is a claim that must be read as one of belonging to the land (Krog 2015) not as a claim that the land belongs to them. For Lynch, the

> decision thus provides incentives for Kenyans (as well as other Africans, and others) to utilize ethnic and cultural narratives of difference and distinction, and notions of ethnically delineated territorial zones or 'traditional homelands' to strengthen their claims to the ownership and control of land. (2013: 42).

Whilst it might be valid to contest such efforts by economically and culturally dominant peoples who have access to state power and resources, to apply this analysis to the subaltern and the marginalised is quite different. In my view, to read Endorois claims as arising through efforts at 'branding' by 'culture brokers' as Lynch (2011: 149, 153) does is to misunderstand the nature of the claims being made. As Kepe and Hall (2018: 134) drawing on Krog (2015) argue in relation to South Africa, what is being sought is 'not merely for a return of land lost, but for a new relationship with land, one that returns to a pre-commodification notion of land, in which land is not merely "owned" but that people identify with and are instead "owned by" the land'. As a result, as the African Commission on Human and Peoples' Rights (2005) has stressed, the objective is to recognise a history of domination and marginalisation. Rather than a claim of 'first people', it is an assertion that a given group has not had access to fruits of development. Claims for recognition cannot be neatly set in opposition to claims for redistribution, as Fraser herself (2000: 108–09) has argued in calling for a more nuanced understanding of her formulation of the 'politics of recognition':

> Not all forms of recognition politics are equally pernicious: some represent genuinely emancipatory responses to serious injustices that cannot be remedied by redistribution alone. Culture, moreover, is a legitimate, even necessary, terrain of struggle, a site of injustice in its own right and deeply imbricated with economic inequality. Properly conceived, struggles for recognition can aid the redistribution of power and wealth and can promote interaction and cooperation across gulfs of difference.

Calls by indigenous groups for recognition can *also* inherently be calls for a different way of distributing resources and power within the state. They have been failed by the post-independence state first by being deprived of access to their most vital means of production (such as grazing cattle) and reproduction (for example, religious and cultural rites), and then by a failure of the courts to recognise their legal struggles as the Ogiek's claim and that of the Endorois in the High Court showed. As Sing'oei (2011) has argued convincingly, the courts showed themselves at something of a loss when confronted by land claims framed by different epistemologies: claims that mobilise evidence of community and history come up against state sanctioned framings of property as properly evidenced by paper and title. In the South African Constitutional Court Salem land claims case (see SA CS 2017), Justice Cameron explicitly set out why the Restitution of Land Act permits a court to admit any relevant evidence, including evidence that would not be admissible in other courts. By deliberately broadening the scope of what is admissible evidence in land claim cases, the law is seeking to address the sorts of ontological suspicion faced by the Ogiek before the Kenyan courts. Sing'oei rightly points to the manifest failure of Kenyan and other African courts to respond adequately to historical land claims which is itself a further aspect of the marginalisation and domination of indigenous peoples. It is important to recognise that claims by indigenous communities do not separate territorial claims from ontological ones. Okoth-Ogendo described this pithily when he wrote:

> The commons are...not constituted merely by territoriality, or by the temporal aggregation of members of any given entity, but are, in addition, characterised by important ontological factors among which is their permanent availability across generations past, present, and future. For those societies which recognise and depend on them, the commons are the creative force in social production and reproduction. (Okoth-Ogendo 2002: 2)

Conclusion

Mawani (2014) has written perceptively of what we might call 'constitutional time', that it is founded on an imagined break with the past and a promise of better future times:

> Figured in a moment of discontinuity and interruption, between the past and future of social and political life, the Constitution is not solely a product of or in time. Rather, it produces, condenses, and disjoins time while remaining explicitly teleological. It encourages the people to cultivate and expand their national solidarities by moving beyond the past, overcoming their individual differences, while striving to fulfill a more promising and just future. (Mawani 2014: 72)

This chapter has argued that current thinking on historical land injustice is dominated by teleological assumptions. I have suggested instead that in order fully to understand land wrongs, we must recognise the complex intertemporalities of past and present in the land domain. Legal and policy approaches to historical land injustices which separate these wrongs from the regular workings of the economy will fail to grasp the complexity and interrelatedness of land grabbing and corruption. I have suggested that it is important to recognise the close and pervasive links between the injustices visited on indigenous people and others and the regular functioning of the economy. Over many years, deep and pervasive connections have developed between land corruption and the regular economy. Addressing historical land wrongs demands that we see how they are imbricated in the political economy of the present day.

8

Taking Justice Seriously[1]

Introduction

In this chapter, I draw together the many questions I have raised and make some tentative suggestions about Kenya's prospects for a better – by which I mean a fairer – future in relation to land. In doing so, I also suggest how the Kenyan example provides us with important insights into African land questions and struggles for justice in the land domain. That future requires us to challenge the regular instrumentalisation of land as a tool of negative political mobilisation. It also requires an end to land's deployment to first create and then deepen ethnic schisms, leading far too often to violence and bloodshed. How might we encourage contestation about land matters such that the full range of possible options is made visible and so that citizens can deliberate on the sort of future they wish to see in the land domain? My aim is to draw out the wider lessons of this book for our understanding of African land issues. To do this, I return to the organising ideas set out in Chapter 1 that have run through the subsequent discussion in order to show how my analyses in this book have cast them in a new or different light. Following this, I suggest a possible agenda for future research on land, organising this around what I describe as the 'not yet' (Armah 1968) of land reform or 'prefigurative' land reform. I ask: in our research and teaching, what might we imagine land reform to be, in ways that might not be achievable in any foreseeable political future but that might enable us to prise open that which has so far been closed to us?

Last words

I have shown that the ideals of the rule of law in the land domain – of transparency and fairness in the administration of land and of a clear

---

[1] See 'Taking Suffering Seriously' (Baxi 1985)

and fair legal and institutional framework governing land relations and land management – are far from being achieved. But more than this, law and legal processes have sometimes been used to obscure and obfuscate. We can see this in the way that the legal profession, far from upholding the rule of law, has been implicated in land grabbing, using professional knowledge, skills and networks to facilitate the illegal and irregular allocation of public land to powerful individuals. So vast has been the scale of this professional misconduct that it is no exaggeration to say that land grabbing could not have occurred on Kenya's enormous scale without the concerted work done by many in the legal profession. Legal knowledge has been mobilised in service of the powerful.

But law has been used to obfuscate in less instrumental ways too. Presenting law as a proposed solution to land problems – whether through constitutional provisions or land laws more directly – has had the effect of blocking important deliberations about what land reform might look like. As I have suggested, the meaning and content of land reform has been strategically reduced to land law reform. Put another way, I have been interested throughout this book with domination not just materially but also at the level of ideas. As I showed in Chapter 2, the term 'land reform' has a long history in Kenya. In its different guises and in different eras, however, it has been deployed as an idea predominantly by those who can govern its meaning. I have suggested that when more insurgent notions of land reform have been asserted they have been carefully and determinedly extinguished. Hegemonic notions of land that valorise individual tenure, private ownership and improvement have not lost their hold. This has had important consequences. By substituting land law reform for what might have been wider and deeper considerations of what land reform might constitute, we have failed to walk more difficult terrain. The intellectual history of insurgent land ideas has yet to be written.

I have sought to show that an institutional approach to change in the land arena has distracted us from discussions of fairness, justice and equitably distribution. I have drawn on a number of scholars of South African constitutional history (Comaroff and Comaroff 2004; Madlingozi 2017; Modiri 2018) who have indeed gone further than this by suggesting that major legal reforms such as new constitutions can have an ideological function. For Modiri (2018: 308):

> Not only does a 'new' constitution purport to ground a transformed polity and define its values and ideals, it also hopes to hold together the always-already fragile civic bonds of the nation. In so doing, the constitution and the discourses and subjects it produces, must repress the difficult issue of the contested foundations and unrealised promises of the new order. It must also monopolise the sphere of public and political engagement unless actively countered by a different, more radical, politics.

Building on this analysis, we can suggest that the joining of land reform with constitutional reform that I described in Chapter 4, far from enabling far-reaching discussions of the meanings and content of land reform, instead functioned to block debate, to prevent engagement with Kenya's history of land wrongs and to substitute law reform for more radical politics.

This book's interdisciplinary insights suggest that we must look beyond formal analyses of the law to understand the wider historical and political context in which land reform is debated, shaped and implemented. I am reminded of Ghai and McAuslan's observation, in explaining their approach to their landmark study of constitutional law and in particular 'law's role in the scramble for Africa' (1970: 34), that what is needed is attention to political, economic and historical context. That remains true today. In the domain of land, legal and other professionals have been concerned with developing and making effective a new architecture of land governance. That architecture deserves to be assessed but what we must not neglect is the significant movement from the margins that has kept up considerable pressure on land issues. They have inherited the mantle of earlier, radical movements who in the immediate post-independence period had challenged a conservative elite on land issues (Bates 1989). Harbeson (2012) and Klopp (2012) were drawing attention to this when they pointed out that it was not the international community but in fact an autochthonous civil society that struggled for the National Land Policy and the constitutional provisions on land. In future scholarship, land must be understood as the key topic around which progressive struggles have been organised. I have sought to show the role that land struggles have played in wider political and constitutional struggles since independence. I have argued that these land struggles have been an integral part of what Atieno-Odhiambo characterised as 'African struggles for civil liberties, human rights, democratic participation, workers' rights, peasant independence, spiritual space, elective representation and civic responsibility' (1995: 2), and have suggested that these struggles cannot only be struggles about the content and working of laws.

This is not to suggest that law has no role to play in discussions of land reform. Clearly, debates would need to take place about what legal mechanisms might be used to achieve the ends of land reform agreed upon. But the first, prior step of deliberative discussions amongst citizens of what is meant by land reform must already have taken place. We have had glimpses of debate: at independence, attempts were made by individuals such as Bildad Kaggia to trace an alternative, more equitable vision of land ownership, just as in South Africa the 1955 Freedom Charter asserted: 'The land shall be shared among those who work it'. The drafting of the National Land Policy was preceded by much debate, driven by civil society seeking to draw attention to the dire state of land relations across the country and to propose solutions (see for example KHRC et al. 1994). But, in general, these have remained subaltern attempts. After the significant achievements of civil society groups in driving the publication of the National Land Policy and the insertion of a land chapter in the Constitution, the tone and content of land law reform discussions quickly became highly centralised as the state sought to regain what it saw as lost ground in the land domain. The lack of transparency and deliberation and the failure to promote participation by the people in debates about land law reform around 2012 which I have described in Chapter 5 were attempts to break the momentum of Kenya's still nascent land movement. Law making in the 2011–12 period was characterised by what Baxi (1985: 132) has called 'administration through secrecy'. The elite succeeded in containing and controlling the process of drafting legislation, successfully turning potentially big questions of equity and fairness into technical matters of governance and legal solutions.

As I have shown, there is a wider international context for this attachment to land law reform. When in the early 1990s, a number of countries in East Africa began to debate land matters and to consider overhauling their legal framework governing land, they were prompted by a seeming rediscovery of the role that law might play in development. The emphasis on law was not new (McAuslan 2003). In the 1960s, the law and development movement had promulgated the idea that law reform could promote economic development in newly independent countries. As an area of scholarship and practice, the birth of law and development coincided with the birth of the developmental state. The state was to have a central role in bringing about economic growth. Scholars of law and development, many of whom were based in African law schools as well as in the United States, sought ideas from a range of disciplines such as economics, development studies and politics to address the question of law's role in development (Adelman and Paliwala 1993; Harrington and Manji 2017). The law and development movement had a practical and pragmatic approach to law (Rose 1998). By the middle of the 1970s, however, the methods and objectives of the movement had begun to be called into question as scholars and practitioners grew sceptical of what they saw as its instrumental, naïve and untheoretical approach (ibid.).

However, in the 1990s, there was a revival of law in development policy making (Carothers 1998). This time, the main concern of technical legal experts was not directly with economic growth, but with the promotion of good governance and the rule of law. In turn, and in the context of new political conditionalities and neo-liberalism, international financial institutions and bilateral donors poured billions into rule-of-law aid and rule-of-law reform (Carothers 1998; Faundez 2009; Manji 2006). This focus on the centrality of the rule of law to development has had a major impact on how land issues have been understood across the sub-continent since the 1990s (Tamanaha 2009; Trubek and Santos 2006). Land reform in East Africa must be understood as part of a wider project for rule-of-law reforms (Manji 2006; McAuslan 2013) but so too must the terms in which it is debated. What is on the table in land reform debates – what we can speak of, what we can envisage as reform – is severely circumscribed by the circumstances out of which new wave land reform (McAuslan 2013) arose. Redistribution has become the bogeyman of land reform. The World Bank, arriving in South Africa as the negotiated settlement was underway, explicitly held out the threat of widespread redistributive demands as a reason to intervene to model a more moderate approach (Klug 2000). Liberal legalism – the promise of strong institutions – has quieted more radical demands – for redistribution or restitution or a reckoning with dispossession (Moyo 2001; Shivji 2009).

Alongside land law reform and the renewed prominence of law as a proposed solution to land problems has come the deeper embedding of the private law model of land described in Chapter 1 in international public policy. Financialisation (Manji 2010), ideologies of improvement (Bhandar 2018), and notions of the ideal, neo-liberal citizen (Shivji 2009) have become powerfully intertwined. Land is represented as a tradeable asset that can and should be used to leverage loans. The ideal citizen is one who relates to land as an asset to be improved, leveraged and traded. The World Bank captured this perspective on land in its Policy Research Report on Land published in 2003. The report strongly advocated formalisation of tenure relations as a desirable objective of land policy. According to the Bank, land does more than simply provide a shelter and a means of livelihood. Access to land affects incentives to make investments, and the ability of the poor to access financial markets. The Bank argued that policies that make it possible to use land as a means to access credit will transform such property from a dead asset into an economic resource (de Soto 2000) As commentators have pointed out, secure formal property rights are widely presented by international financial institutions as a pre-condition for economic growth and poverty reduction (Trebilcock and Davis 2009) and as fundamental to establishing the rule of law in the developing world (Carothers 2006).

This approach to land is not new for Kenya. Through the Swynnerton Plan, introduced in 1954 with the aim of consolidating landholdings in order to stimulate cash crop production, the country had long been the poster child of this approach to tenure (van Arkadie 2016). It could be argued that in fact Kenya stood to one side of the global rediscovery of private formal tenure and titling as a priority of international donors in the 1990s. It was not part of the wave of land reforms that took place in the 1990s and which included Tanzania and Uganda (McAuslan 2013) where an emphasis on secure formal property rights and developed land and mortgage markets formed a major part of legislative reform for at least a decade (Manji 1998). Such legislative reforms were portrayed as prerequisites for economic growth, poverty reduction and establishment of the rule of law. Formalisation of tenure and monetisation of land relations went hand in hand as part of a 'market-friendly' approach to land described by McAuslan (2013: 2), as 'the globalisation of land markets'. Kenya, long viewed by the international community as a preeminent example of success in promoting individual tenure (in spite of evidence to the contrary: see Nyamu-Musembi 2007), came to land reform somewhat later and with a different trajectory. As I showed in Chapter 4, the momentum for changes in the land sector was harnessed to broader demands for constitutional change and its 'principal driver' was, as Harbeson (2012: 17) has pointed out, not external demands coming from the international community but rather internal pressure. The efforts of civil society over a long period of two decades brought about Kenya's new land policy and its new land laws. For Harbeson: 'At least with respect to land tenure relations, Kenya's constitutional moment has consisted of comprehensive and possibly conflicting promises to itself' (2013: 29).

Kenya did not however escape the broader tendency of neo-liberal policies to present development solutions as technocratic and apolitical (Perry-Kessaris 2009). I have shown that Kenya's land reform efforts have confirmed Kennedy's thesis that there is an unarticulated hope amongst law and development practitioners and academics that working within a strictly legal framework can substitute for, and thus avoid confrontation with, 'perplexing political and economic choices' (2003: 168). On land matters, Kenya has not thus far begun to confront the deeply perplexing choices before it. It has certainly placed 'law, legal institution building, the techniques of legal policy making and implementation – the 'rule of law' broadly conceived – front and centre' (ibid.: 18). It has excluded, rather than encouraged, contestation over economic and political choices. It is no doubt the case that it has relied on putting its faith in the law as a way to substitute for contestation. This approach has enabled it to 'settle on the legal choices embedded in one legal regime as if they were the only alternative' (ibid.: 168). The analysis I have presented in this book suggests that Kennedy is surely right to argue that the rule of law 'promises ... a domain of expertise, a program for action, which obscures the need for distributional choices or for clarity about how distributing things one way rather than another will, in fact, lead to development' (ibid.: 155).

It is important however to note one countervailing trend. Pulling against this prioritisation of private tenure has been an increasing awareness in international policy prescriptions of both the tenacity and the viability of customary tenure. Strongly discouraged and disparaged by the World Bank and others throughout the 1990s, customary land tenure has come to be more clearly understood. Since around 2010, there has been a revision in thinking on this form of tenure and a discernible move away from an evolutionary model of land relations which takes private tenure as a desirable and inevitable endpoint. Instead, there has been some acceptance that customary relations over land have endured and that their features and workings need both to be studied and to be afforded protection. In turn, customary, community and communal land – the terms widely used interchangeably – can be said to be the one domain in land policy in which a profound rethink has occurred in the 2010s. Here, ideas of what is a suitable (or 'modern') form of land tenure have shifted remarkably: since the 1990s, we have gone from international and national land policy prescriptions which deprecated community land to one in which such tenure regimes are viewed as valuable, workable and even desirable. Nyamu-Musembi (2007) provided an early insight into this trend in thinking about customary tenure when she distinguished between colonial-era attitudes to customary land rights and later approaches in international land policy emanating from the World Bank and, in particular, advocates of land rights formalisation led by the economist Hernando de Soto (see Manji 2006). Drawing on Chanock (1991) and Klug (1995), Nyamu-Musembi (2007: 1463) noted that, whereas in the colonial period a negative 'portrayal of African customary tenure was necessary to give the impression that no defined rights were implicated in the expropriation of African lands for European settlement', by the 1990s advocates of formalisation were nonetheless prepared to concede that 'informally held property rights are quite well defined and upheld within each narrow setting, and only need to be represented in a form that outsiders (such as the state and financial institutions) recognise' (ibid.). The importance of legal interventions in this form of tenure is not limited to Kenya. Changes relating to community land now exist or are under discussion in Benin, the Democratic Republic of the Congo, Ghana, Kenya, Liberia, Malawi, Mali, Morocco, Namibia, Senegal, Sierra Leone, South Africa and Zambia (Alden Wily 2017). According to Alden Wily (ibid.) there is at last a recognition that community tenure should be afforded respect and protection as opposed to being seen as a backward form of tenure that would die out over time and be replaced with individual property rights.

I have argued that an adequate assessment of the prospects for land justice in Kenya requires that we consider not just historical questions of land injustice but also their continued effects in the present day. Taking my cue from the language used in the Investigation of Historical Land Injustices Regulations (National Land Commission 2017) which distinguish between historical and present land injustice, I argued that we should scrutinise the possible contours of 'present land injustices'. This would mean recognising not just that land injustices continue to be visited upon the less powerful in the present day (for example, in the form of land grabbing), although this is manifestly the case. I also argued that the term 'present land injustices' can constitute the starting point of a discussion on a broader conceptual issue. This is that we cannot continue to interpret land wrongs such as land grabbing as irregular, episodic and exceptional. Instead, we need to rethink the scope of our investigation to ask: how do land wrongs underpin the economy as a whole? Rather than being sealed off from the wider economy, I suggest that land injustices underpin its very structure, provide much of its impetus and energy and deeply affect how it is organised.

An agenda for future research

What might be the contours of a future research agenda on land that is informed by theoretical insights drawn from a range of disciplines? That research agenda needs scholarship on land issues to move beyond the empirical and explanatory. I would suggest that it needs to be founded in a nuanced understanding of the history of ideas. Who determines how we talk about land? How have hegemonic ideas about citizens' relationships to land taken hold and how has this caused us to lose sight of other alternatives? In the land domain, thinking about 'project Kenya' (Musila 2012), requires us to consider 'writing history's silences' (ibid.). In Chapter 1, I attempted to reveal some of these silences and suggested that it has taken the post-colonial state's 'sustained enactment' (Blomley 2003: 114) of these ideas to ensure that the dominant model of land – one which valorises private land ownership – has become 'common sense' (Harrington 2017). I have argued that, beyond narrow studies of legal rules, we must pay attention to the structural parameters within which such rules operate. This is an approach to law which does not eschew politics and history but rather puts them at the centre of legal studies. I have argued that greater attention must be paid to legal history, and in particular to the history of ideas. An important example in the land domain would be the writing of the intellectual histories of Kenya's land radicals, a history which has been largely submerged (but see Ng'weno and Tharao 2007; and more widely Patel 2006). That task must fall not just to writers but also to filmmakers and playwrights (Gikandi and Wachanga 2018; Irungu 2012; Maloba 2017; Sibi-Okumu 2014).

Such a widened agenda for legal research will have important implications for teaching law and for the shape and content of law curricula, and should inform debates on the role and place of the law school (Shako 2019). It should inform policy making and debates about law reform. I have suggested so far that legal history should lie at the heart of any project to revitalise legal research and teaching. But there is also an important future-oriented aspect to emphasise. Here we can draw on projects which have sought to challenge settled law in imaginative and creative ways, such as the ongoing feminist judgments projects in which groups of feminist academics and practitioners draft alternative feminist judgments in landmark cases (see for example Hodson and Lavers 2019). Similarly, feminist projects that describe themselves as 'prefigurative' have proposed that imagining and even drafting legislative proposals and discussing projects for law reform that may yet be a long way off the political agenda can have important political effects. Cooper (2018) has described this as a 'form of rehearsal, exploring the implications of a particular legal pathway well in advance of any official uptake ... teasing out the issues for more radical reform may inform how governments and social movements think about it'. Faced with the distinct likelihood that a law reform proposal is not achievable in the current political and economic context, this approach nonetheless argues that the power of prefigurative law reform projects lie in their potential, as 'experimental projects' to unsettle 'current possibilities' (ibid.). As I have shown, unsettling prevailing ideas of Kenya's property regime is an urgent task.

Conclusion

Given 'law's complicity with political oppression, violence and racism' (Douzinas and Gearey 2005: 1; see also Ghai and McAuslan 1970) it is curious the extent to which Kenya has come to rely upon law as the solution to land problems. That reliance has been explored in this book as partly explicable in the context of a wider global inclination for the rule of law and constitutionalism. In the land arena, this wider inclination for legal solutions has seen numerous African countries resort to law as a way to address land inequality and land grievances of all sorts. I have called that approach into question. Arguing that the label 'post-apartheid' is fundamentally misconstrued, Modiri has challenged us to 'consciously eschew constitutional optimism' and instead to be 'cognisant of the limits and limitations of the law in bringing about decommodification of basic necessities, redistribution of resources' (2018: 297). Throughout this book, I have argued that an adequate grasp of land wrongs can only be achieved through an interdisciplinary approach to land issues. A legal approach alone will not suffice. This has important implications for policy making and for law reform, as well as for legal research and legal education. In particular, approaches to legal education that are highly doctrinal (Shako 2019) and that train students to focus exclusively on legal rules with little attention to political and economic context and especially to legal history, will not produce the sort of critical land law scholarship I have shown is needed.

Albertyn (2018), drawing on Sheppard (2010), has made the case for a broad socio-legal method of approaching rights violations, arguing that attention to context is necessary if we are to grasp how inequalities are reproduced. According to Albertyn:

> substantive equality should not only focus on substantive outcomes and concrete effects (impact) but also on the 'structures, processes, relationships and norms' that reproduce hierarchy, marginalisation, exclusion and inequality in everyday life (context). This 'prompts an inquiry into both the actual realities and conditions of inequality, and the social, political and institutional processes that account for its reproduction'. (2018: 466–67, citing Sheppard 2010: 4)

A starting point for critical land law scholarship, research and teaching is to recognise the moral harms done by an enduring system of land wrongs. As this book has shown, policy makers cannot ignore these structural realities. Neither must law makers and those charged with interpreting the law: they too must recognise the limits of law in bringing about material change.

Rose (2019 n.p.) has written in relation to the ongoing trauma of dispossession in South Africa, that '[t]here will be no political emancipation for anyone till we all recognise the corpse still lying on the road, the continuing injustice, the work that remains to be done'. This book is a small contribution to such work.

Bibliography

Publications

Ackerman, B. (1997), 'The Rise of World Constitutionalism', *Virginia Law Review*, 83(4), pp. 771–97.

Ackerman, B. (2000), 'The New Separation of Powers', *Harvard Law Review*, 113(3), pp. 634–725.

Ackerman, B. (2019), *Revolutionary Constitutions: Charismatic Leadership and the Rule of Law* (Cambridge MA: Harvard University Press).

Adelman, S. and Paliwala, A., eds (1993), *Law and Crisis in the Third World* (London: Hans Zell).

Africa National Congress (1955), 'The Freedom Charter', 26 June, www.historicalpapers.wits.ac.za/inventories/inv_pdfo/AD1137/AD1137-Ea6-1-001-jpeg.pdf, accessed 2 September 2019.

Ahmed, S. (2013), 'Making Feminist Points', Feministkilljoys, 11 September, http://feministkilljoys.com/2013/09/11/making-feminist-points, accessed 22 April 2015.

Albertus, M. (2015), *Autocracy and Redistribution: The Politics of Land Reform* (Cambridge UK: Cambridge University Press)

Albertyn, C. (2018), 'Contested Substantive Equality in the South African Constitution: Beyond Social Inclusion Towards Systemic Justice', *South African Journal on Human Rights*, 34(3), pp. 441–68.

Alden Wily, L. (2017), 'Customary Tenure: Remaking Property for the 21st Century', *Comparative Property Law Global Perspectives*, eds Graziadei, M. and Smith, L. (Cheltenham UK; Northampton MA, USA: Edward Elgar Publishing), pp. 458–77.

Alden Wily, L. (2018a), 'Compulsory Acquisition as a Constitutional Matter: The Case in Africa', *Journal of African Law*, 62(1), pp. 77–103.

Alden Wily, L. (2018b), 'Risks to the Sanctity of Community Lands in Kenya: A Look at New Legislation with Reference to Forestlands', *Land Use Policy*, 75, pp. 661–72.

Alden Wily, L. (2018c), 'The Community Land Act in Kenya Opportunities and Challenges for Communities', *Land*, 7(1), pp. 1–25.

Amin, S. (2000), *Capitalism in the Age of Globalization: The Management of Contemporary Society* (London: Zed Books).

Amutabi, M.N. (2002), 'Crisis and Student Protest in Universities in Kenya', *African Studies Review*, 45(2), pp. 157–78.

Anderson, D.M. (2005a), *Histories of the Hanged: The Dirty War in Kenya and the End of Empire* (New York: WW Norton).

Anderson, D.M. (2005b), '"Yours in the Struggle for Majimbo": Nationalism and the Party Politics of Decolonisation in Kenya 1955–64', *Journal of Contemporary History*, 40(3), pp. 547–64.Anderson, D.M. (2011), 'Mau Mau in the High Court and the "lost" British Empire Archives: Colonial Conspiracy or Bureaucratic Bungle?' *Journal of Imperial and Commonwealth History*, 39(5), pp. 699–716.

Anderson, D.M. (2015), 'Guilty Secrets: Deceit, Denial, and the Discovery of Kenya's "Migrated Archive"', *History Workshop Journal*, 80(1), pp. 142–60.

Andrew, N. (2016), 'The Importance of Land in Rethinking Rural Transformation, Agrarian Revolution and Unfinished Liberation in Africa', *Review of African Political Economy*, 43(1), pp. 130–44.

Armah, A.K. (1968), *The Beautyful Ones are Not Yet Born* (London: Heinemann).

Ashfort, A. (1990), 'Reckoning Schemes of Legitimation: On Commission of Inquiry as Power/Knowledge Forms', *Journal of Historical Sociology*, 3(1), pp. 17–35.

Atieno, B. (2016), 'Assessing the Effectiveness of the National Land Commission in Addressing Irregular and Illegal Allocation of Land in Kenya', Unpublished LL.M. (University of Nairobi).

Atieno-Odhiambo, E.S. (1987), 'Democracy and the Ideology of Order in Kenya', *The Political Economy of Kenya*, ed. Schatzberg, M.G. (New York: Praeger), pp. 177–201.

Atieno-Odhiambo, E.S. (1995), 'The Invention of Kenya', *Decolonization and Independence in Kenya 1940–1993*, eds Ogot, B.A. and Ochieng, W.R. (London: James Currey), pp. 1–3.

Atieno-Odhiambo, E.S. (2002), 'Hegemonic Enterprises and Instrumentalities of Survival: Ethnicity and Democracy in Kenya'*African Studies*, 61(2), pp. 223–49.

Ayieko, F. (2009), 'Land Barons in High-Level Lobbying over Kenya's 999-Year Leases', *The East African*, 7 February, www.theeastafrican.co.ke/news/-/2558/525862/-/view/printVersion/-/5dh5lvz/-/index.html, accessed 24 March 2020.

Bassett, E.M. (2017), 'The Challenge of Reforming Land Governance in Kenya Under the 2010 Constitution', *Journal of Modern African Studies*, 55(4), pp. 537–66.

Bates, R. (1989), *Beyond the Miracle of the Market: The Political Economy of Agrarian Development in Kenya* (Cambridge UK: Cambridge University Press).

Baxi, U. (1985), 'Taking Suffering Seriously: Social Action Litiga-tion in the Supreme Court of India', *Third World Legal Studies*, 4(6). pp. 108–32.

Baxi, U. (2003), 'Global Development and Impoverishment', *Oxford Handbook of Legal Studies*, eds Cane, P. and Tushnet, M. (Oxford: Oxford University Press), pp. 455–82.

Berman, B. (2004), 'Ethnicity, Bureaucracy, Democracy: The Politics of Trust', *Ethnicity and Democracy in Africa*, eds Berman, B., Eyoh, D. and Kymlicka, W. (Oxford: James Currey).

Berman, B.J., Cottrell, J. and Ghai, Y.P. (2009), 'Patrons, Clients, and Constitutions: Ethnic Politics and Political Reform in Kenya', *Canadian Journal of African Studies/Revue Canadienne des études Africaines*, 43(3), pp. 462–506.

Bernstein, H. (2002), 'Land Reform: Taking a Long(er) View', *Journal of Agrarian Change*, 1, pp. 433–63.

Berry, S. (2002), 'Debating the Land Question in Africa', *Comparative Studies in Society and History*, 44(4), pp. 638–68.

Berry, S. (2004), 'Reinventing the Local? Privatization, Decentralization and the Politics of Resource Management: Examples from Africa', *African Study Monographs*, 25(2), pp. 79–101.

Bhandar, B. (2018), *Colonial Lives of Property: Law, Land and Racial Regimes of Ownership* (Durham NC: Duke University Press).

Blomley, N. (2003), *Unsettling the City: Urban Land and the Politics of Property* (London: Routledge).

Bojosi, K. and Wachira, G.M. (2006), 'Protecting Indigenous Peoples in Africa: An Analysis of the Approach of the African Commission on Human and Peoples' Rights', *African Human Rights Law Journal*, 6(2), pp. 382–406.

Boone, C. (2011), 'Politically Allocated Land Rights and the Geography of Electoral Violence: The Case of Kenya in the 1990s', *Comparative Political Studies*, 44(10), pp. 1311–42.

Boone, C. (2012), 'Land Conflict and Distributive Politics in Kenya', *African Studies Review*, 55(1), pp. 75–103.

Boone, C. (2014), *Property and Political Order in Africa: Land Rights and the Structure of Politics* (Cambridge UK: Cambridge University Press).

Boone, C., Dyzenhaus, A., Manji, A., Gateri, C., Ouma, S., Owino, J.K., Gargule, A. and Klopp, J. (2019), 'Land Law Reform in Kenya: Devolution, Veto Players and the Limits of an Institutional Fix', *African Affairs*, 118(471), pp. 215–37.

Bosire, L.K. and Lynch, G. (2014), 'Kenya's Search for Truth and Justice: The Role of Civil Society', *International Journal of Transitional Justice*, 8(2), pp. 256–76.

Branch, D. (2009), *Defeating Mau Mau, Creating Kenya: Counterinsurgency, Civil War and Decolonisation* (Cambridge UK and New York: Cambridge University Press).

Branch, D. (2011), *Kenya: Between Hope and Despair, 1963–2011* (London and New Haven CT: Yale University Press).

Branch, D. and Cheeseman, N. eds (2008), 'Election Fever: Kenya's Crisis', *Special Edition of the Journal of Eastern African Studies*, 2(2), pp. 165–367.

Branch, D., Cheeseman, N. and Gardner, L., eds (2010), *Our Turn to Eat: Politics in Kenya since 1950* (Berlin: LIT Verlag).

Brennan, J. (2008), 'Lowering the Sultan's Flag: Sovereignty and Decolonization in Coastal Kenya', *Comparative Studies in Society and History*, 50(4), pp. 831–61.

Brown, S. (2004), 'Theorising Kenya's Protracted Transition to Democracy', *Journal of Contemporary African Studies*, 22(3), pp. 325–42.

Browne, A. and Leonardi C. (2018), 'Introduction: Valuing Land in Eastern Africa', Special issue: Land, *Journal of Critical African Studies*, 10(1), pp. 1–13.

Bruce, B. and Lonsdale, J. (1992), *Unhappy Valley: Conflict in Kenya and Africa, Book 2: Violence and Ethnicity* (London: James Currey).

Bush, R., Bujra, J. and Littlejohn, G. (2011), 'Editorial: The Accumulation of Dispossession', *Review of African Political Economy*, 38 pp. 187–92.

Byres, T.J. (2004), 'Introduction: Contextualizing and Interrogating the GKI Case for Redistributive Land Reform', *Journal of Agrarian Change*, 4(1&2), pp. 1–16.

Carothers, T. (1998), 'The Rule of Law Revival', *Foreign Affairs*, 77, pp. 95–106.

Carothers, T. (2006), 'The Rule of Law Revival', *Promoting the Rule of Law Abroad: In Search of Knowledge*, ed. Carothers, T. (Washington: Carnegie Endowment for International Peace).

Chanock, M. (1991), 'A Peculiar Sharpness: An Essay on Property in the History of Customary Law in Colonial Africa', *Journal of African History*, 32(1), pp. 65–88.

Cheeseman, N. (2008), 'The Kenya Elections of 2007: An Introduction', *Journal of Eastern African Studies*, 2(2), pp. 166–84.

Chibundu, M. (1997), 'Law in Development: On Tapping, Gourding and Serving Palm-Wine', *Case Western Reserve Journal of International Law*, 29(1), pp. 167–258.

Cliffe, L. (2001), 'The Struggle for Land in Africa', LUCAS Annual African Studies Lecture, *Leeds African Studies Bulletin* 64, pp. 9–44.

Cliffe, L., Alexander, J., Cousins, B. and Gaidzanwa, R. (2011), 'An Overview of Fast Track Land Reform in Zimbabwe: Editorial Introduction', *The Journal of Peasant Studies*, 38(5), pp. 907–38.

Clough, M. and Jackson, K. (1975), *Mau Mau Syllabus* (Standard, CA: Mimeographed).

Coetzee, C. (2018), 'Unsettling the Air-Conditioned Room', African Literature Association Keynote Lecture, Washington DC, 25 May.

Coldham, S. (1978a), 'Effects of Registration of Title Upon Customary Land Rights in Kenya', *Journal of African Law*, 22(2), pp. 91–111.

Coldham, S. (1978b), 'Land Control in Kenya', *Journal of African Law*, 22(1). pp. 63–77.

Coldham, S. (1979), 'Land Tenure Reform in Kenya: The Limits of the Law', *Journal of Modern African Studies*, 17(4), pp. 615–27.

Comaroff, J. and Comaroff, J.L. (2004), 'Policing Culture, Cultural Policing: Law and Social Order in Postcolonial South Africa', *Law & Social Inquiry*, 29(3), pp. 513–45.

Cooper, D. (1998), *Governing Out of Order: Space, Law and the Politics of Belonging* (London: Rivers Oram Press).

Cooper, D. (2018), 'Acting as if Other Law Reform Options were Already on the Table?' The Future of Legal Gender: A critical law reform project, https://futureoflegalgender.kcl.ac.uk/author/k1769086, accessed 24 March 2020.

Cottrell, J. and Ghai, Y.P. (2007), 'Constitution Making and Democratization in Kenya (2000–2005)', *Democratization*, 14(1), pp. 1–25.

Cottrell, J. and Ghai, Y.P. (2018), 'The Contribution of the South African Constitution to Kenya's Constitution', *Constitutional Triumphs, Constitutional Disappointments: A Critical Assessment of the 1996 South African Constitution's Local and International Influence,* eds Dixon, R. and Roux, T. (Cambridge UK: Cambridge University Press), pp. 252–93.

Cross, C. (1992), 'An Alternative Legality: The Property Rights Question in Relation to South African Land Reform', *South African Journal of Human Rights*, 8(3), pp. 305–31.

Cutler, A.C. (2002), 'Historical Materialism, Globalization, and Law: Competing Conceptions of Property', *Historical Materialism and Globalization*, eds Rupert, M. and Smith, H. (London: Routledge), pp. 230–56.

D'Arcy, M. and Nistotskaya, M. (2019), 'Intensified Local Grievances, Enduring National Control: The Politics of Land in the 2017 Kenyan Elections', *Journal of Eastern African Studies*, 13(2), pp. 294–312.

Daily Nation (2016), 'Court Clarifies Roles of Lands Ministry and NLC', 28 January, www.nation.co.ke/lifestyle/dn2/Court-clarifies-roles-of-lands-ministry-and-NLC/957860-3051986-64gs5v/index.html, accessed 17 March 2020.

Daniel, L. (2019), 'EFF manifesto launch 2019: Five main talking points', *The South African*, 2 February, www.thesouthafrican.com/eff-manifesto-launch-2019-talking-points, accessed 31 August 2019.

De Feyter, S. (2015), '"They are Like Crocodiles Under Water": Rumour in a Slum Upgrading Project in Nairobi, Kenya', *Journal of Eastern African Studies*, 9(2), pp. 289–306.

de Jong, F. (2016), 'At Work in the Archive: Introduction to Special Issue', *World Art*, 6(1), pp. 3–17.

de Soto, H. (2000), *The Mystery of Capital: Why Capitalism Triumphs in the West and Fails Everywhere Else* (London: Black Swan).

de Sousa Santos, B. (2002), *Toward a New Legal Common Sense: Law, Globalization, and Emancipation* (London: Butterworths).

Derrida, J. (1996), *Archive Fever: A Freudian Impression*, translated by Eric Prenowitz (Chicago: Chicago University Press).

Diepeveen, S. (2010), '"The Kenyas We Don't Want": Popular thought over constitutional review in Kenya, 2002', *The Journal of Modern African Studies*, 48(2), pp. 231–58.

Dooley, T. (2016), 'Land and Politics in Independent Ireland, 1923–48: The Case for Reappraisal', *Irish Historical Studies*, 34(134), pp. 175–97.

Douglas, S., 'Constitutions are Not Enough: Museums as Law's Counter-archive', *Law, Memory, Violence: Uncovering the Counter-Archive*, eds Motha, S. and Van Rijswyk, H. (London: Routledge, 2016), pp. 140–53.

Douzinas, C. and Gearey, A. (2005), *Critical Jurisprudence: The Political Philosophy of Justice* (Oxford: Hart Publishing).Economic Freedom Fighters (2019), 'EFF Elections Manifesto', www.asclibrary.nl/docs/374320462.pdf, accessed 26 September 2019, 1–32.

Elkins, C. (2005), *Britain's Gulag: The Brutal End of Empire in Kenya* (London: Jonathan Cape).

Ellis, S. (1989), 'Tuning in to Pavement Radio' *African Affairs*, 88(352), pp. 321–30.

Englert, B. and Daley, P. eds (2008), *Women's Land Rights and Privatization in Eastern Africa* (Oxford: James Currey).

Fanon, F. (2001 [1961]), *The Wretched of the Earth* (London: Penguin).

Faundez, Julio (2010), 'Rule of Law or Washington Consensus: The Evolution of the World Bank's Approach to Legal and Judicial Reform', *Law in the Pursuit of Development*, ed. Perry-Kessaris, A. (Abingdon and New York: Routledge), pp. 180–201.

Fraser, A. (2007), 'Land Reform in South Africa and the Colonial Present', *Social & Cultural Geography*, 8(6), pp. 835–51.Fraser, N. (2000), 'Rethinking Recognition', *New Left Review*, 3, pp. 107–20.

Furedi, F. (1989), *The Mau Mau War in Perspective* (London: James Currey).

Gathii, J.T. (2007), 'Imperialism, Colonialism and International Law', *Buffalo Law Review*, 54(4), pp. 1013–66.

Gathii, J.T. (2016), *The Contested Empowerment of Kenya's Judiciary 2010–2015: A Historical Institutional Analysis* (Nairobi: Sheria Publishing House).Ghai, J. (2012), 'This is No Way to Reform the Land Law', *The Star*, 18 April.

Ghai, J. (2017), 'Constitutionalism: African Perspectives', Kameri Mbote, P. and Odote, C., *The Gallant Academic: Essays in Honour of HWO Okoth Ogendo* (Nairobi: University of Nairobi Press).

Ghai, Y.P. (1987), 'Law, Development and African Scholarship', *Modern Law Review*, 50, pp. 750–76.

Ghai, Y.P. (2002), *Reviewing the Constitution: A Guide to the Kenya Constitution* (Nairobi: Constitution of Kenya Review Commission).

Ghai, Y.P. (2009), 'Creating a New Constitutional Order: Kenya's Predicament', *Governance, Institutions and the Human Condition*, eds Gachenga, E., Franceschi, L., Akech, M. and Lutz, D. (Nairobi: Strathmore University Press), pp. 28–45.

Ghai, Y.P. (2014), 'Constitutions and Constitutionalism: The Fate of the 2010 Constitution', *Kenya: The Struggle for a New Constitutional Order*, eds Murunga, G., Okello, D. and Sjögren, A. (London: Zed Books).

Ghai, Y.P. and Cottrell, J. (2015), 'The State and Constitutionalism in Post-Colonial Societies in Africa', *Law's Ethical, Global and Theoretical Contexts: Essays in Honour of William Twining*, eds Baxi, U., McCrudden, C. and Paliwala, A. (Cambridge UK: Cambridge University Press).

Ghai, Y.P. and McAuslan, P. (1970), *Public Law and Political Change in Kenya* (New York: Oxford University Press).

Gikandi, S. and Wachanga, N. eds (2018), *Ngugi: Reflections on his Life of Writing* (Woodbridge UK: James Currey).

Ginsburg, T. (2000), 'Does Law Matter for Economic Development? Evidence from East Asia', *Law and Society Review*, 34(3), pp. 829–56.

Ginsburg, T., Melton, J. and Elkins, Z. (2009), *The Endurance of National Constitutions*, Olin Working Paper No. 511 (Cambridge UK: Cambridge University Press; Chicago IL: University of Chicago Law & Economics, see https://ssrn.com/abstract=1536925.

Githongo, J. (2019), 'Towards an Anti-corruption Strategy for Kenya: The Private Sector's Role', Presentation to the National Anti-Corruption Plan: Private Sector Stakeholder Consultation, Nairobi, 17 October 2000.

Gluckman, M. (1955), *The Judicial Process Amongst the Barotse of Northern Rhodesia* (Manchester: Manchester University Press).

Gregory, D. (2004), *The Colonial Present: Afghanistan, Palestine, Iraq* (Oxford: Blackwell).

Griffin, K., Khan, A. and Ickowitz, A. (2002), 'Poverty and Distribution of Land', *Journal of Agrarian Change*, 2(3), pp. 279–330.

Guha, R. (1996), *A Rule of Property for Bengal: An Essay on the Idea of Permanent Settlement* (Durham NC: Duke University Press).

Guyer, J. (2004), *Marginal Gains: Monetary Transactions in Atlantic Africa* (Chicago IL: University of Chicago Press).

Hall, R. and Cousins, B. (2019), 'Land Reform is at a Crossroads', *Daily Maverick*, 1 February, www.dailymaverick.co.za/article/2019-02-01-land-reform-is-at-a-crossroads, accessed 26 September 2019.

Hall, R. and Thembela, K. (2017), 'Elite Capture and State Neglect: New

Evidence on South Africa's Land Reform', *Review of African Political Economy*, 44(151), pp. 122–30.

Hanlon, J., Manjengwa, J. and Smart, T. (2012), *Zimbabwe Takes Back Its Land* (Boulder CO: Lynne Rienner).

Harbeson, J. (1971), 'Land Reforms and Politics in Kenya, 1954–70', *Journal of Modern African Studies*, 9(2), pp. 231–51.

Harbeson, J. (1973), *Nation-Building in Kenya: The Role of Land Reform* (Evanston, IL: Northwestern University Press).

Harbeson, J. (2012), 'Land and the Quest for a Democratic State in Kenya: Bringing Citizens Back', *African Studies Review*, 55(1), pp. 15–30.

Harrington, J. (2014), 'Access to Essential Medicines in Kenya: Intellectual Property, Anti-counterfeiting and the Right to Health', *Law and Global Health: Current Legal Issues Volume 16*, eds Freeman, M., Hawkes, S. and Bennett, B. (Oxford: Oxford University Press).

Harrington, J. (2017), *Towards a Rhetoric of Medical Law* (London: Routledge).

Harrington, J. and Manji, A. (2011), 'Alimentary Satire and the Politics of Corruption in Kenya', British Institute of Eastern Africa Annual Lecture, British Academy, London, November 2011.

Harrington, J. and Manji, A. (2013), 'Satire and the Politics of Corruption in Kenya', *Social and Legal Studies*, 22(1), pp. 3–23.

Harrington, J. and Manji, A. (2013), 'Satire and the Politics of Corruption in Kenya', *Social & Legal Studies*, 22(1), pp. 3–23.

Harrington, J. and Manji, A. (2017), 'The Limits of Socio-Legal Radicalism: Social and Legal Studies and Third World Scholarship', *Social and Legal Studies*, 26(6), pp. 700–715.

Harrington, J. and O'Hare, A. (2014), 'Framing the National Interest: Debating Intellectual Property and Access to Essential Medicines in Kenya', *The Journal of World Intellectual Property*, 17(1–2), pp. 16–33.

Harris, C. (1993), 'Whiteness as Property', *Harvard Law Review*, 106, pp. 1707–91.

Harvey, D. (2005), *A Brief History of Neoliberalism* (Oxford: Oxford University Press).

Haugerud, A. (1983), 'The Consequences of Land Tenure Reform among Smallholders in the Kenya Highlands', *Rural Africana*, 15/16, pp. 65–90.

Hegel, G.W.F. (1956), *The Philosophy of History*, translated by J. Sibree (New York: Dover Books).

Hirst, T. and Lamba, D. (1994), *The Struggle for Nairobi: A Documentary Comic Book* (Nairobi: Mazingira Institute).

Hodson, L. and Lavers, T. (2019), *Feminist Judgments in International Law* (Oxford: Hart Publishing).

Holtham, G. and Hazelwood, A. (2010), *Aid and Inequality in Kenya: British Development Assistance to Kenya* (London: Routledge).

Hornsby, C. (2013), *Kenya: A History Since Independence* (London: I.B. Tauris).

Hughes, L. (2006), *Moving the Masai: A Colonial Misadventure* (London: Palgrave).

Hunt, D. (1984), *The Impending Crisis in Kenya: The Case for Land Reform* (London: Ashgate).

Illiffe, J. (2005), *Honour in African History* (Cambridge UK: Cambridge University Press).

Irungu, F.M. (2016), 'Cinematographic Techniques of Hilary Ng'weno's *The Making of a Nation*', LL.M. Thesis (Kenyatta University).

Iyayi, F. (1986), 'The Primitive Accumulation of Capital in a Neo-Colony: The Nigerian Case', *Review of African Political Economy*, 35: 27–39.

James, D. (2006), 'White Power, Black Redress: The Racial Politics of Land Restitution and Land Reform', Paper Presented at Conference on Land, Memory, Reconstruction and Justice: Perspectives on Land Restitution in South Africa, Cape Town, 13–15 September 2006.

Juma, L. and Okpaluba, C. (2012), 'Judicial Intervention in Kenya's Constitutional Review Process', *Washington University Global Studies Law Review*, 11(2), pp. 287–364.

Juma, M.K. (2009), 'African Mediation of the Kenyan Post-2007 Election Crisis in Kenya's Uncertain Democracy: The Electoral Crisis of 2008', *Journal of Contemporary African Studies*, 27(3), pp. 407–30.

Kaggia, B. (1975), *Roots of Freedom 1921–1963: The Autobiography of Bildad Kaggia* (Nairobi: East African Publishing House).

Kamau, J. (2009), 'PC Mahihu's Signature Was All that One Needed to Own a Prime Beach Plot', *Daily Nation*, 13 November, www.nation.co.ke/news/1056-685750-jk2od9z/index.html, accessed 31 August 2019.

Kamau, J. (2016), 'When Ministers, Civil Servants got 100 Acres and Farm House for Free', *Sunday Nation*, 21 February, www.nation.co.ke/oped/opinion/Ministers-got-farm-houses-for-free/440808-3086058-s7yor6/index.html, accessed 29 August 2019.

Kamencu, M. (2013), 'Student Activism in the University of Nairobi and Democratic Space 1970–1992', LLM thesis, Department of History, University of Nairobi.

Kameri-Mbote, P. and Kindiki, K. (2009), 'Trouble in Eden: How and Why Unresolved Land Issues Landed "Peaceful Kenya" in Trouble in 2008', *Forum for Development Studies*, 1, pp. 167–93.

Kameri-Mbote, P. and Odote C. (2017), *The Gallant Academic: Essays in Honour of HWO Okoth-Ogendo* (Nairobi: University of Nairobi Press).

Kanongo, T. (1987), *Squatters and the Roots of Mau Mau 1905–1963* (London: James Currey).

Kantai, P. (2007), 'In the Grip of the Vampire State: Maasai Land Struggles in Kenyan Politics', *Journal of Eastern African Studies*, 1(1), pp. 107–22.

Kanyinga, K. (2000), 'Re-distribution from Above: The Politics of Land Rights and Squatting in Coastal Kenya', Research Report No. 115, Uppsala: Nordiska Afrikainstitutet.

Kanyinga, K. (2005), 'Speaking to the Past and the Present: The Land Question in the Draft Constitution of Kenya', *The Anatomy of Bomas: Selected Analysis of the 2004 Draft Constitution of Kenya*, eds Kindiki, K. and Ambani, O. (Nairobi: Claripress), pp. 25–56.

Kanyinga, K. (2009), 'The Legacy of the White Highlands: Land Rights, Ethnicity and the Post-2007 Election Violence in Kenya', *Journal of Contemporary African Studies*, 27(3), pp. 325–44.

Kanyinga, K. (2011), 'Stopping a Conflagration: The Response of Kenyan Civil Society to the Post-2007 Election Violence', *Politikon: South African Journal of Political Studies*, 38(1), pp. 85–109.

Kanyinga, K. (2017), 'Demystifying the Politics of Land Tenure: Okoth-Ogendo and the Concept of Land in Africa', *The Gallant Academic: Essays in Honour of H.W.O. Okoth-Ogendo*, eds Kameri-Mbote, P. and Odote, C. (Nairobi: University of Nairobi School of Law), pp. 185–204.

Kanyinga, K. and Long, J. (2012), 'The Political Economy of Reforms in Kenya: The Post-2007 Election Violence and a New Constitution', *African Studies Review*, 55(1), pp. 31–51.

Karanja, S.K. (2010), 'Land Restitution in the Emerging Kenyan Transitional Justice Process', *Nordic Journal of Human Rights*, 28(2), pp. 177–201.

Kariuki, F., Ouma, S. and Ng'etich, R. (2016), *Property Law* (Nairobi: Strathmore University Press).

Keenan, S. (2013), 'Property as Governance: Time, Space and Belonging in Australia's Northern', *The Modern Law Review*, 76(3), pp. 464–93.

Kekering, C. and Mabazira, C. eds (2017), *Friend of the Court and the 2010 Constitution: the Kenyan Experience and Comparative State Practice on Amicus Curiae* (Rome: International Development Law Organization).

Kennedy, D. (2003), 'Laws and Developments', *Law and Development: Facing Complexity in the 21st Century*, eds Hatchard, J. and Perry-Kessaris, A. (London: Cavendish), pp. 9–17.

Kenny, S. (2017), '"Specimens Calculated to Shock the Soundest Sleeper": Deep Layers of Anatomical Racism Circulated On-Board the Louisiana Health Exhibit Train', *Bodies Beyond Borders: Moving Anatomies, 1750–1950*, eds Wils, K., De Bont, R. and Au, S. (Leuven: Leuven University Press), pp. 163–93.

Kepe, T. and Hall, R. (2018), 'Land Redistribution in South Africa: Towards Decolonisation or Recolonisation?' *Politikon*, 45(1), pp. 128–37.

Kershaw, G. (1972), 'The Land is the People', Ph.D Thesis (University of Chicago).

Kershaw, G. (1997), *Mau Mau from Below* (Oxford: James Currey).

Kimari, W. (2018), 'Activists, Care Work, and the 'Cry of the Ghetto' in Nairobi, Kenya', *Nature*, 4(23), pp. 1–7.

Kitching, G. (1980), *Class and Economic Change in Kenya: The Making of an African Petite-Bourgeoisie, 1905–70* (New Haven CT: Yale University Press).

Kituo cha Sheria, Mazingira Institute, Katiba Institute, Akiba Mashinani Trust et al. (2012), 'The Land Bills 2012: Proposals for a Framework Chapter and Review of the Published Versions of the Bills', Presented to the Parliamentary Committee on Land and Natural Resources and the Technical Drafting Committee on the Land Bills (Nairobi: Mazingira Institute with support from Rooftops Canada/ Abri International and Canadian International Development Agency).

Klopp, J. (2000), 'Pilfering the Public: The Problem of Land Grabbing in Contemporary Kenya', *Africa Today*, 47(1), pp. 7–26.

Klopp, J. (2002), 'Can Moral Ethnicity Trump Political Tribalism? The Struggle for Land and Nation in Kenya', *African Studies*, 61(2), pp. 269–94.

Klopp, J. (2008), 'Remembering the Muoroto Uprising: Slum Demolitions, Land and Democratization in Kenya', *African Studies*, 67(3), pp. 295–314.

Klopp, J. (2012), 'Deforestation and Democratization: Patronage, Politics and Forests in Kenya', *Journal of Eastern African Studies*, 6(2), pp. 351–70.

Klopp, J. and Lumumba, O. (2017), 'Reform and Counter-Reform in Kenya's Land Governance', *Review of African Political Economy*, 44(154), pp. 577–94.

Klopp, J. and Orina, J.R. (2002), 'University Crisis and Student Activism in Kenya', *African Studies Review*, 45(1), pp. 43–76.

Klug, H. (1995), 'Defining the Property Rights of Others: Political Power, Indigenous Tenure and the Construction of Customary Law', Working Paper No. 23, Johannesburg: Centre for Applied Legal Studies, University of Witwatersrand.

Klug, H. (2000), *Constituting Democracy: Law, Globalism and South Africa's Political Reconstruction* (Cambridge UK: Cambridge University Press).

Klug, H. (2018), 'Decolonisation, Compensation and Constitutionalism: Land, Wealth and the Sustainability of Constitutionalism in Post-Apartheid South Africa', *South African Journal on Human Rights*, 34(3), pp. 469–91.

Kramon, E. and Posner, D. N. (2011), 'Kenya's New Constitution', *Journal of Democracy*, 22(2), pp. 89–103.

Krog, A. (2015), 'Baas van die plaas/Izwe lethu: Essay in Fragments and Two Villanells Exploring Different Relationships to Land in Some

Indigenous Poetic Texts', *Land Divided, Land Restored: Land Reform in South Africa in the 21st Century*, eds Cousins, B. and Walker, C. (Cape Town: Jacana), pp. 206–31.

Kuria, G.K. (1995), 'The Role of Land in the Constitutional Process', Paper Presented at the Forum on 'Land Rights, Utilization and Equity Under a New Constitution', Nairobi, 14 June 1995 (unpublished).

Kyle, K. (1999), *The Politics of Independence of Kenya* (Basingstoke: Palgrave Macmillan).

Laher, R. and Sing'oei, K. eds (2014), *Indigenous People in Africa: Contestations, Empowerment and Group Rights* (Africa Institute of South Africa).

Le Roux, M. and D. Davis (2019), *Lawfare: Judging Politics in South Africa* (Johannesburg: Jonathan Ball Publishers).

Lee, J.J. (1989), *Ireland, 1912–1985: Politics and Society* (Cambridge UK: Cambridge University Press).

Leo, C. (1984), *Land and Class in Kenya* (Toronto: University of Toronto Press).

Leys, C. (1975), *Underdevelopment in Kenya: The Political Economy of Neo-Colonialism, 1964–1971* (London: Heinemann; Berkeley: University of California Press).

Lindenmayer, E. and Kaye, J.L. (2009), *A Choice for Peace? The Story of Forty-One Days of Mediation in Kenya* (New York: International Peace Institute).

Lonsdale, J. (1986), 'The Depression and the Second World War in the Transformation of Kenya', *Africa and the Second World War*, eds Rathbone, R. and Killingray, D. (London: Palgrave Macmillan).

Loughlin, M. (2017), 'The Rise and Fall of Urban Law 1968–1988', *Land Law and Urban Policy in Context: Essays on the Contribution of Patrick McAuslan*, ed. Zartaloudis, T. (London: Birkbeck Law Press), pp. 129–50.

Lucey, D.S. (2011), *Land, Popular Politics and Agrarian Violence in Ireland: The Case of County Kerry, 1872–86* (Dublin: University College Dublin Press).

Lumumba, O. (2017), 'The Role of Civil Society in Land Reforms in Kenya: The Kenya Land Alliance', *The Gallant Academic: Essays in Honour of HWO Okoth-Ogendo*, eds Kameri-Mbote, P. and Odote, C. (Nairobi: University of Nairobi Press), pp. 171–84.

Lumumba, P.L.O. and Franceschi, L.G. (2010), *The Constitution of Kenya, an Introductory Commentary* (Nairobi: Strathmore University Press).

Lund, C. and Boone, C. (2013), 'Introduction: Land Politics in Africa – Constituting Authority Over Territory, Property and Persons', *Africa*, 83(1), pp. 1–13.

Luxemburg, R (2003 [1913]), *The Accumulation of Capital* (London: Routledge).

Lynch, G. (2006), 'The Fruits of Perception: "Ethnic Politics" and the Case of Kenya's Constitutional Referendum', *African Studies*, 65(2), pp. 233–70.

Lynch, G. (2008), 'Courting the Kalenjin: The Failure of Dynasticism and the Strength of the ODM Wave in Kenya's Rift Valley Province', *African Affairs*, 107(429), pp. 541–68.

Lynch, G. (2012), 'Becoming Indigenous in the Pursuit of Justice: The African Commission on Human and Peoples' Rights and the Endorois', *African Affairs*, 111(442), pp. 24–45.

Lynch, G. (2014), 'Electing the "Alliance of the Accused": The Success of the Jubilee Alliance in Kenya's Rift Valley', *Journal of Eastern African Studies*, 8(1), pp. 93–114.

Lynch, G. (2016), 'What's in a Name? The Politics of Naming Ethnic Groups in Kenya's Cherangany Hills', *Journal of Eastern African Studies*, 10(1), pp. 208–27.

Lynch, G. (2018), *Performances of Injustice: The Politics of Truth, Justice and Reconciliation in Kenya* (Cambridge UK: Cambridge University Press).

MacAuslan P. (2000), 'Only the Name of the Country Changes: The Diaspora of European Land Law in Commonwealth Africa', *Evolving Land Rights, Policy and Tenure in Africa*, eds Toulmin, C. and Quan, J. (London: IIED and NRI), pp. 75–96.

Macharia, R. and Ghai, Y.P. (2017), 'The Role of Participation in the Two Kenya Constitution-Building Processes of 2000–2005 and 2010: Lessons Learnt?' *Public Participation in African Constitutionalism*, eds Abbiate, T., Bockenforde, M. and Federico, V. (London: Routledge).

Madlingozi, T. (2017), 'Social Justice in a Time of Neo-Apartheid Constitutionalism: Critiquing the Anti-Black Economy of Recognition, Incorporation and Distribution', *Stellenbosch Law Review*, 28(1), pp. 123–47.

Maingi, G.W. (2015), 'Public Participation: Engaging Citizens in Policy Making', *National Values and Principles of the Constitution*, eds Ghai, Y.P. and Cottrell, J. (Nairobi: Katiba Institute).

Maliti, T. (2015), 'Kenyan President and Chief Justice Apologize for Past Injustices', *International Justice Monitor*, 9 April, www.ijmonitor.org/2015/04/kenyan-president-and-chief-justice-apologize-for-past-injustices, accessed 31 August 2019.

Maloba, W.O. (2017), *The Anatomy of Neo-Colonialism in Kenya: British Imperialism and Kenyatta, 1963–1978* (London: Palgrave Macmillan).

Malombe, D. (2013), 'Taking Back Gains; Marching Towards Constitutionalism', Kenya Human Rights Commission, panel discussion to mark the 3rd Anniversary of the Promulgation of the Constitution of Kenya 2010, Mazingira Institute, 27 August 2013.

Manji, A. (1998), 'Gender and the Politics of the Land Reform Process in Tanzania', *The Journal of Modern African Studies*, 36(4), pp. 645–67.

Manji, A. (1999), 'Imagining Women's "Legal World": Towards a Feminist Theory of Legal Pluralism in Africa', *Social & Legal Studies*, 8(4), pp. 435–55.

Manji, A. (2005), '"The Beautyful Ones" of Law of Law and Development', *International Law: Modern Feminist Approaches*, eds Buss, D.E. and Manji, A. (Oxford: Hart Publishing), pp. 159–71.

Manji, A. (2006), *The Politics of Land Reform in Africa* (London: Zed Books).

Manji, A. (2010), 'Eliminating Poverty? "Financial Inclusion", Access to Land, and Gender Equality in International Development', *Modern Law Review*, 73(6), pp. 985–1004.

Manji, A. (2012), 'The Grabbed State: Lawyers, Politics and Public Land in Kenya', *Journal of Modern African Studies*, 50(3), pp. 467–92.

Manji, A. (2014), 'The Politics of Land Reform in Kenya 2012', *African Studies Review*, 57(1), pp. 115–30.

Manji, A. (2015), *Whose Land is it Anyway? The Failure of Land Law Reform in Kenya*, (video), Africa Research Institute: Africa Research Institute, https://youtu.be/ulfjgRx_CBg?list=PLm3vRPZVAmFx-Pi5dKJ7fEjhQxBgAAj0VV, (accessed 25 March 2020).

Manji, A. (2017a), 'Land Law', *Great Debates in Gender and the Law*, ed. Auchmuty, R., Great Debates in Law series (Basingstoke: Palgrave Macmillan).

Manji, A. (2017b), 'Patrick McAuslan, Land Law and Development', *Land Law and Urban Policy in Context: Essays on the Contributions of Patrick McAuslan*, ed. Zartaloudis, T. (London: Routledge/ Birkbeck Law Press), pp. 171–88.

Manji, A. (2017c), 'Property, Conservation, and Enclosure in Karura Forest, Nairobi', *African Affairs*, 116(463), pp. 186–205.

Marx, K. (1976 [1867]), *Capital: A Critique of Political Economy*, Vol. 1 (Harmondsworth: Penguin).

Maughan-Brown, D. (1985), *Land, Freedom and Fiction: History and Ideology in Kenya* (London: Zed Books).

Mawani, R. (2014), 'Law as Temporality: Colonial Politics and Indian Settlers', *UC Irvine Law Review*, 4(1), pp. 65–96.

Mbondenyi, M.K., Asaala, E.O., Kabau, T. and Waris, A. eds (2015), *Human Rights and Democratic Governance in Kenya: A Post-2007 Appraisal* (Pretoria: Pretoria University Law Press).

McAuslan, P. (2003), *Bringing the Law Back In: Essays in Land Law and Development* (Aldershot: Ashgate).

McAuslan, P. (2006), 'Legal Pluralism as a Policy Option: Is it Desirable? Is it Doable?' *Land Rights for African Development from Knowledge to Action*, CAPRi, UNDP and ILC (Washington DC: CAPRi Policy Brief), pp. 9–10.

McAuslan, P. (2007a), 'Improving Tenure Security for the Poor in Africa', Working Paper No. 8, UN Food and Agriculture Organisation (FAO), May, www.fao.org/3/a-k1797e.pdf, accessed 2 September 2019.

McAuslan, P. (2007b), 'Land Law and the Making of the British Empire', *Modern Studies in Property Law Volume 4*, ed. Cooke, E. (Oxford: Hart Publishing), pp. 239–62.

McAuslan, P. (2013), *Land Law Reform in Eastern Africa: Traditional or Transformative?* (London: Routledge).

McClintock, A. (1992), 'The Angel of Progress: Pitfalls of the Term "Post-Colonialism"', *Social Text*, 31/32, pp. 84–98.

McEldowney, J. (2017), 'Policy and Development: Perspectives from Public Law and Political Thought – a 21st Century Odyssey', *Land Law and Urban Policy in Context: Essays on the Contribution of Patrick McAuslan*, ed. Zartaloudis, T. (London: Birkbeck Law Press), pp. 189–219.

McNeilly, K. (2019), 'Are Rights Out of Time? International Human Rights Law, Temporality, and Radical Social Change', *Social & Legal Studies*, 28(6), pp. 817–38.

Meek, C.K. (1946), *Land Law and Custom in the Colonies* (London: Oxford University Press).

Meiksins Wood, M. (2003), *Empire of Capital* (London: Verso).

Merryman, J.H. (1977), 'Comparative Law and Social Change: On the Origins, Style, Decline and Revival of the Law and Development Movement', *American Journal of Comparative Law*, 25(3), pp. 457–83.

Monte, E.P. (2018), 'Representations of Land in Kenyan Song', *Journal of Critical African Studies* Special issue: Valuing Land in Eastern Africa, 10(1), pp. 14–30.

Motha, S. and van Rijswijk, H. (2016), 'Introduction: Developing a Counter-Archival Sense', *Law, Violence, Memory: Uncovering the Counter-Archive*, eds Motha, S. and van Rijswijk, H. (Abingdon UK: Routledge).

Moyo, S. (2001), 'The Land Occupation Movement and Democratisation in Zimbabwe: Contradictions of Neo-Liberalism', *Millennium: Journal of International Studies*, 30(2), pp. 311–30.

Moyo, S. (2003), 'The Land Question in Africa: Research Perspectives and Questions', Draft paper presented at CODESRIA Conferences on Land Reform, the Agrarian Question and Nationalism in Gaborone, Botswana and Dakar, Senegal.

Moyo, S. (2011), 'Three Decades of Agrarian Reform in Zimbabwe', *Journal of Peasant Studies*, 38(3), pp. 493–531.

Moyo, S. and Yeros, P. (2005), 'The Resurgence of Rural Movements under Neoliberalism', *Reclaiming the Land: The Resurgence of Rural Movements in Africa, Asia and Latin America*, eds Moyo, S. and Yeros, P. (London: Zed Books), pp. 8–64.

Mueller, S. (1998), 'The Political Economy of Kenya's Crisis', *Journal of Eastern African Studies*, 2(2), pp. 85–210.

Muigua, K., Wamukoya, D. and Kariuki, F. (2015), *Natural Resources and Environmental Justice in Kenya* (Nairobi: Glenwood Publishers).

Mulevu, E. (2014), 'A Critical Analysis of the Extent to which the National Land Commission Addresses the Land Question in Kenya', LL.M. Thesis (University of Nairobi).

Mullei, P. (1988), 'Social Security in Kenya', *International Social Security Review*, 41(4), pp. 433–7.

Murray, C. (2006), 'The Human Rights Commission et al.: What is the Role of South Africa's Chapter 9 Institutions', *Potchefstroom Electronic Journal*, 2, pp. 1–26.

Murunga, G.R. (2009), 'The Kenyan General Election: Troubling Propaganda in an Intellectual Garb', *CODESRIA Bulletin*, 1–2, pp. 16–22.

Murunga, G.R. and Nasong'o, S.W. (2006), 'Bent on Self Destruction: The Kibaki Regime in Kenya', *Journal of Contemporary African Studies*, 24(1), pp. 1–28.

Murunga, G.R. and Nasong'o, S.W. eds (2007), *Kenya: The Struggle for Democracy* (London: Zed Books).

Musila, G.A. (2009), 'Phallocracies and Gynocratic Transgressions: Gender, State Power and Kenyan Public Life', *Africa Insight*, 39(1), pp. 39–57.

Musila, G.A. (2012), 'Writing History's Silences: Interview with Parselelo Kantai', *Kunapipi*, 34(1), pp. 71–80.

Musila, G.A. (2015), *A Death Retold in Truth and Rumour: Kenya, Britain and the Julie Ward Murder* (Woodbridge UK: James Currey).

Musila, G.A. (2017), 'Navigating Epistemic Disarticulations', *African Affairs*, 116(465), pp. 692–704.

Musila, G.A. (2018), 'MaKhumalo's Spaza Shop || Lena Moi's Dance', African Studies Association UK (ASAUK) Keynote Lecture, University of Birmingham, 11 September.

Mutua, M. (1997), 'Hope and Despair for a New South Africa: The Limits of Rights Discourse' *Harvard Human Rights Journal*, 10, pp. 63–114.

Mutua, M. (2004), 'Republic of Kenya Report of the Task Force on the Establishment of a Truth, Justice and Reconciliation Commission', *Buffalo Human Rights Law Review*, 10, pp. 15–214. https://digitalcommons.law.buffalo.edu/cgi/viewcontent.cgi?article=1120&context=bhrlr, accessed 19 March 2020.

Mutua, M. (2008), *Kenya's Quest for Democracy: Taming Leviathan* (Kampala: Fountain Publishers).

Mutunga, W. (1999), *Constitution-Making from the Middle: Civil Society and Transition Politics in Kenya, 1992–1997* (Harare: Mwengo).

Mutunga, W. (2018), 'Pan-African Jurisprudence for the Liberation of Africa', Lecture delivered at the Institute of African Studies, University of Ghana, 27 June.

Mwanzia, M. (2012), 'Team Meets to Fine-Tune Land Bills', *The Standard*, 4 April https://www.standardmedia.co.ke/article/2000055535/n-a, accessed 2 April 2020.

Mwathane, I. (2018a), 'Land Commission has Failed, it's Time for Soul Searching', *Daily Nation*, 14 July, www.nation.co.ke/oped/opinion/Land-commission-has-failed--it-s-time-for-soul-searching/440808 4661624-mi5gihz/index.html, accessed 30 August 2019.

Mwathane, I. (2018b), 'Mwathane: The Good, Bad and Ugly News that Defined Land Sector in 2018', *Kenyan Tribune*, 28 December 2018, https://kenyantribune.com/mwathane-the-good-bad-and-ugly-news-that-defined-land-sector-in-2018, accessed 30 August 2019.

Mwongela, K. (2013), 'Student Activism in the University of Nairobi and Democratic Space 1970–1992', Master of Arts Thesis (University of Nairobi).

Ngugi, J. (2002), 'The Decolonization-Modernization Interface and The Plight of Indigenous Peoples in Post-Colonial Development Discourse in Africa', *Wisconsin International Law Journal*, 20, pp. 297–352.

Ng'weno, H. and Tharao, J. (2007), 'Hilary Ng'weno's *The Making of a Nation*: A Political History of Kenya (DVD), NTV Kenya (Nairobi: Nation Media Group).

Nkosi, L. (2016), 'The Republic of Letters after the Mandela Republic', *Writing Home: Lewis Nkosi on South African Writing*, eds Stiebel, L. and Chapman, M. (Durban: University of KwaZulu Natal Press), pp. 240–58.

Nyamu-Musembi, C. (2007), 'De Soto and Land Relations in Rural Africa: Breathing Life into Dead Theories about Property Rights', *Third World Quarterly*, 28(8), pp. 1457–78.

Nyong'o, P.A. ed. (1992), *Thirty Years of African Independence: The Lost Decades* (Nairobi: Academy Science Publishers).

Odinga, O. (1967), *Not Yet Uhuru: The Autobiography of Oginga Odinga* (New York: Hill and Wang).

Odote, C. (2013), 'Kenya: The New Environment and Land Court', *IUCN Academy of Environmental Law E Journal*, 4(1), pp. 171–7.

Odote, C. (2017), 'The Conundrum of Institutional Arrangements to Govern Community Land in Kenya', *The Gallant Academic: Essays in Honour of HWO Okoth-Ogendo,* eds Kameri-Mbote, P. and Odote, C. (Nairobi: University of Nairobi Press), pp. 119–48.

Ogot, B. (1976), *Hadith 5: Economic and Social History of East Africa* (Nairobi: East African Literature Bureau).

Ogot, B. (1996), 'The Construction of a National Culture', *Decolonization and Independence in Kenya 1940–1993,* eds Ogot, B. and Ochieng, W. (London: James Currey), pp. 214–38.

Ogot, B. (1999), *Building on the Indigenous: Selected Essays, 1981–1998* (Kisumu, Kenya: Anyange Press).

Ogot, B. and Zeleza, T. (1988), 'Kenya: The Road to Independence and After', *Decolonisation and African Independence*, eds Prosser, G. and Louis, R. (New Haven, CT: Yale University Press), pp. 401–26.

Ohenjo, N. (2018), 'Kenya's Castaways: The Ogiek and National Development Processes', Minority Rights Group International Microstudy, https://minorityrights.org/publications/kenyas-castaways-the-ogiek-and-national-development-processes-march-2003, accessed 24 March 2020.

Ojwang, J.B. (1990), *Constitutional Development in Kenya: Institutional Adaptation and Social Change* (Nairobi: Acts Press).

Ojwang, J.B. (2013), *Ascendant Judiciary in Africa: Reconfiguring the Balance of Power in a Democratizing Order* (Nairobi: Strathmore University Press).

Okoth-Ogendo, H.W.O. (1975), 'Property Theory and Land Use Analysis: An Essay in the Political Economy of Ideas', *Journal of Eastern African Research and Development*, 1, pp. 37–53.

Okoth-Ogendo, H.W.O. (1976), 'African Land Tenure Reform', *Agricultural Development in Kenya: An Economic Assessment*, eds Heyer, J., Maitha, J. and Senga, W. (Nairobi: Oxford University Press).

Okoth-Ogendo, H.W.O. (1979), 'The Imposition of Property Law in Kenya', *The Imposition of Law*, eds Harrell-Bond, B.E. and Burman, S. (New York: Academic Press).

Okoth-Ogendo, H.W.O. (1989), 'Some Issues of Theory in the Study of Tenure Relations in African Agriculture', *Africa*, 59(1), pp. 6–17.

Okoth-Ogendo, H.W.O. (1991), *Tenants of the Crown: The evolution of Agrarian Law and Policy in Kenya* (Nairobi: ACTS Press).

Okoth-Ogendo, H.W.O. (1993a), 'Agrarian reform in Sub-Saharan Africa: An Assessment of State Responses to the African Agrarian Crisis and their Implications for Agricultural Development', *Land in African Agrarian Systems*, eds Basset, T. and Crummey, D. (Madison: University of Wisconsin Press).

Okoth-Ogendo, H.W.O. (1993b), 'Constitutions without Constitutionalism: Reflections on an African Political Paradox', eds Greenberg, D., Karz, S.N., Oliviero, B. and Wheatley, S.C., *Constitutionalism and Democracy: Transitions in the Contemporary World* (Oxford: Oxford University Press).

Okoth-Ogendo, H.W.O. (1998), 'Land Policy Reforms in East and Southern Africa: A Comparative Analysis of Drivers, Processes, and Outcomes', paper delivered at an International Conference on Land Policy, Cape Town, 27–29 January 1998.

Okoth-Ogendo, H.W.O. (2000), 'Legislative Approaches to Customary Tenure and Tenure Reform in East Africa', *Evolving Land Rights, Policy and Tenure in Africa*, eds Toulmin, C. and Quan, J. (London: International Institute of Environment and Development).

Okoth-Ogendo, H.W.O. (2002), 'The Tragic African Commons: A Century of Expropriation, Suppression and Subversion', *Land Reform and Agrarian Change in Southern Africa*, 24 (Programme for Land and Agrarian Studies, School of Government, University of the Western Cape), pp 1–17.

Okoth-Ogendo, H.W.O. (2007), 'The Last Colonial Question: An Essay in the Pathology of Land Administration Systems in Africa', Keynote Presentation at a Workshop on Norwegian Land Tools Relevant to Africa, Oslo, 3–4 May 2007, https://learning.uonbi.ac.ke/courses/GPR203_001/document/Property_Law_GPR216-September,_2014/Articles/HWOOkoth-Ogendo_THELASTCOLONIALQUESTION.pdf, accessed 29 August 2019.

Olima, W.H.A. (1997), 'The Conflicts, Shortcomings, and Implications of the Urban Land Management System in Kenya', *Habitat International*, 21(3), pp. 319–31.

Onoma, A. (2010), *The Politics of Property Rights Institutions in Africa* (New York: Cambridge University Press).

Opiyo, P. (2012), '"Mischief" in Land Bills Sparks Alarm', *The Standard*, 20 February, www.standardmedia.co.ke/article/2000052473/mischief-in-land-bills-sparks-alarm, accessed 2 April 2020.

Ouma, S. (2019), 'Jurisdictional Minefields, Jurisdictional Fetishes and Incompatibilities with the Rule of Law', paper presented at the Second Biennial Conference on Law and Society in Africa, Cairo, Egypt, 3 April 2019.

Ouma, S. and Manji, A. (2019), 'A Lost Opportunity: Can the National Land Commission Reclaim Its Original Mandate and Regain the Public's Trust?' www.theelephant.info/features/2019/02/28/a-lost-opportunity-can-the-national-land-commission-reclaim-its-original-mandate-and-regain-the-publics-trust, accessed 24 March 2020.

Patel, Z. (2006). *Unquiet: The Life and Times of Makhan Singh* (Nairobi: Zand Graphics).

Perry-Kessaris, A., ed. (2009). *Law in the Pursuit of Development: Principles into Practice?* (London: Routledge, Cavendish).

Peters, P. (2004), 'Inequality and Social Conflict over Land', *Journal of Agrarian Change*, 4(3), pp. 269–314.

Platzky, L. and Walker, C. (1985), *The Surplus People: Forced Removals in South Africa* (Johannesburg: Ravan Press).

Posner, R. (1998), 'Creating a Legal Framework for Economic Development', *The World Bank Research Observer*, 13(1), pp. 1–11.

Rocha, J., Brown, E. and Cloke, J. (2011), 'Of Legitimate and Illegitimate Corruption: Bankruptcies in Nicaragua', *Critical Perspectives on International Business*, 7, pp. 159–76.

Rose, C. (1998). 'The "New" Law and Development Movement in the Post-Cold War Era: A Vietnam Case Study', *Law & Society Review*, 32, pp. 93–140.

Rose, J. (2019), 'One Long Scream: Jacqueline Rose on Trauma and Justice in South Africa', *London Review of Books*, 41(10), pp. 10–14, www.lrb.co.uk/the-paper/v41/n10/jacqueline-rose/one-long-scream, accessed 18 March 2020.

Roux, T. (2009), 'Land Restitution and Reconciliation in South Africa',

Justice and Reconciliation in Post-Apartheid South Africa, eds Du Bois, F. and Du Bois-Pedain, A. (New York: Cambridge University Press), pp. 144–71.

Saul, J.S. (2012), 'Transition in South Africa: Choice, Fate ... or Recolonisation?' *Critical Arts*, 26(4), pp. 588–605.

Scott, J. (1999), *Seeing Like a State: How Certain Schemes to Improve the Human Condition have Failed* (New Haven CT and London: Yale University Press).

Shako, F. (2018), 'Need to Reform Legal Education in Kenya', *The Nation*, 3 April, www.nation.co.ke/oped/opinion/Need-to-reform-legal-education-in-Kenya-/440808-4368860-87mu68z/index.html, accessed 25 March 2020.

Sharma, A. and Gupta, A. (2006), *The Anthropology of the State: A Reader* (Oxford: Blackwell).

Sheppard, C. (2010), *Inclusive Equality: The Relational Dimensions of Systemic Discrimination in Canada* (Montreal: McGill-Queen's University Press).

Shihata, I.F.I. (1997), *Complementary Reforms: Essays on Legal, Judicial and Other Institutional Reforms Supported by the World Bank* (Boston MA: Kluwer Law International).

Shipton, P. (1988), 'The Kenyan Land Tenure Reform: Misunderstandings in the Public Creation of Private Property', *Land and Society in Contemporary Africa*, eds Downs, R. and Reyna, S. (Hanover: University Press of New England), pp. 91–135.

Shivji, I.G. (1991), *State and Constitutionalism: An African Debate on Democracy* (Harare: Southern African Research and Documentation Centre).

Shivji, I.G. (1997a), 'Guest Editor's Introduction: Not Yet Uhuru', *Change*, 5(2–3).

Shivji, I.G. (1997b), 'Contradictory Perspectives on Rights and Justice in the Context of Land Tenure Reform in Tanzania', paper presented to a meeting of the Academic Staff Council, University of Dar es Salaam, March 1997.

Shivji, I.G. (2009), *Accumulation in an African Periphery: A Theoretical Framework* (Dar es Salaam: Mkuki na Nyota).

Shivji, I.G. and Kapinga, W.B. (1997), 'Implications of the Draft Bill for the Land Act', *Change* (Dar es Salaam), 5, pp. 48–63.

Sibi-Okumu, J. (2014), *Kaggia: A Play* (Nairobi: Phoenix Theatre).

Sihanya, B.M. (2011), 'Constitutional Implementation in Kenya 2010–2015: Challenges and Prospects', Friedrich-Ebert-Stiftung Occasional Paper 5, pp. 1–42.

Sing'oei, K. (2011), 'Engaging the Leviathan: National Development, Corporate Globalisation and the Endorois' Quest to Recover their Herding Grounds', *International Journal on Minority and Group Rights*, 18(4), pp. 515–40.

Slaughter, J. and Wenzel, J. (2018), 'Theory', *Critical Terms of the Study of Africa*, eds Desai, G. and Masquelier, A. (Chicago and London: University of Chicago Press), pp. 302–16.

Slye, R. (2018), *The Kenyan TJRC: An Outsider's View from the Inside* (Cambridge UK: Cambridge University Press).

Sorrenson, M.P.K., *Land Reform in the Kikuyu Country* (London and Nairobi: Oxford University Press, 1967).

Southall, R. (2005), 'The Ndung'u Report: Land and Graft in Kenya', *Review of African Political Economy*, 32(103), pp. 142–51.

Spalling, B. (1992), *Development with Equity in the 1990s: Policies and Alternatives* (Madison WI: Global Studies Research Programme).

Stichter, S. (1982), *Migrant Labour in Kenya: Capitalism and African Response 1895–1975* (Harlow: Longman).

Stoler, A.L. (2002), 'Colonial Archives and the Arts of Governance', *Archival Science*, 2(1–2), pp. 87–109.

Swainson, N., *The Development of Corporate Capitalism in Kenya* (London: James Currey, 1980).

Swynnerton, R.J.M., *A Plan to Intensify the Development of African Agriculture in Kenya* (Nairobi: Government Printer, 1954).

Syagga, P. (2006), 'Land Ownership and Uses in Kenya: Policy Prescriptions from an Inequality Perspective', *Readings on Inequality in Kenya: Sectoral Dynamics and Perspectives*, ed. Society for International Development (SID) (Nairobi: SID).

Syagga, P. (2015), 'Public Land, Historical Land Injustices and the New Constitution', Working Paper No. 9, Nairobi: Society for International Development (SID). Tamanaha, B. (2012), *On the Rule of Law: History, Politics, Theory* (Cambridge UK: Cambridge University Press).

Teitel, R (1997), 'Transitional Jurisprudence: The Role of Law in Political Transformation', *Yale Law Journal*, 106, pp. 2009–82.

Throup, D. (1987), 'The Construction and Destruction of the Kenyatta State', *The Political Economy of Kenya*, ed. Schatzberg, M.G. (New York: Praeger), pp. 23–53.

Throup, D. and Hornsby, C. (1998), *Multi-party Politics in Kenya: The Kenyatta & Moi States & the Triumph of the System in the 1992 Election* (Oxford: James Currey).

Toulmin, C. and Quan, J. eds (2000), Evolving Land Rights, Policy & Tenure in Africa (London: IIED).

Trebilcock, M. and Davis, K. (2009), 'Property Rights and Development: The Contingent Case for Formalization', University of Toronto Faculty of Law, Legal Studies Research Series No. 08-10.

Trubek, D. and Galanter, M. (1974), 'Scholars in Self-Estrangement: Some Reflections on the Crisis in Law and Development', *Wisconsin Law Review*, 4, pp. 1062–1101.

Trubek, D. and Santos, A. eds (2006), *The New Law and Economic Development: A Critical Appraisal* (New York: Cambridge University Press).

Trubek, D.M. and Galanter, M. (1974), 'Scholars in Self-Estrangement: Some Reflections on the Crisis in Law and Development Studies in the United States', *Wisconsin Law Review*, 4, pp. 1062–1103.

Tuma, E. (1965), *Twenty-Six Centuries of Agrarian Reform: A Comparative Analysis* (Berkeley: University of California Press).

Upham, F. (2001), 'Ideology, Experience and the Rule of Law in Developing Societies', paper presented at a Roundtable on the Rule of Law, at the Carnegie Endowment, Washington DC, 5 September 2001.

Van Arkadie, B. (2016), 'Reflections on Land Policy and the Independence Settlement in Kenya', Special issue: Land, Liberation and Democracy: A Tribute to Lionel Cliffe, *Review of African Political Economy*, 43, pp. 60–68.

van der Walt, A. (2009), *Property in the Margins* (Oxford: Hart Publishing).

von Benda-Beckmann, F. (2003 [1993]), Scapegoat and Magic Charm: Law in Development Theory and Practice, *An Anthropological Critique Of Development: The Growth of Ignorance*, ed. Hobart, M. (London and New York: Routledge).

Vyas, Y., Kibwana, K., Owiti, O. and Wanjala, S. (1994), *Law and Development in the Third World* (Nairobi: Faculty of Law).

wa Gīthīnji, M. and Holmquist, F. (2012), 'Reform and Political Impunity in Kenya: Transparency without Accountability', *African Studies Review*, 55(1), pp. 53–74.

wa Thiong'o, N. (2009), *Something Torn and New: An African Renaissance* (New York: Basic Civitas Books).

Wachanga, N. (2018), 'Ngugi at Work', *Ngugi: Reflections on his Life of Writing*, eds Gikandi, S. and Wachanga, N. (Woodbridge UK: James Currey).

Waddilove, Hannah (2019), 'Support or Subvert? Assessing Devolution's Effect on Central Power during Kenya's 2017 Presidential Rerun', *Journal of Eastern African Studies*, 13(2), pp. 334–52.

Walker, C., Bohlin, A., Hall, R. and Kepe, T. (2003), *Land, Memory, Reconstruction, and Justice: Perspectives on Land Claims in South Africa* (Athens OH: Ohio University Press).

Walsh, R. (2015), 'A Review of *Property in the Margins* by AJ van der Walt', *King's Law Journal*, 21(3), pp. 591–96.

Wanjala, S. ed. (2000), *Essays on Land Law: The Reform Debate in Kenya* (Nairobi: University of Nairobi Press).

Warah, R. (2019), 'Cloak-And-Dagger Intrigues: An Insider's Account of Why the TJRC Report Was Delayed', *The Elephant*, 7 May, www.theelephant.info/op-eds/2019/05/07/cloak-and-dagger-intrigues-an-insiders-account-of-why-the-tjrc-report-was-delayed, accessed 31 August 2019.

Wasserman, G. (1973), 'Continuity and Counter-Insurgency: The Role of Land Reform in Decolonizing Kenya, 1962–70', *Canadian Journal of African Studies*, 7(1), pp. 133–48.

Wasserman, G. (1976), *Politics of Decolonization: Kenya Europeans and the Land Issue 1960–65* (Cambridge UK: Cambridge University Press).

White, L. (2000), *Speaking with Vampires: Rumor and History in Colonial Africa* (Berkeley: University of California Press).

Williams, D. (1999), 'Constructing Economic Space: The World Bank and the Making of Homo Economics', *Millennium: Journal of International Studies*, 28(1), pp. 79–99.

Willis, J. and Gona, G. (2013), 'Pwani C Kenya? Memory, Documents and Secessionist Politics in Coastal Kenya', *African Affairs*, 112(446), pp. 48–71.

Wolfe, P. (1999), *Settler Colonialism* (London and New York City: Continuum International Publishing Group).

Wolfe, P. (2006), 'Settler Colonialism and the Elimination of the Native', *Journal of Genocide Research*, 8(4), pp. 387–409.

Wrong, M. (2009), *It's Our Turn to Eat* (London: Harper Perennial).

Reports

AfriCOG (African Centre for Open Governance) (2009), 'Mission Impossible: Implementing the Ndung'u Report', 10 June, https://africog.org/old2019site/mission-impossible-implementing-the-ndung-u-report, accessed 29 August 2019.

BBC News (2004), 'UK Envoy's Speech on Kenyan Corruption', *BBC News*, 14 July. http://news.bbc.co.uk/1/hi/world/africa/3893625.stm, accessed 3 January 2019.

Business Advocacy Fund (2008), 'Withdrawal of the Draft National Land Policy', 29 February, www.businessadvocacy.org/isue006a.html, accessed 29 August 2019. CKRC – Constitution of Kenya Review Commission (2001a), 'Reviewing the Constitution' (Nairobi: CKRC).

CKRC – Constitution of Kenya Review Commission (2001b), 'The Constitutional Review Process in Kenya: Issues and Questions for Public Hearings' (Nairobi: CKRC).

CKRC – Constitution of Kenya Review Commission (2001c), 'Making Informed Choices: A Curriculum for Civic Education for Marginalised Communities, Constitution and Reform Education Consortium, Ecumenical Civic Education Programme, and the Gender Consortium' (Nairobi: CKRC).

CKRC – Constitution of Kenya Review Commission (2004), 'A Summary of Land Policy Principles Drawn from the Commission of Inquiry into the Land Law System of Kenya ('Njonjo Commission')', Proceedings of the National Civil Society Conference on Land Reform and the Land Question, 2 April (Nairobi: CKRC), http://mokoro.co.uk/

wp-content/uploads/kenya_summary_ land_policy_principles.pdf, accessed 31 August 2019.

CKRC – Constitution of Kenya Review Commission (2005a), 'Civic Education for the Referendum: CKRC Curriculum' (Nairobi: CKRC), 5 September, www.katibainstitute.org/Archives/images/CKRC/CK/Special%20Working%20Documents/The%20CE%20Curriculum.pdf, accessed 2 September 2019.

CKRC – Constitution of Kenya Review Commission (2005b), *Final Report of the Constitution of Kenya Review Commission* (Nairobi: CKRC).

Colony and Protectorate of Kenya (1958), *Report of the Working Party on African Land Tenure, 1957–1958* (Nairobi: Government Printers).

East Africa Royal Commission (1955), *East Africa Royal Commission Report 1953–1955*, (London: Her Majesty's Stationery Office) http://kenyalaw.org/kl/fileadmin/CommissionReports/E-A-Royal-Commission-1953-1955.pdf, accessed 30 August 2019.

KLF – Kenya Landowners Federation (2007), 'An Overview of the Draft National Land Policy (DNLP)', April, www.mng5.com/papers/klfOverview.pdf, accessed 29 August 2019.

Kenya National Assembly (2018), 'Investigations of Historical Land Injustices Regulations 2017 Hansard', 28 March, www.parliament.go.ke/sites/default/files/2017-05/Hansard_Report_-_Wednesday_28th_March_2018P.pdf, accessed 31 August 2019.

Kenya Ministry of Devolution and Planning & Council of Governors (2016), 'County Public Participation Guidelines', January, http://devolutionasals.go.ke/wp-content/uploads/2018/03/County-Public-Participation_Final-1216-2.pdf, accessed 31 August 2019.

KHRC – Kenya Human Rights Commission (2011), 'Lest We Forget: The Faces of Impunity in Kenya', www.khrc.or.ke/mobile-publications/civil-political-rights/30-lest-we-forget-the-faces-of-impunity-in-kenya/file.html, accessed 24 March 2020.

KHRC – Kenya Human Rights Commission (n.d.), 'Redress for Historical Land Injustices in Kenya: A brief for Proposed Legislation for Historical Land Injustices', www.khrc.or.ke/publications/114-redress-for-historical-land-injustices-in-kenya/file.html, accessed 24 March 2020.

KHRC – Kenya Human Rights Commission, Law Society of Kenya and International Commission of Jurists (1994), *The Kenya We Want: Proposals for a Model Constitution* (Nairobi: LSK, ICJ-Kenya and KHRC).

KNCHR (Kenya National Commission on Human Rights) and KLA (Kenya Land Alliance) (2006), *Unjust Enrichment: The Making of Land Grabbing Millionaires* (Nairobi: KHCHR and KLA).KNDR – Kenya National Dialogue and Reconciliation (2008), 'Statement of Principles on Long-Term Issues and Solutions', The Kenya National

Dialogue and Reconciliation, mediated by Kofi Annan, Chair, Panel of Eminent African Personalities.

KNDR – Kenya National Dialogue and Reconciliation (2009), 'Monitoring Project Agenda Item 4: Long-Standing Issues and Solutions – Draft Report on Status of Implementation' January, https://docplayer. net/amp/158580305-Kndr-documents-agenda-item-four-draft -report-on-status-of-implementation.html, accessed 24 March 2020.

Maina, W. (2019), 'State Capture: Inside Kenya's Inability to Fight Corruption', State of the Nation Report by the Africa Centre for Open Governance (AfriCOG), 26 May, https://africog.org/wp-content/ uploads/2019/05/STATE-CAPTURE.pdf, accessed 26 September 2019.

Minority Rights International (2018), 'World Directory of Minorities and Indigenous Peoples – Kenya: Hunter and Gatherers', January, London, www.refworld.org/docid/49749cf84a.html, accessed 29 August 2019.

National Land Commission (2014), *The National Land Commission Report 2013* (Nairobi: National Land Commission).

National Land Commission (2017), 'Investigation of Historical Land Injustices Regulations', L.N. No. 258.

Republic of Kenya (1966), *Report of the Mission on Land Consolidation and Registration in Kenya 1965–1966* (Nairobi: Government Printers).

Republic of Kenya (2002), *Report of the Commission of Inquiry into the Land Law Systems of Kenya on Principles of a National Land Policy Framework, Constitutional Position of Land and New Institutional Framework for Land Administration* (Nairobi: Government Printers).

Republic of Kenya (2008), *Report of the Commission into Post-Election Violence* (Nairobi: Government Printers).

Republic of Kenya (2009a), *Report of the Commission into Illegal and Irregular Allocations of Land* (Nairobi: Government Printers).

Republic of Kenya (2009b), *Sessional Paper 2 of 2009 on National Land Policy* (Nairobi: Government Printers).

Republic of Kenya (2009c), *Sessional Paper 3 of 2009 on National Land Policy* (Nairobi: Government Printers).

Republic of Kenya (2012a), Commission for the Implementation of the Constitution (CIC), Second Annual Report. Nairobi: Government Printers.

Republic of Kenya (2012b), National Land Commission Act, http:// kenyalaw.org:8181/exist/kenyalex/actview.xql?actid=No.%20 5%20of%202012, accessed 19 March 2020.

Republic of Kenya (2013), *Report of the Truth, Justice and Reconciliation Commission* (Nairobi: Government Printers).

RIPOCA – Human Rights, Power and Civic Action in Developing Societies (funded by Norwegian Research Council) (2010), 'Kenya Land

Alliance CASE Study', February, www.jus.uio.no/smr/english/research/projects/ripoca/workshop-april-2010/Kenya_Org_study_Kenya_Land_Alliance_Feb%202010.pdf, accessed 30 August 2019.

Sing'Oei, K. (2012), 'Kenya at 50: Unrealised Rights of Minorities and Indigenous Peoples', 8 March (London: Minority Rights Group), www.ogiekpeoples.org/images/downloads/Minority-and-indigenous-people-report.pdf, accessed 30 August 2019.

Society for International Development (SID) (2010), *Public Land, Historical Land Injustices and the New Constitution* (Nairobi: SID).TJRC – Truth, Justice and Reconciliation Commission (2003), 'Makau Task Force Report', *II. Pre-TJRC Documents 6*, 26 August, https://digitalcommons.law.seattleu.edu/tjrc-pre/6, accessed 31 August 2019.

TJRC – Truth, Justice and Reconciliation Commission (2008a), 'Act and Amendments (TJRC) – TJRC Act 2008 (as Amended)', *I. Core TJRC Related Documents 25*, https://digitalcommons.law.seattleu.edu/tjrc-core/25, accessed 31 August 2019.

TJRC – Truth, Justice and Reconciliation Commission (2008b), 'Concerns About the TJRC Bill (Amnesty International)', *VII. Academic and Civil Society Analysis*, 21 May, https://digitalcommons.law.seattleu.edu/cgi/viewcontent.cgi?article=1026&context=tjrc-academic, accessed 31 August 2019.

TJRC – Truth, Justice and Reconciliation Commission (2013), *The Final Report of the TJRC* (Nairobi: Government Printer).

TJRC – Truth, Justice and Reconciliation Commission (2018), *Report of the Kenya Truth, Justice and Reconciliation Commission*, https://digitalcommons.law.seattleu.edu/tjrc, accessed 24 March 2020

Transparency International (TI), (2011), *Bribe Payers Index* (Berlin: TI).

Ufungamano Initiative (2004), *Proposed Draft Constitution of the Republic of Kenya*.United Kingdom Government (2013), *Colonial Administration Records (migrated archives): Kenya Land Transfer Programme* (London: The National Archives).

United Republic of Tanzania, Ministry of Land, Housing and Urban Development (1994), *Report of the Presidential Commission of Inquiry into Land Matters. Volume I: Land Policy and Land Tenure Structure, and Volume II: Selected Land Disputes and Recommendations* (Uppsala: Scandinavian Institute of African Studies).

World Bank (2013), *Doing Business* (International Bank for Reconstruction and Development / World Bank).

Cases

Centre for Minority Rights Development (Kenya) and Minority Rights Group on Behalf of Endorois Welfare Council v. Kenya (2010), African Commission on Human and Peoples' Rights, 4 February, www.

hrw.org/news/2010/02/04/kenya-landmark-ruling-indigenous-land-rights, accessed 25 March 2020.

Centre for Minority Rights Development (CEMIRIDE) and Minority Rights Group International (MRG) (on behalf of the Endorois) v. Kenya (Feb. 2010), African Commission on Human and Peoples' Rights, Communication (decision on merits), Communication 276/2003.

Doctors for Life International v. Speaker of the National Assembly and Others (2006) ZACC 11; 2006 (12) BCLR 1399 (CC); 2006 (6) SA 416 (CC).

Hassan Hashi Shirwa and Another v. Swaleh Mohamed and 7 Others, Malindi ELCC No. 41B of 2012.

In the Matter of the National Land Commission, Supreme Court of Kenya Advisory Opinion Reference No. 2 of 2014.

National Land Commission v. Attorney General and Others, Advisory Opinion Reference No. 2 of 2014.

Ol le Njogo and others v. Attorney General of the EAP (1914) 5 EALR 70.

Port Elizabeth Municipality v Various Occupiers (2005) 1 (SA) 217 (CC).

Re Speaker of the Senate, Supreme Court Advisory Opinion Reference No. 2 of 2013.

Robert N. Gakuru & Others v. Governor Kiambu County & 3 others (2014) Eklr.

S. and Others v. Van Rooyen and Others (General Council of the Bar of South Africa Intervening), [2002] ZACC 8; 2002 (5) SA 246; 2002 (8) BCLR 810.

Salem Party Club and Others v. Salem Community and Others (CCT26/17) (2017) ZACC 46; 2018 (3) BCLR 342 (CC); 2018 (3) SA 1 (CC) (11 December 2017).

Wainaina v Murito (1923) 9 KLR 102.

William Ngasis and Others v. Baringo County Council and Others, Miscellaneous Civil CASE No. 183 of 2000.

Index

Eastern Africa Series

EASTERN AFRICAN STUDIES

These titles published in the United States and Canada by Ohio University Press

www.ingramcontent.com/pod-product-compliance
Lightning Source LLC
Chambersburg PA
CBHW070325270326
41926CB00017B/3766